SEPTEMBER 1, 1939

A BIOGRAPHY OF A POEM

SEPTEMBER 1, 1939

IAN SANSOM

4th ESTATE • London

4th Estate
An imprint of HarperCollins*Publishers*
1 London Bridge Street
London SE1 9GF

www.4thEstate.co.uk

First published in Great Britain in 2019 by 4th Estate

1

Unpublished writings by W. H. Auden are quoted with the
permission of the Estate of W. H. Auden.

'September 1, 1939' from *Another Time* by W. H. Auden
(1940, Faber & Faber).

A catalogue record for this book is
available from the British Library

ISBN 978-0-00-755721-9

Typeset in ITC Giovanni and Monotype Bembo
Printed and bound in Great Britain by
CPI Group (UK) Ltd, Croydon

MIX
Paper from
responsible sources
FSC™ C007454

For N. J. Humphrey

CONTENTS

WOW!

At just after five o'clock on 11 June 1956, W. H. Auden stood up to give his inaugural lecture as Oxford Professor of Poetry at the Sheldonian Theatre, the very heart of the university, adjacent to the Bodleian and the Clarendon Building, opposite Blackwell's bookshop on Broad Street, and a short walk from Auden's old college, Christ Church.

It was a warm afternoon. Auden, famously crumpled, had enjoyed, I imagine, a good lunch and was sweating in his thick black MA gown with its distinctive, gaudy crimson shot-silk hood. He was buzzing: he had long since adopted a strict chemical daily routine to enable him to work more efficiently. These 'labor-saving devices', in what he called his 'mental kitchen', included not only strategic quantities of alcohol, coffee and tobacco, but also the amphetamine Benzedrine, as a pick-me-up at breakfast, and the barbiturate Seconal, to bring him down at night. 'If you ever get that depressed unable-to-concentrate feeling, try taking Benzidrine [sic] Tablets,' he advised his friend Annie Dodds, 'but not too many.'

The Sheldonian was full: the audience were expectant. The University Chancellor, the Vice-Chancellor and the Proctors were in full fig – black gowns, gold lace, white tie. The undergraduates and graduate students wore subfusc and were crammed into the high-tiered seating under the lurid sunburst-orange ceiling fresco by King Charles II's court painter Robert Streater, which depicts Truth descending upon the Arts and Sciences like the wolf on the fold, dispelling ignorance from the university.

It was quite a return.

In 1928 Auden had left Oxford with a miserable Third in English, and his appointment as professor was not without controversy. The university elects its Professor of Poetry unusually – indeed, uniquely – by a vote among its graduates, and Auden remained a divisive figure in England. The two other candidates were Harold Nicolson, a well-connected author, diplomat, politician and husband to Vita Sackville-West, and G. Wilson Knight, an eminent and massively prolific Shakespeare scholar, author of both the standard work on Shakespearean tragedy, *The Wheel of Fire* (1930), and the bestselling *The Sceptred Isle: Shakespeare's Message for England at War* (1940).

Nicolson and Wilson Knight had obvious merits – they were sensible, distinguished, learned individuals. And they were easily and identifiably *English*. Auden, in contrast, was an eccentric, remote, supernational sort of a figure, a poet celebrity, English-born but now a self-proclaimed New Yorker who had developed a strange, drawling mid-Atlantic accent – recently further complicated after he'd had his few final teeth removed and been fitted with dentures – and who made a living 'on the circuit', touring American campuses delivering his lectures and reading his poems. He saw himself as a kind of itinerant preacher:

An air-borne instrument I sit,
Predestined nightly to fulfil
Columbia-Giesen-Management's
Unfathomable will,

By whose election justified,
I bring my gospel of the Muse
To fundamentalists, to nuns,
to Gentiles and to Jews.

(Auden, 'On the Circuit')

Auden's usual touring schedule did not include the English Midlands. The closest he came was spending his summers in bohemian fashion on the Italian island of Ischia with his lover Chester Kallman. ('They engaged a handsome local boy known as Giocondo', notes one biographer, 'to look after the house, and possibly also to provide sexual services.') Though popular among undergraduates, who weren't entitled to vote, Auden was not considered a serious candidate for the professorship by the more senior members of the university.

There was also the small matter of his having abandoned England in 1939, and having taken the oath of allegiance and become an American citizen in 1946, something he was never allowed to forget, and for which he was certainly never forgiven. On learning of Auden's death in 1973, the novelist Anthony Powell was rendered almost speechless with joy and disgust, declaring, 'I'm *delighted* that *shit* has gone … It should have happened years ago … Scuttling off to America in 1939 with his boyfriend like a … like a …' In 1956, memories of the war were still fresh. G. Wilson Knight had served as a dispatch rider in World War I, and in World War II Nicolson had been parliamentary secretary at the Ministry of Information. Auden's war record was rather less distinguished. When he had left England in 1939, questions were asked in Parliament about his departure: he was a disappointment to the nation. When he arrived back in London at the end of the war, wearing his honorary US Army major's uniform, as part of his role in the US Strategic Bombing Survey, people were appalled.

But if England wasn't too sure about Auden, Auden wasn't at all sure he wanted to spend too much time in England delivering the one lecture per term required by the university statutes. 'The winter months', he wrote to Enid Starkie, the flamboyant, publicity-seeking, cigar-smoking Rimbaud scholar who had proposed him as a candidate, 'are those in which I earn enough dollars to allow me [...] to devote myself to the unprofitable occupation of writing poetry. I do not see any way in which I could earn the equivalent if I had to reside in England during that period.' Nonetheless, he allowed his nomination to go forward.

On Thursday, 9 February 1956, the result was announced.

Wilson Knight had attracted just 91 votes. Nicolson had secured 192. And Auden topped the poll with 216. He was therefore elected as professor, succeeding his old friend Cecil Day Lewis.

'You have chosen for your new Professor', Auden began his inaugural lecture – typically teasing and self-effacing – 'someone who has no more right to the learned garb he is wearing than he would have to a clerical collar.' Setting out the terms of his professorship, he went on:

> Speaking for myself, the questions which interest me most when reading a poem are two. The first is technical: 'Here is a verbal contraption. How does it work?' The second is, in the broadest sense, moral: 'What kind of a guy inhabits this poem? What is his notion of the good life or the good place? His notion of the Evil One? What does he conceal from the reader? What does he conceal even from himself?'

This book does a very simple thing. It asks Auden's two obvious questions of his own poem 'September 1, 1939'. How does it work? And what kind of a guy inhabits this poem?

In a sense, the first question is easy to answer. 'September 1, 1939' consists of 99 lines, written in trimeters, divided into nine eleven-line stanzas with a shifting rhyme scheme, each stanza being composed of just one sentence, so that – as the poet Joseph Brodsky has usefully pointed out – the thought unit corresponds exactly to the stanzaic unit, which corresponds also to the syntactic and grammatical unit. Which is neat.

Too neat.

Because, of course, this is only the beginning of an understanding of how the poem works. It takes us only to the very edge of the poem, to the outskirts of its territory. In order properly to understand 'September 1, 1939', we would have to investigate why Auden chose this rigorous, cramped, bastard form – and not, for example, an elegant villanelle, or a sestina, or a double sestina, traditional and virtuoso forms at which he excelled. And why did he begin a poem with an 'I', undoubtedly the most depressing and dreary little pronoun in the English language? And who is this 'I'? And why do they 'sit' in one of the dives – why aren't they standing? And how are they sitting? At a table? And where is this dive? And why is it a 'dive'? And what exactly were the 'clever hopes' of this 'low dishonest decade'? And why so many double adjectives? And so on and so on. This book will attempt to follow the route of some of these obvious but necessary questions, mapping the poem word by word, line by line and phrase by phrase.

And as for the 'guy' who inhabits this poem? What is his notion of the good life or the good place? What is his notion of the Evil One? What does he conceal from the reader? What does he conceal from himself?

These are also good questions.

'September 1, 1939' is an important poem, I believe, and worthy of scrutiny, because it provides us with a rare glimpse of a writer in the act of reinventing himself, at a culminating moment in world affairs. Like *Ulysses* and *The Waste Land*, like *Guernica* and *The Rite of Spring*, this poem is a snapshot of the artist *in extremis*, working at the farthest reaches of his capacities.

But 'September 1, 1939' is not only one of those rare coincidences in literature in which the force of history meets personal psychology and ideology, to produce something truly marvellous – it also represents a moment of crisis, where the great pressures at work both outside and inside the poem force certain flaws to become apparent. Not only that, it's a poem whose troubled history involves its own self-destruction and reinvention: it therefore represents the art object as living organism, something that grows and changes, that is understood, misunderstood, appropriated, abandoned, recycled and reused, again and again. Above all, it is a poem that still reverberates with meaning and controversy, a poem that readers return to at times of personal and national crisis: it turns out that the 'guy' who inhabits Auden's poem is us.

The aim of this book, then, is to demonstrate how a poem gets produced, consumed and incorporated into people's lives – how, in the words of another of Auden's great poems, 'In Memory of W. B. Yeats', the work of a poet becomes 'modified in the guts of the living', and not just modified, but colonised, metabolised, metastasised. It is a record of how and why we respond to great art.

Or, at least, it is a record of how and why *I* have responded to this particular example of great art, and of how the work of this particular poet has become modified in these particular guts –

modified, metabolised and metastasised. There has been so much written about Auden by so many people – brilliant and insightful people – over so many years, that the best I can do is to try and explain the impact that reading and studying this poem has had on me. Not because there's anything particularly interesting about me – on the contrary – but because I might usefully represent the common reader, the sensual man-in-the-street, the entirely average individual with a rather unusual interest in a particular work of art.

In the end, I hope that this book amounts to more than a record of my own peculiar tastes and notions and gives expression to that common sense of awe and inadequacy that we might all experience in the presence of great art, for how can one possibly begin to cope with someone like Auden, who was clearly a genius, and with something like this, which is clearly a masterpiece? What can one possibly say, except … 'Wow!'?

SEPTEMBER 1, 1939

I sit in one of the dives
On Fifty-Second Street
Uncertain and afraid
As the clever hopes expire
Of a low dishonest decade:
Waves of anger and fear
Circulate over the bright
And darkened lands of the earth,
Obsessing our private lives;
The unmentionable odour of death
Offends the September night.

Accurate scholarship can
Unearth the whole offence
From Luther until now
That has driven a culture mad,
Find what occurred at Linz,
What huge imago made
A psychopathic god:
I and the public know
What all schoolchildren learn,
Those to whom evil is done
Do evil in return.

Exiled Thucydides knew
All that a speech can say
About Democracy,
And what dictators do,
The elderly rubbish they talk
To an apathetic grave;
Analysed all in his book,
The enlightenment driven away,
The habit-forming pain,
Mismanagement and grief:
We must suffer them all again.

Into this neutral air
Where blind skyscrapers use
Their full height to proclaim
The strength of Collective Man,
Each language pours its vain
Competitive excuse:
But who can live for long
In an euphoric dream;
Out of the mirror they stare,
Imperialism's face
And the international wrong.

Faces along the bar
Cling to their average day:
The lights must never go out,
The music must always play,
All the conventions conspire
To make this fort assume
The furniture of home;
Lest we should see where we are,
Lost in a haunted wood,
Children afraid of the night
Who have never been happy or good.

The windiest militant trash
Important Persons shout
Is not so crude as our wish:
What mad Nijinsky wrote
About Diaghilev
Is true of the normal heart;
For the error bred in the bone
Of each woman and each man
Craves what it cannot have,
Not universal love
But to be loved alone.

From the conservative dark
Into the ethical life
The dense commuters come,
Repeating their morning vow,
'I *will* be true to the wife,
I'll concentrate more on my work',
And helpless governors wake
To resume their compulsory game:
Who can release them now,
Who can reach the deaf,
Who can speak for the dumb?

All I have is a voice
To undo the folded lie,
The romantic lie in the brain
Of the sensual man-in-the-street
And the lie of Authority
Whose buildings grope the sky:
There is no such thing as the State
And no one exists alone;
Hunger allows no choice
To the citizen or the police;
We must love one another or die.

Defenceless under the night
Our world in stupor lies;
Yet, dotted everywhere,
Ironic points of light
Flash out wherever the Just
Exchange their messages:
May I, composed like them
Of Eros and of dust,
Beleaguered by the same
Negation and despair,
Show an affirming flame.

YOUR LEAST
FAVOURITE AUDEN
POEM?

INTERVIEWER: What's your least favourite Auden poem?
AUDEN: 'September 1, 1939.'

> Michael Newman, interview with
> W. H. Auden, *The Paris Review* (1972)

Me too.

*

I have been trying to write a book about W. H. Auden for
twenty-five years.

It could not be described as a cost-effective enterprise.

It may not have been the best use of my time.

The poet cannot understand the function of money in
modern society because for him there is no relation
between subjective value and market value; he may be
paid ten pounds for a poem which he believes is very
good and took him months to write, and a hundred
pounds for a piece of journalism which costs him but a
day's work.

> (Auden, 'The Poet & The City')

A lot can happen to someone in twenty-five years – though it hasn't really happened to me. I have overcome no addictions. I have suffered no serious mental or physical breakdowns. There were no major achievements, no terrible lows: I am, in all regards, average to the point of being dull. There is, alas, no backstory to this story. This is not one of *those* books.

It is not a book about grief.

It is not a book about loss.

It is not a book about some great self-realisation.

I did not go – I have not been – on any kind of a journey with W. H. Auden.

I do not believe that Auden provides readers with the key to understanding life, the universe and everything. Reading Auden has not made me happier, healthier, or a better or more interesting person.

Perhaps the only strange or remarkable thing to have happened to me over the past twenty-five years is that I have been trying to write a book about W. H. Auden.

The only possible conclusion, I suppose, after all this time, is either that I haven't been trying hard enough, or that I'm simply not up to the job.

Or, possibly, both.

*

Completed finally in my early fifties, in vain and solitary celebration, this – whatever this is – turns out to be proof against itself.

For decades I had imagined writing a big book about Auden's life and work, a truly great book, a *magnum opus*.

I have managed instead to write a short book about just one of his poems. At the very moment of its completion, the work turns out to be evidence of failure. *Opus minus*.

In the end, one feels only depletion, disgust and disappointment, the sense that one has once again turned manna into gall, the everlasting taste of bitterness.

*

(I am reading the collected poems of Bertolt Brecht, in translation. I come across this, 'Motto':

> This, then, is all. It's not enough, I know.
> At least I'm still alive, as you may see.
> I'm like the man who took a brick to show
> How beautiful his house used once to be.

This book is my brick: it is proof of how beautiful the house might have been.)

*

Auden wrote all of his prose, he claimed, because he needed the money.
  I have written all of my prose because I am not a poet.
  And I needed the money.

> Underneath the abject willow,
>   Lover, sulk no more;
> Act from thought should quickly follow:
>   What is thinking for?
> Your unique and moping station
>   Proves you cold;
>   Stand up and fold
> Your map of desolation.
>   (Auden, 'Underneath the abject willow')

Twenty-five years, though – can you imagine? – twenty-five years of failing to write a book.

*

It's perhaps not entirely uncommon.

There are, of course, individuals who write great books at great speed, and with great success, and to great acclaim – Auden's first book with Faber was published when he was just twenty-three and he went on to produce a book about every three years for the rest of his life. The truth is, it takes most of us years to get a book published, and even then those books end in massive failure: neglected, overlooked and forgotten.

(My own books, it should probably be admitted, have all ended in massive failure: neglected, overlooked and forgotten. It's nature's way. There's a critic, Franco Moretti, notorious in literary studies, who has pioneered the study of literature as a kind of data set, and he has an essay, 'The Slaughterhouse of Literature', which is all about clues in detective literature, and which is an excellent essay, though I'm less interested in his thoughts about clues in detective literature than I am in his redolent title phrase – which he stole from Hegel, actually – because it acknowledges what is rarely acknowledged, which is the hard, painful truth that to study literature, never mind to participate in it, is to become a witness to the sheer horrors of literary history, as savage and violent as all history. 'The majority of books disappear forever –' writes Moretti, 'and "majority" actually misses the point: if we set today's canon of nineteenth-century British novels at two hundred titles (which is a very high figure), they would still be only about *0.5 percent* of all published novels. And the other 99.5 percent?' I am one of the 99.5 per cent: I am one of the living dead, the Great Unread. This book too will undoubtedly end up in the slaughterhouse, as it should and as it must.)

*

This book I began long before I had written or even contemplated writing any of my other books. It was the first – and it may be the last. It may be time to admit defeat, to admit to my own obvious lack of whatever it was that Auden had, which was just about everything. In Auden, one might say – if it didn't sound so dramatic, if it didn't sound like I was trying to talk things up by talking myself down – in Auden was my beginning and in Auden is my end.

*

One might, I suppose, console oneself with the knowledge that even some of Auden's books were not entirely successful: *Academic Graffiti, City Without Walls.*

But to dwell on the minor faults and failings of the great is hardly a comfort.

It is merely another sign of one's own inadequacies.

The greater the equality of opportunity in a society
becomes, the more obvious becomes the inequality of
the talent and character among individuals, and the more
bitter and personal it must be to fail, particularly for
those who have some talent but not enough to win them
second or third place.

(Auden, 'West's Disease')

But surely – surely? – literature is not a competition. Literature is not a sport. One cannot measure oneself by the usual standards of success.

The writer who allows himself to become infected by the
competitive spirit proper to the production of material
goods so that, instead of trying to write *his* book, he tries
to write one which is better than somebody else's book
is in danger of trying to write the absolute masterpiece
which will eliminate all competition once and for all
and, since this task is totally unreal, his creative powers
cannot relate to it, and the result is sterility.

(Auden, 'Red Ribbon on a White Horse')

Let's not kid ourselves.

It *is* a competition.

It *is* a sport.

One *does* measure oneself by the usual standards of success.

When writing about any great writer – or indeed about
anyone who has achieved great things – one can't help but
compare oneself.

*

(Throughout his life, Philip Larkin often measured himself
against Auden. Auden, for him, was the Truly Great Man: Philip
Larkin *loved* Auden. When he bought a car in 1984, for example,
an Audi, he said he liked the name 'because it reminds me of
Auden'. In a letter to a friend in 1959, extolling the virtues of
Auden's poem 'Night Mail', he wrote in horrible realisation,
'HE'D BE ABOUT SEVEN YEARS YOUNGER THAN ME,' but
then quickly added, 'I reckon he'd shot his bolt by the age of 33,
actually.' Again, when Larkin was awarded the Queen's Medal for
Poetry in 1965, he told an interviewer, 'Take this Queen's Medal.
I'm 42, but he got it for "Look, Stranger!" when he was 30. Mind
you, I feel he was played out as a poet after 1940.' This scuttering
between despair and disdain is typical of Larkin in general but it

is also typical of his attitude towards Auden in particular. He prefaced a home-made booklet of poems in 1941 with the gulping confession 'I think that almost any single line by Auden would be worth more than the whole lot put together.' When, in 1972, Auden's bibliographer Barry Bloomfield asked Larkin if he might be his next subject, Larkin expressed both delight and dismay: Bloomfield 'has switched to me now Auden's gone', he told his friend Anthony Thwaite; 'I am not much more than a five-finger exercise after Auden,' he apologised to Bloomfield.)

*

If Philip Larkin was no more than a five-finger exercise compared to Auden, then this – this! – is, what? At the very best, a one-note tribute?

*

Polyphony
↓
Monophony
↓
Penny whistle and kazoo

*

Parnassus after all is not a mountain,
    Reserved for A.1. climbers such as you;
It's got a park, it's got a public fountain.
    The most I ask is leave to share a pew
    With Bradford or with Cottam, that will do.
                                (Auden, 'Letter to Lord Byron')

*

Park?
Fountain?
Pissoir.

*

Perhaps one of the only things the rest of us share with the truly great writers is the sense of struggle, the sense of inadequacy.

Flaubert: 'Sometimes when I find myself empty, when the expression refuses to come, when, after having scrawled long pages, I discover that I have not written one sentence, I fall on my couch and remain stupefied in an internal swamp of *ennuis*.'

Gerard Manley Hopkins: 'Birds build – but not I build; no, but strain, / Time's eunuch, and not breed one work that wakes.'

Katherine Mansfield: 'For the last two weeks I have written scarcely anything. I have been idle; I have *failed*.'

We all know that feeling, that sense of despair and woe-is-me and all-I-taste-is-ashes, and all-I-touch-has-turned-to-dust.

Great writers, it seems, are not necessarily those who are most confident about their own capacities or skills. They are more often keenly aware that words are failing them, and that they are failing words. Like us, they find it difficult.

*

Or rather, most of them find it difficult: Auden was convinced of his own skills and capacities from an early age and went on to fulfil and exceed his early promise.

(His tutor at Oxford, Nevill Coghill, recalled Auden announcing his intention to become a poet. Jolly good, said Coghill – or something donnish to that effect – that should help with understanding the old technical side of Eng. Lit., eh, old chap? 'Oh no, you don't understand,' replied Auden – or again, words to that effect – 'I mean a great poet.')

He seems never to have been lacking in confidence. He seems always to have been convinced not merely of his brilliance but of his sovereignty.

'Evidently they are waiting for Someone,' he told his friend Stephen Spender.

He was that Someone.

*

And me, who am I?

If nothing else, one of the things I have realised over the course of the past twenty-five years, in trying to write a book about W. H. Auden, is the obvious fact that I AM NOT W. H. AUDEN.

*

Other people realise they're not their heroes much earlier, but I was in the slow learners' class in school and seem to be a slow learner still.

I think I probably believed that one day – through sheer will-power and determined slog, through dogged persistence and self-discipline – I might somehow overcome my weaknesses and become an artist of some significance.

It is only recently that I have come to accept my true role and status, which is, obviously, naturally, inevitably, as an utterly insignificant bit-part player in the world of literary affairs.

This is the real trouble with studying major writers: it reminds one of one's minority status.

(Great Lies of Literature No. 1: reading great literature is good for the soul. The truth: reading the greats does not just uplift; it also casts down.)

*

F. R. Leavis once described E. M. Forster, when compared with Henry James, as 'only too unmistakably minor' – though Forster accurately remarked of James that though he might have been a 'perfect novelist', it wasn't a 'very enthralling type of perfection'. It hardly needs stating that I'm not in James's league, nor in Forster's – but, alas, the real truth is that I'm not even in Leavis's league, which is a league no one in their right mind would want to be in anyway, a league whose entry requirements include anger, bitterness and envy. (He was not a great fan of Auden, Leavis, particularly not his irony, which he described as 'self-defensive, self-indulgent or merely irresponsible'. God, one wonders, what would F. R. Leavis make of this?) Reading Leavis, it is clear that I am only too unmistakably minor even in relation to him writing about Forster writing about James – a gnat on a flea on the shoulders of giants. Forster has an essay, 'The C Minor of that Life', whose title is an allusion to Browning's poem 'Abt Vogler', the last line of which begins 'The C Major of this life'. This life is neither C Major nor Minor, but C very much Diminished.

*

(This book, clearly, is not just about Auden. It's about everything else I've been thinking and reading while I've been thinking and reading Auden, and which has influenced my thinking and reading of Auden. As Mr Weller long ago explained to his son, Sam – the archetypal Cockney geezers – in *The Pickwick Papers*: 'Ven you're a married man, Samivel, you'll understand a good many things as you don't understand now; but vether it's worth while goin' through so much, to learn so little, as the charity-boy said ven he got to the end of the alphabet, is a matter o' taste. I rayther think it isn't.')

*

Other things I have come to realise, in passing, as I have been trying to write a book about W. H. Auden, over the course of the past twenty-five years:

- Despite what you may have heard, one's talents do not necessarily grow and develop over time. One's character does not necessarily blossom. Things do not necessarily work out. The unique gift that you might have thought you had to offer the world does not necessarily become apparent to you or to anyone else. There is not just the possibility of loss and waste and failure: failure and waste and loss are *inevitable*. (William Empson, in that wonderful remark about Gray's 'Elegy', in *Some Versions of Pastoral* – my absolute favourite among all of Empson's wonderful remarks: 'And yet what is said is one of the permanent truths; it is only in degree that any improvement of society could prevent wastage of human powers; the waste even in a fortunate life, the isolation even of a life rich in intimacy, cannot but be felt deeply, and is the central feeling of tragedy.')
- There are many individuals whose natural talents far exceed your own.
- There are many individuals whose natural talents may seem far less than your own and yet who will inevitably succeed far beyond your own small successes.
- There will always be something, someone, some circumstance pushing you to the side of your life, something obscuring the view, something preventing you from doing what you thought you might do or being who you thought you might be. For me, that

something, that someone, was Auden: for me, Auden was the problem as well as the solution. Perhaps this is always the case with the people who really matter: wives, husbands, lovers, friends.

*

So what is the final justification for this book, which has taken so long, for so little apparent reason, and which obviously amounts to so little – 70,000 words, give or take, expended in trying to explain Auden's 99-line poem?

*

I can't really claim, as is now often claimed by those attempting to write about their relationship to other – often, conveniently, dead – writers, that this is a record of a 'relationship'. If it is a relationship, it is clearly a very odd sort of relationship, since I never met Auden and realistically never would have met Auden, and if I had done, it seems doubtful we would have got on. He could never have been, for me, as he was for the poet John Hollander, and for many others, 'Like a clever young uncle' or 'like a wise old aunt': I am not someone blessed with such uncles or such aunts. My actual uncle Dave was a minicab driver; my auntie worked at Yardley's. There have been, for me, no mentors: there has been no extending of the hand, no leg-up, no hand-me-downs. (In *Ulysses*, Mr Deasy asks Stephen what an Englishman is proud of – 'I will tell you, he said solemnly, what is his proudest boast, I paid my way ... I paid my way. I never borrowed a shilling in my life. Can you feel that? I owe nothing? Can you?' It's true.) But then, in fairness, I was never really protégé material. My relationship with Auden – had there been anything like a relationship – would have been at best a very vague acquaintanceship, a relationship from a great distance, a one-sided sort of relationship, not so much teacher-to-pupil or guru-to-disciple, as master to his valet.

> I am beginning to lose patience
> With my personal relations:
> They are not deep
> And they are not cheap.
>
> (Auden, 'Case Histories')

This book does not therefore record my 'relationship' with Auden – I have no relationship with Auden in any meaningful sense – so much as my relationship with language, or my relationship with language through Auden. Auden as the *OED*, as *Roget's*, as *Brewer's*, *Fowler's*, *Webster's*, the *Encyclopaedia Britannica*, and *Partridge's Usage and Abusage* and *Dictionary of Slang and Unconventional English* – all of them, combined.

*

('Is it one of those How So-and-So Changed My Life type of books?' asks a friend. 'No,' I say. 'That's a shame,' they say. 'People really like those sorts of books.' 'It's more about my relationship with language, and literature, and ideas,' I say. 'Hmm,' says my friend. 'Well, good luck with that.')

*

One of Auden's great ambitions was to be included in the *OED* – 'that inestimable successor to Holy Writ', as the critic I. A. Richards called it – with his words and phrases listed as coinages and exemplars. It was an ambition he fulfilled many times over, being credited with more than 100 significant usages, including the phrase 'Age of Anxiety' (defined, in the second edition of the

OED, as 'the title of W. H. Auden's poem applied as a catch-phrase to any period characterized by anxiety or danger'), the adjective 'entropic', and the noun 'agent' (abbreviated from 'secret agent'). According to the biographer Humphrey Carpenter, describing Auden's study in his house in Kirchstetten, 'The most prominent object in the workroom was a set of the *Oxford English Dictionary*, missing one volume, which was downstairs, Auden invariably using it as a cushion to sit on when at table – as if (a friend observed) he was a child not quite big enough for the nursery furniture.'

*

(The missing volume – Auden's hardback dictionary cushion – was, according to Carpenter, volume X of the *OED*: (Sole–Sz). Which might provide a nice alternative title for this book, would it not? *Sole–Sz*, a title which offers an obvious homophonic pun on 'sole' and which also usefully alludes to Roland Barthes' *S/Z*, that impossibly complicated book about Balzac's story 'Sarrasine', which was once required reading on every grad course in literary theory, with its typologies of interacting SEM codes and SYM codes, and REF, and ACT and HER codes, and which therefore might suggest that this book too is a work of great theoretical sophistication. Maybe not.)

*

So, not a book about my relationship with Auden. A book about my relationship with language.

*

But we all know – we don't have to be a Roland Barthes to know – that there can be no simple explanation in language of our relationship with language. It's like using a mirror to look at a mirror. Words are insufficient to do justice to words, let alone to everything else.

So the enterprise is doomed again.

*

This is all entirely obvious, I suppose, to most people. And barely needs stating.

All I can safely say, then, is that it has taken me twenty-five years to work out the entirely obvious.

And these are my notes.

In literature, as in life, affectation, passionately adopted and loyally persevered in, is one of the chief forms of self-discipline by which mankind has raised itself by its own bootstraps.

(Auden, 'Writing')

JUST A TITLE

> The reason (artistic) I left England […] was precisely to
> *stop* me writing poems like 'September 1, 1939', the most
> dishonest poem I have ever written.
>> (Auden, letter to Naomi Mitchison, 1 April 1967)

'September 1, 1939'.

If you know anything about the poem – and you may well know more about it than I do, in which case I should warn you, this is probably not the book for you, it's a book for my friends and my cousins, for everyone who has ever said to me, 'W. H. Who? September the What?' – you will know that it was a poem that over the course of his lifetime Auden variously revised and then disowned. It is a poem with a long and troubled history. It is a poem that has undergone a lot of changes. Perhaps that's part of its appeal: it is a poem with another life, an afterlife. It is a poem, like a person, that comes with a lot of baggage.

Even the title changed. We may know it as 'September 1, 1939', but on first publication, in the American magazine the *New Republic*, on 18 October 1939, it was 'September – 1939'; in Auden's collection *Another Time* (1940) it then became simply number four in a sequence of 'Occasional Poems', thus, 'IV. September 1, 1939'; and not until subsequent versions and revisions did it appear as both '1st September 1939' and 'September 1, 1939'.

Auden had a strong habit of revision. (He had strong habits generally: drug habits, writing habits.) He liked to change the titles of his poems, just as he liked to change all other aspects of his poems: 'Palais des Beaux Arts' became 'Musée des Beaux Arts'; 'The Territory of the Heart' became 'Please Make Yourself at Home' became 'Like a Vocation'; 'The Leaves of Life' became 'The Riddle'; et cetera, et cetera; the list is very long.

Not everyone approved of all these rethinks and rewrites, of course. A lot of people thought them arrogant, or foolish, or merely eccentric. The poet and critic Randall Jarrell thought Auden's revisions were not only arrogant, foolish and eccentric; he thought they were morally reprehensible: 'Auden is attempting to get rid of a sloughed-off self by hacking it up and dropping the pieces into a bathtub full of lye,' he wrote, figuring Auden both as a snake, and as an acid-bath murderer.

(If not the greatest critic of poetry in the twentieth century, Randall Jarrell was certainly the greatest reviewer of poetry in the twentieth century, and to be a great reviewer of anything you need to be given to peculiarly vivid language: Clive James writing on television was given to peculiarly vivid language; Anthony Lane writing on films in the *New Yorker*; Dorothy Parker; Virginia Woolf, oddly. But Jarrell was undoubtedly the greatest, the most vivid of all, and he had what one might generously describe as a love–hate relationship with Auden. According to fellow poet John Berryman, Jarrell knew Auden's mind 'better than anyone ought to be allowed to understand anyone else's', even when Auden was in two minds.)

*

But those tiny little adjustments to the title of this poem, do they really matter?

*

Yes.

No.

Of course.

Not really.

Same as anything else.

Does it matter if you leave out that little pinch of salt in your recipe? Would it matter if I was called Samson, instead of Sansom, or Sampson? Simpson? Ivan, not Ian? Ivor? Ifor? Oscar?

(Some years ago, invited to give a reading at a library, I was introduced as C. J. Sansom – the bestselling author of historical crime fiction, and no relation. When I explained that I was not, alas, C. J. Sansom, two women in the audience got up and left. Which was fine, really. The other half of the audience remained.)

> I mentioned that I was afraid I put into my journal too
> many little incidents. JOHNSON: 'There is nothing, Sir,
> too little for so little a creature as man. It is by studying
> little things that we attain the great art of having as little
> misery and as much happiness as possible.'
> (Boswell, *The Life of Samuel Johnson, LL.D.*, 1791)

If one were a certain kind of critic I suppose one might note that a poem titled 'September 1, 1939' clearly, deliberately recalls Yeats's poem 'September 1913', signalling that this is a poem written in response to another. (In his poem 'In Memory of W. B. Yeats', Auden calls Yeats 'silly like us', which he certainly was:

silly like us for believing that we might be able to simplify and sum things up.)

One would also note that a poem titled 'September 1, 1939' clearly announces itself as an American poem: Americans write Month/Day/Year; in the UK we normally write Day/Month/Year.

One might note further that to use a date as a title perhaps suggests that the poem might be something like a diary entry, setting certain expectations and a tone. It suggests that the poem might have been composed or conceived on that specific date, for example – such as Wordsworth's famous sonnet 'Composed upon Westminster Bridge, September 3, 1802' (which was in fact originally published as 'Composed upon Westminster Bridge, September 3, 1803', which rather suggests that it might be foolish simply to read dates in poems as facts in a poet's life, not least because the *actual* date of Wordsworth's crossing Westminster Bridge, according to his sister Dorothy's journal entry, was 31 July 1802).

(One might speculate further, parenthetically, that a minor artist is someone who is very precisely not prepared to risk breaking and bending the rules a little. A definition of the minor artist – the non-Wordsworth, the un-Auden – is that they are not prepared to fiddle around with inconvenient details like dates and facts and figures. As everyone knows, Tennyson got it wrong in 'The Charge of the Light Brigade' when he wrote, 'Into the jaws of Death, / Into the mouth of Hell / Rode the six hundred' – it was closer to 700 who rode into the jaws of death. But when challenged on the point, Tennyson is said to have remarked, 'Six is much better than seven hundred metrically, so keep it.' Poets are not historians, or statisticians.)

One might suggest, furthermore, that a poem whose title appears to commemorate some famous historic event is not necessarily a poem written with the sole intent of commemorating that event. Even Yeats, that great commemorator, who loved to use dates for titles – 'September 1913', written after the Dublin lock-out, and 'Easter, 1916' – wasn't writing manifestos or reports. The titles may be significant but they are hardly a full explanation. Yeats's poem 'Nineteen Hundred and Nineteen', for example, was originally titled 'Thoughts Upon the Present State of the World', which suggests exactly the kind of meandering activity that is going on in much of his work, which is then given shape and focus by the addition of a date and title, rather than proceeding in a straight line either from or towards it.

Which might lead one, finally, towards the conclusion that though a title may appear to come first, very often it may in fact come last: a poem's title may be a post hoc rationalisation. It might also be a false sign.

Or, ultimately, just a title.

*

Anyway.

I'm not that kind of critic.

*

September 1, 1939, as it happens, was a Friday.

Auden had just returned to New York from his road-trip honeymoon with his young lover Chester Kallman. For almost three months – 'the eleven happiest weeks of my life' – they had criss-crossed the nation, from New York to Washington, New Orleans, New Mexico, Arizona and Nevada and on to California. 'C is getting quite a tan', Auden told Chester's father, 'and I scribble away.'

But now the summer of love was over. 'At 32½ I suppose I shall not change physically very much for some time except in weight which is now 154lbs [...] I am happy, but in debt [...] I have no job. My visa is out of order. There may be a war. But I have an epithalamion to write and cannot worry much.'

(*There may be a war. But I have an epithalamion to write and cannot worry much.* It's reassuring, isn't it, that like us – whatever else was happening – Auden *had stuff on.* I remember when the Berlin Wall came down, and it was the end of the Cold War and the beginning of a New World Order, and I was in my early twenties and I was working as a farm labourer up in the Craigantlet Hills, just outside Belfast, and I'd listen to the news on the radio in the morning, but it was like listening to news from another planet: I was busy; I had work to do; I *had stuff on.* It's the whole point of Auden's poem 'Musée des Beaux Arts', which is about Brueghel's painting *The Fall of Icarus*: 'About suffering they were never wrong, / The Old Masters: how well they understood / Its human position; how it takes place / While someone else is eating or opening a window or just walking dully along.' It turns out that I have spent a lifetime walking dully along, unable and unwilling to recognise the extraordinary and the other while it's happening all around me. Like Auden's description of the dogs in his poem, I have simply ambled on, leading my doggy life. Attending to Auden is probably the closest I've ever come to stopping and noticing something truly amazing, an actual Icarus, a boy falling out of the sky.)

*

On the long Greyhound bus journey back to New York on Tuesday, 29 August, Auden wrote to a friend in England, 'There is a radio on this coach, so that every hour or so, one has a violent pain in one's stomach as the news comes on. By the time you get this, I suppose, we shall know one way or the other ...'

In fact, people knew already: *everybody* knew already.

*

In his novel *Coming up for Air*, published in June 1939, George Orwell has his narrator remark:

> I can see the war that's coming [...] There are millions of others like me. Ordinary chaps that I meet everywhere, chaps I run across in pubs, bus drivers and travelling salesmen for hardware firms, have got a feeling that the world's gone wrong. They can feel things cracking and collapsing under their feet.

Auden may have been enjoying his holiday in the sun, but things had been cracking and collapsing for some time.

*

'Europe', writes Antony Beevor in his panoramic history *The Second World War* (2012), 'did not stumble into war on 1 September 1939.' She had been walking steadily towards it for years. In *The Shape of Things to Come*, published in 1933, H. G. Wells had predicted a total war by 1940: 'The tension had risen to a point at which disaster seemed like relief and Europe was free to tear itself to fragments.'

The fragmentation had not begun months or years before: it had begun decades before.

*

A. J. P. Taylor, in his account in *The Origins of the Second World War* (1961), claimed that a second world war 'had been implicit since the moment when the first war ended': it became explicit at exactly 4.30 a.m. on 1 September 1939, when the German panzer divisions which had been gathering on the Polish border began their advance, and the first air raids began. By the time the Soviets invaded northern China in September 1945 – the last campaign of the Second World War – almost 50 million people throughout the world had died, more than half of them civilians; approximately 1000 deaths per hour, every hour, for six years.

*

1 September 1939 inaugurated an entirely new kind of war. World War I had been fought by infantrymen moving slowly, heroically and predictably into battlefields prepared for war: 'They fell with their faces to the foe', in the words of Laurence Binyon's famous poem 'For the Fallen'. But on 1 September, Hitler unleashed 'blitzkrieg' – lightning war, impersonal war, war that was intended to lead to *Vernichtungsschlacht*, annihilation. First came the air attacks and bombing raids, then the motorised infantry and the tanks, followed by the SS Death's Head regiments who conducted what were euphemistically referred to as 'police and security' measures to ensure what Himmler called the 'radical suppression of the incipient Polish insurrection in the newly occupied parts of Upper Silesia'. Within a week, Cracow, with a population of a quarter of a million, was under German control. Twenty-four thousand SS troops had moved into Poland, by train, by plane and on foot; the massacres of civilians began. Villages and towns were set alight. There were public executions.

*

The front-page headline of the *New York Times* on Friday, 1 September 1939 tapped it all out in telegraphese: 'GERMAN ARMY ATTACKS POLAND; CITIES BOMBED, PORT BLOCKADED; DANZIG IS ACCEPTED INTO REICH'. With their trochaic-patterned strong-stressed syllables, one might almost rearrange the lines into verse:

German army attacks Poland;
Cities bombed, port blockaded;
Danzig is accepted into Reich.

The lead column then begins with the words 'BRITISH MOBILIZING'.

Indeed they were – and had been for some time.

*

In England, ever since the Munich Agreement of September 1938, trenches had been dug, air-raid shelters constructed and barrage balloons floated above London. The pictures from the National Gallery had been packed up and sent off to Wales. Most of the British Museum's treasures were safely stored in an underground tunnel in Aberystwyth. Rationing was being planned.

*

And meanwhile, back in America … what exactly was Auden up to?

We know roughly what he was up to.

*

On 12 June 2013, the British Library acquired an Auden manuscript at Christie's in London for £47,475. It was Auden's diary for August and November 1939, written in a 'National' notebook, made in the USA, 'this book contains eye-ease paper, "Easy on the Eyes".' The diary is incorrectly dated, by Auden, 'August 1938'. The entry for 1 September begins 'Woke with a headache after a night of bad dreams in which C [Chester Kallman] was unfaithful. Paper reports German attack on Poland.' There follow several pages of notes on scientific and political subjects – beginning with 'Good News,' [underlined]. 'A scanning microscope has been invented.'

('A scanning microscope' is another way of describing a poem.)

*

At 9.30 p.m. on 1 September, the British government issued an ultimatum to the Nazis to withdraw from Poland.

At 9 a.m. on 3 September, a second ultimatum was issued to the German Foreign Office in Berlin: Sir Nevile Henderson, the British Ambassador, read out the ultimatum to a deserted room.

And then finally, at 11.15 a.m. on 3 September, the British prime minister, Neville Chamberlain, broadcast to the nation on the BBC. The country, he announced, was at war:

> This morning the British Ambassador in Berlin handed
> the German Government a final note stating that, unless
> we heard from them by eleven o'clock that they were
> prepared at once to withdraw their troops from Poland,
> a state of war would exist between us. I have to tell you
> now that no such undertaking has been received, and
> that consequently this country is at war with Germany.

Also on 3 September, the American president, Franklin Roosevelt, made his own radio broadcast, of a very different kind: 'Let no man or woman thoughtlessly or falsely talk of America sending its armies to European fields. At this moment there is being prepared a proclamation of American neutrality.' There would be, Roosevelt promised, 'no blackout of peace in the United States'.

(The proclamation, the American neutrality, the promise of no blackout of peace: Roosevelt's words seem to echo in the words of Auden's poem, which indeed contains a 'proclaim', a 'neutral' and the famous ironic points of light. How many poems, one wonders, are plucked from the ether, and how many from the airwaves? Poets are like thieves and spies; they're always listening in. It's like that film *The Lives of Others*, the one about the spy in East Germany, eavesdropping with his headphones on. Poems are the words of others – the words of us all. There's a poem by Denise Riley, 'Lure, 1963', for example, which is composed of snatches of half-remembered pop lyrics – 'The Great Pretender' by The Platters, 'The Wanderer' by Dion, 'It's in His Kiss' by Betty Everett. One of the truly great works of literary criticism, John Livingston Lowes's *The Road to Xanadu: A Study in the Ways of the Imagination*, a study of the work of Coleridge, basically consists of Lowes eavesdropping on Coleridge's eaves-droppings, tracing every image to its source in Coleridge's read-ing. As a model, Lowes is probably best avoided: the book is pretty much unreadable; *The Road to Xanadu* contains too many detours.)

*

('Does your book have an argument?' asks my editor. 'It's more a series of detours,' I say. 'And cul-de-sacs. And dead ends. And stoppings-short.' 'Like a journey?' 'Sort of like a journey.' This is not a journey. And I am no John Livingston Lowes. This is either the beginning of the preparations for a journey, or the aftermath.)

*

In London, in the days leading up to 1 September, according to *The Times*, things were 'largely normal':

London at this time of tension has retained its usual appearance to a remarkable extent, but there are differences which the continuing crisis has made unavoidable. In the streets one of the most obvious is the banking of sandbags which now shields many buildings. Londoners are carrying on much the same as usual, except that every one is contributing something towards ensuring complete preparedness for any emergency. No worried casualties in a war of nerves are to be seen; the population remain calm, hopeful, and resolute.

('London Largely Normal: Calm in Time of Tension, Defence Activities', *The Times*, Thursday, 31 August 1939)

Calm, hopeful, resolute? Maybe it was. I don't know.

My family were all Londoners. I wish I could have asked them what it was like, but they had things to do. They were busy.

*

On 1 September 1939, my father was busy being evacuated:

The Government decision that evacuation should begin to-day as a precaution was made known yesterday in the following announcement by the Minister of Health, Mr. Elliot, and the Secretary of State for Scotland, Mr. Colville, which was broadcast several times during the day: — It has been decided to start evacuation of the school children and other priority classes as already arranged under the Government scheme to-morrow (Friday, September 1) [...] Mothers and other persons in charge of children below school age should take hand luggage with the same equipment for themselves and their children as for school children. The names of the children should be written on strong paper and sewn on to their clothes. No one can take more than a little hand luggage.

('Evacuation To-Day: Official Advice to Parents,
"A Great National Undertaking"',
The Times, Friday, 1 September 1939)

And my grandfather – who knows? He may well have been busy with the rest of the East End, all those cheerful Cockney geezers preparing for war:

East London is prepared, and the people living in this lively, crowded, industrially important part of the capital are justifiably proud of what they have done towards completing the nation's defences. A tour of East London yesterday was a stirring and heartening experience. At one point, not far from the docks, a piece of waste land had fallen into the hands of a big squad of willing and tireless workers, whose picks and spades were quickly supplying fillings for thousands of sandbags. Stripped to the waist, the men dug vigorously, pausing only now and then to make a fellow-worker laugh with a cheerful quip.

('Cheerfulness in East London: Voluntary Help,
Willing and Tireless Workers',
The Times, Friday, 1 September 1939)

The whole scene sounds highly unlikely, frankly – a fantasy of the *Times* reporter – but on the other hand I can certainly imagine him, my grandfather, George Sansom, stripped to the waist, filling sandbags, ready with a cheerful quip. He was a boxer, a tough guy, a sweet man, and born the same year as Auden, coincidentally, 1907, though his life and Auden's could not have been more different. When Auden was moving from prep school to boarding school, George Sansom was leaving school to go and work at Windsor and Newton paint manufacturers in east London. When Auden was going up to Oxford, George Sansom was going off to work in a factory making orange boxes. And while Auden sat out the war, safe in New York, he served in the Merchant Navy. The year Auden died, George Sansom was retiring from the Post Office, where he'd worked as a postman for most of his adult life. Auden died in Austria, where he'd bought a home on the proceeds of book sales and awards. My grandfather died in Essex, having moved from his council flat in Poplar into sheltered accommodation on a busy main road in Romford. At Auden's funeral, they played Siegfried's Funeral March from *Tristan und Isolde*. After my granddad's funeral at the crematorium, when all the family got together to clear out the flat, I was not surprised to find that there were no books in the house, not a single one, and that he owned only the clothes he stood up in, some bed linen, a few pots and pans, and three LPs: the Massed Bands of the Royal Marines; an Elvis Christmas album; and *The Best of Pavarotti*. His life savings were exactly one hundred and one pounds. When Auden speaks on others' behalf in this poem, as he so often liked to do – 'I and the public', 'We must suffer them all again', 'our wish', 'We must love one another or die' – I wonder if he thought he was speaking on behalf of people like my grandfather. If he did, my grandfather certainly would not have thanked him for it.

*

(I make no apology for bringing in these family matters here, though I'll try not to make a habit of it. Auden's reviews and essays are defiantly personal, of course – but that's always been a perk of the privileged; they're allowed to be defiantly personal, because of who they are. They've earned it. The rich and the famous, we assume, and they assume, are just more interesting than the rest of us. They have permission to do and say what they want. Auden begins an early review, for example, 'If the business of a reviewer is to describe the contents of the books he reviews and to appraise their value, this is not going to be a review.' Well, in that case: this is not going to be a book.)

Anyway, all of this is just to be clear at the outset that a lot was happening on 1 September 1939.

And a lot is happening in 'September 1, 1939'.

1

I sit in one of the dives
On Fifty-Second Street
Uncertain and afraid
As the clever hopes expire
Of a low dishonest decade:
Waves of anger and fear
Circulate over the bright
And darkened lands of the earth,
Obsessing our private lives;
The unmentionable odour of death
Offends the September night.

I ≠ A

The first words of the poem: I sit.

  It's hardly a stirring start, is it?

  Who on earth begins a poem from a seated position?

  And who sits?

  Auden sits?

*

There is no reason to assume that the 'I' who is sitting here at the beginning of the poem is necessarily the poem's author, Wystan Hugh Auden, who was born in York on 21 February 1907, the youngest of three brothers, son of George Augustus Auden, a doctor, and Constance Rosalie Auden (née Bicknell), who had trained as a nurse and who loved opera and who doted on her precocious son. (Of his parents, Auden remarked that 'Ma should have married a robust Italian who was very sexy [...] Pa should have married someone weaker than he and utterly devoted to him. But of course, if they had, I shouldn't be here.')

The 'I' *could* be this Auden – the Auden who we know attended Gresham's School in Holt in Norfolk and who in 1925 went up to Christ Church, Oxford, graduating three years later with an inglorious Third, and who in the late 1920s and 1930s worked variously as a teacher, a reviewer and as a documentary filmmaker with the GPO Film Unit. It could be the Auden who

48

travelled to Weimar Berlin and to Iceland, and who went to
Spain to support the newly formed Republican government,
where he witnessed the brutalities of the civil war and where he
wrote some of his most famous poems, 'A Communist to Others'
and 'Spain 1937', poems which, as with 'September 1, 1939', he
later disowned, describing them as 'dishonest'.

It could be – couldn't it? – this Auden, the Auden who in
January 1939 sailed to America with his friend the playwright
Christopher Isherwood, their departure seen by many in England
as a betrayal of their country in its hour of need, and the Auden
who soon after arriving in New York met the eighteen-year-old
Chester Kallman, who became his lifelong companion and
lover. (They exchanged rings and behaved to all intents and
purposes as a married couple – for better and for worse – even
though in 1935 Auden had already married Erika Mann, the
daughter of the novelist Thomas Mann, in order to assist her
escaping Nazi Germany, an act he described as a 'bugger's duty'.)

It could be him: the Auden who lived his adult life mostly in
New York, teaching at various colleges and universities, who in
1945 served as a major in the US Air Force in their Strategic
Bombing Survey, and who in 1946 became a US citizen. It could
be the Auden who was Professor of Poetry at Oxford from 1956
to 1961, the Auden who summered on the Italian island of
Ischia, the Auden who bought a house in Kirchstetten in Austria
and who published during his lifetime more than a dozen books
of poetry, as well as volumes of essays, plays and libretti, the very
Auden who died in Vienna on 29 September 1973, the death
certificate giving the cause of death as 'hypertrophy of the heart'.

It could be that Auden.

But probably not.

*

There is no need to assume it is Auden who is sitting here at the beginning of the poem, any more than we need assume that the often sad and lonely 'I' in Shakespeare's sonnets, in sonnet 29, say ('When, in disgrace with fortune and men's eyes, / I all alone beweep my outcast state'), is necessarily or entirely the William Shakespeare of Stratford-upon-Avon, who may or may not have been the author of the plays that bear his name and who famously left his wife Anne his second-best bed; or that the wildly jubilant 'I' of Walt Whitman's 'I Sing the Body Electric' is the big-bearded bard from Long Island; or that when we read at the beginning of Anne Sexton's poem 'Double Image' that 'I am thirty this November' we can safely assume that Sexton herself was thirty that November, though she was and we do, we almost always assume that the speaker of a poem, the voice on the page, is indeed the 'I' of the poet.

*

It's definitely not Auden.

*

It's Auden.

> The artist must be in his work as God is in creation,
> invisible and all-powerful; one must sense him
> everywhere but never see him.
> > (Gustave Flaubert, letter to Mademoiselle
> > Leroyer de Chantepie, 18 March 1857)

This is what we do know: an 'I' is not always a self; an 'I' is not a proxy for a person.

> We feel that in the cases in which 'I' is used as subject, we
> don't use it because we recognise a particular person by
> his bodily characteristics; and this creates the illusion that
> we use this word to refer to something bodiless, which,
> however, has its seat in our body. In fact *this* seems to be
> the real ego, the one of which it was said, 'Cogito ergo
> sum'.
>
> (Ludwig Wittgenstein,
> *The Blue and Brown Books*, 1958)

(This is one of the things that poems do for us: they present us with an 'I' that is not a body – but which may be a person. Or if not a person, an ego. Or if not an ego, then a thinking machine. The 'I' is a function. It is an algorithm. A process. The 'I' is – or can be – simply the poem.)

*

You can tie yourself in all sorts of philosophical knots with this sort of thing, obviously: who am I, what is 'I', is 'I' an unchanging object through time and space? But this way metaphysics and ontology lies – which is a route I cannot follow. I am not equipped.

A better, blunter, bluffer question might be not 'Who am I?' or 'Who is "I"?', but rather 'Who cares?'

To which the honest answer is probably: no one. No one cares at all.

Not even if you're W. H. Auden.

Which is, of course, why we write 'I'.

I says 'I am'.

*

Or 'I Am!'

> I am! yet what I am none cares or knows,
>   My friends forsake me like a memory lost;
> I am the self-consumer of my woes,
>   They rise and vanish in oblivious host,
> Like shades in love and death's oblivion lost;
> And yet I am! and live with shadows tost.
>
> (John Clare, 'I Am!')

John Clare wrote this poem in Northampton General Lunatic Asylum, where he spent the last twenty years of his life. Clare – or the 'I' of the poem – clearly feels alone and isolated, the 'self-consumer' of his woes. 'And yet I am!' he writes. It is in this act of defiance, in the act of writing, that he lives.

*

Writing, for many people – for those of us who keep diaries no one will ever read; for those of us who write only for ourselves and perhaps a few others; as for those who pursue literary fame for its own end; and indeed even for those, like Auden, who seem destined for true greatness and are proclaimed geniuses by the world at large – writing, for all of us, in different ways, is a way of saying, 'And yet I am!' Writing is a form of self-proclamation, of self-avowal.

(Philip Roth describes the urge to live on paper in his novel *Exit Ghost*: 'Isn't one's pain quotient shocking enough without fictional amplification, without giving things an intensity that is ephemeral in life and sometimes even unseen? Not for some. For some very, very few that amplification, evolving uncertainly out of nothing, constitutes their only assurance, and the unlived, the surmise, fully drawn in print on paper, is the life whose meaning comes to matter most.' To write is to live the unlived.)

To write is to reveal oneself.

*

It is also a wonderful disguise. Poets, like all other writers, are liars, confabulators and cheats – just read a biography of a poet. Any poet. They're all the same: poets are self-pleasuring beings who like to play around with their 'I', just as they like to play around with everything else.

*

With his 'I' at the beginning of this poem, Auden is donning a disguise. He is putting on a mask.

*

In middle age his face indeed became a mask – a 'wedding cake left out in the rain' is how he liked to describe it. He looked, he said, like 'an unmade bed'. That face, that ruined, piteous, covetable, comfortable face – 'I have a face of putty,' he told Stephen Spender, 'I should have been a clown' – has long been a source of fascination to writers and artists. The philosopher Hannah Arendt remarked that it was 'as though life itself had delineated a kind of face-scape to make manifest the "heart's invisible furies"'. (Humboldt, in Saul Bellow's *Humboldt's Gift*, is described as having 'developed in his face all the graver, all the more important human feelings'. Wouldn't you just love a face, like Auden's, like Humboldt's, in which you had developed all the more important human feelings?) According to Randall Jarrell, Auden looked 'like a disenchanted lion'. The poet Gavin Ewart charted his appalled fascination with Auden's face – what another poet, John Hollander, calls simply 'The Face' – in a poem titled 'Auden':

Photographed, he looked like Spencer Tracy
or even Danny Kaye –
in the late Forties. But later it was wiser
to look the other way.

A young David Hockney, asked to sketch a portrait of Auden, was absolutely horrified: 'I kept thinking, if his face looks like this, what must his balls look like?'

*

Whatever it looks like, whatever it appears to be, perhaps all we can be sure of is that the 'I' in the work of a poet is a complex act of self-dramatisation, a performance. The 'I' in a poem may appear to be referring to something – to someone – but we need not postulate the poet's self as its referent. The 'I' in a poem is not necessarily a proxy for a name.

The I ≠ Auden.

*

I ≠ A.

*

'I' is a persona. Though the persona may of course be Auden: it may be a clever double bluff; 'I' am I; either I am the mask, or the mask has eaten into the face, the performance having become the true self. Henry David Thoreau, at the beginning of *Walden*, reminds his readers that even when the 'I' appears to be absent it's always there, hiding: 'In most books, the I, or first person, is omitted; in this it will be retained; that, in respect to egotism, is the main difference. We commonly do not remember that it is, after all, always the first person that is speaking.'

Writers are always hiding in plain sight.
Madame Bovary, c'est moi.

*

(A couple of years ago I published a book of short stories. Everyone assumed they were autobiographical. Some were auto-biographical. But not the ones that people thought.)

*

Whether we know it or not, we bring great expectations to a poem: we are conditioned to expect something from a poem, as soon as it declares itself a poem, and even more so when an 'I' declares itself at the beginning of a poem. A poetic 'I' implies a particular kind of poem, a lyric poem, the kind of poem we are familiar with from school, a poem which usually promises and delivers intense personal emotions presented in the first person. M. H. Abrams, who was one of those literary critics everyone used to read and now almost no one has heard of – the fate of all critics – defined the Romantic lyric poem as a meditation that 'achieves an insight, faces up to a tragic loss, comes to a moral decision, or resolves an emotional problem'. This is the kind of poem we know what to do with.

So what are we going to get here, in 'September 1, 1939'? An insight? A reckoning? A decision? A resolution?

*

In 'September 1, 1939' we get all of that, and more – which is exactly the trouble, and what Auden hated about the poem, which he described as 'the most dishonest' he had ever written.

*

But we're getting ahead of ourselves. Let's just assume for a moment – as we naturally do – that the 'I' here is an unproblematic person, that the 'I' here is Auden.

Fine.

*

Who the hell is W. H. Auden?

THE MODERN POET

'It's odd to be asked today what I saw in Auden,' replied the American poet John Ashbery to a wet-behind-the-ears interviewer in 1980. 'Forty years ago when I first began to read modern poetry no one would have asked – he was *the* modern poet.'

*

In his 1937 'Letter to W. H. Auden', the poet Louis MacNeice addressed his friend, 'Dear Wystan, I have to write you a letter in a great hurry and so it would be out of the question to try to assess your importance. I take it that you are important.'

*

He was more than important: he was an absolute star. In his book *The Personal Principle* (1944), the literary critic D. S. Savage claimed that during the 1930s Auden was 'the centre of a cult' and, in a telling phrase, described Auden's position thus: 'A new star had arisen, it seemed, in the English sky.' John Berryman recalled that even in America 'by 1935 … the Auden climate had set in strongly'. What Tom Driberg in the *Daily Express* called 'awareness of Auden' was everywhere: it affected things generally; as Boswell breathed the Johnsonian 'oether', so the 1930s breathed the air of Auden. When the *London Mercury* was published for the last time on the eve of the Second World War, Stephen Spender summed things up in an article titled 'The Importance of W. H. Auden': 'Auden's poetry is a phenomenon, the most remarkable in English verse of this decade.'

*

Now, to be clear: not everyone admired Auden. Some people despised him. Hugh MacDiarmid thought him a 'complete wash-out'. Truman Capote, when asked what he thought of Auden's poetry, replied, 'Never meant nothin' to me.' (Though – note – even MacDiarmid, in his polemical autobiographical prose work *Lucky Poet* (1943), attempting to define 'The Kind of Poetry I Want', had to devote much of his time to defining 'the kind of poetry I don't want', i.e. 'the Auden–Spender–MacNeice school'.) The argument against Auden is certainly worth stating and goes something like this:

'W. H. Auden is to blame for everything that went wrong with English poetry in the late twentieth century. Absurdly over-praised when young, he remained naive and immature both as a person and as a poet, his preciosities and youthful good looks becoming vile and monstrous. He was dictatorial in his approach and his opinions, imprisoned by his own intelligence, intellectually dishonest, irresponsible and incoherent, atrociously showy in diction and lexical range, technically ingenious rather than profound, pathetically at the mercy of contemporary cultural and political fashions and ideas, facetious, frivolous, self-praising, self-indulgent, vulgar and ultimately merely quaint: the ruined schoolboy; an example, indeed the ultimate example, the epitome, the exemplum, not of mastery but of Englishness metastasised. Auden undoubtedly thought he was *it* and the next big thing, when in fact he was *It*: the disease, the enemy, The Thing.'

*

This sort of argument has been thoroughly rehearsed down through the years by readers such as F. R. Leavis, and Randall Jarrell (during the hate phase of his love–hate relationship), and Philip Larkin (ditto), and Hugh MacDiarmid, and William Empson. One would perhaps expect all of them to complain – they were world-class complainers – but when someone like Seamus Heaney, *that* Seamus Heaney, the Seamus Heaney, a poet and critic with perfect manners, whose kindness and generosity knew almost no bounds, when even Seamus Heaney, in a review of Auden's *Collected Poems*, writes dismissively of Auden's 'educated in-talk' and of his tone 'somewhere between camp and costive', one might begin to think that there is indeed a serious case to be made against him. Maybe Auden was just a coterie poet; maybe he was just a flash in the pan; a poet merely of his class and his place and his time. William Empson has a poem, 'Just a Smack at Auden', which is certainly very funny, mocking Auden's 1930s doom-mongering ('Treason of the clerks, boys, curtains that descend, / Lights becoming darks, boys, waiting for the end'), but Heaney's summation of Auden's achievement as 'a writer of perfect light verse' is potentially more wounding.

(We may well return to the question of 'light' verse later. But an obvious question has to be, does great literature necessarily have to be 'heavy'? Does it have to be serious and difficult? Does it have to be exhausting and challenging and exceptional? Does every book have to be a pick-axe breaking the frozen sea in our souls? Sometimes it's nice – isn't it? – to hear the sound of a swizzle stick tinkling away at the ice.)

*

Anyway, and nonetheless, and despite the quibbles and the doubts, it would be safe to say that in the 1930s, for those whom it affected, the Auden phenomenon was as disturbing as it was remarkable. The title of Geoffrey Grigson's contribution to the special 1937 *New Verse* Auden double issue, 'Auden as a Monster', is indicative of the fear and excitement generated by Auden's reputation. 'Auden does not fit. Auden is no gentleman. Auden does not write, or exist, by any of the codes, by the Bloomsbury rules, by the Hampstead rules, by the Oxford, Cambridge, or the Russell Square rules,' enthused Grigson; Auden's poetry, he claimed, had a 'monstrous' quality. Other contributors to *New Verse* were similarly impressed by Auden's peculiar strength and power: Edwin Muir described Auden's imagination as 'grotesque'; Frederic Prokosch described his talents as 'immense'; Dylan Thomas described him as 'wide and deep'; Bernard Spencer claimed that he 'succeeds in brutalizing his thought and language'.

*

Auden was clearly regarded – as great writers often are by their contemporaries – as somehow superhuman, or rather subhuman, inhuman, freakish. (Stephen Spender, in his *Journals*, recalls being accused of making Auden 'sound a bit inhuman': 'This did ring a bell,' he writes, 'because I remember when we were both young thinking of him as *sui generis*, not at all like other people and of an inhuman cleverness. I did not think of him as having ordinary human feelings.')

*

(I tend to fall into this trap today, with writers I know and admire: they are just not, I think, like me. They are different; they are special; they are odd. Which is both true, as it happens, and entirely false.)

*

With its emphasis on Auden's 'monstrous' qualities, his physicality, his animality, his otherness, the *New Verse* double issue inaugurated a significant theme in subsequent figurations of Auden. In numerous books, reviews, essays and poems, Auden is figured as a kind of predatory Übermensch, possessing great physical prowess and preternatural powers. The English poet Roy Fuller, for example, described him as a 'legendary monster', an 'immense father-figure','ransacking the past of his art'. The poet Patrick Kavanagh claimed that 'a great poet is a monster who eats up everything. Shakespeare left nothing for those who came after him and it looks as if Auden is doing the same.' Such language can't help but admire as much as be appalled.

Auden is a hero.

Auden is a monster.

*

His intelligence was superlative and frightening. (He was 'the greatest mind of the twentieth century', according to the Russian poet Joseph Brodsky. 'At one or another time there must be five or six supremely intelligent people on earth,' writes Howard Moss in his book *Minor Monuments*. 'Auden was one of them.')

His appearance was outlandish. ('I was struck by the massive head and body and these large, strong, pudgy hands, […] the fine eyes did not look at oneself or at any individual but directly at concepts,' wrote the critic G. S. Fraser.)

And his troubled career was strangely exemplary. (Seamus Heaney's decision to leave Northern Ireland and move to Wicklow in 1972, for example, was read by some critics as a symbolic gesture similar to Auden's move to America in 1939.)

He was a creature to be feared as well as admired, an obstacle to be negotiated as well as an inspiration.

'He set standards so lofty that I developed writer's block,' recalls the poet Harold Norse in his *Memoirs of a Bastard Angel: A Fifty-Year Literary and Erotic Odyssey* (1989).

Even now he remains a barrier. This book, for example: both blocked and enabled by Auden, a classic example of reading in abeyance, a testament to his posthumous power, and a confession and demonstration of my own lowly subaltern status and secondariness.

*

(My interest in Auden, like anyone's interest in any poet, any writer or artist, any great figure who has achieved and excelled in a field in which one wishes oneself to achieve and excel, represents an expression of awe, and disappointment, and self-disgust – and goodness knows what other peculiar and murky impulse is lurking down among the dreck at the bottom of one's psyche. My interest in Auden represents perhaps a desire, if not actually to be Auden, then at least to be identified with Auden. My grandfather used to sing a song, 'Let me shake the hand that shook the hand of Sullivan', referring to John L. Sullivan, the one-time world heavyweight champion. How much literary criticism, one wonders, is in fact a vain attempt to shake the hand of Sullivan? *U & I* is the title of the novelist Nicholson Baker's book about his – non-existent – relationship with John Updike, for example. An alternative title for this effort might be *A & I*. But this implies an addition. Better: *I – A*?)

The continual cracking of your feet on the road makes a
certain quantity of road come up into you.

(Flann O'Brien, *The Third Policeman*)

'Biographers are invariably drawn to the writing of a biography
out of some deep personal motive,' according to Leon Edel, the
biographer of Henry James. Freud's famous criticism of biogra-
phers was that they are 'fixated on their heroes in a quite special
way', and that they devote their energies to 'a task of idealiza-
tion, aimed at enrolling the great man among the class of their
infantile models – at reviving in him, perhaps, the child's idea
of his father'.

I don't think I am reviving in Auden an idea of the father. But
it's possible that I might be reviving in him an idea of the uncle.
The kind of uncle I never had.

(Auden was, by all accounts, an excellent uncle. He sponsored
war orphans to go to college. He supported the work of Dorothy
Day's homeless shelter for the Catholic Worker Movement. He
did not stint in doing good.)

*

He was many things to many people. As every critic notes,
Auden's book *The Double Man* (1941) begins with an epigraph
from Montaigne, 'We are, I know not how, double in ourselves,
so that what we believe we disbelieve, and cannot rid ourselves
of what we condemn.'

*

But he wasn't really double, any more than anyone is double:
anyone, everyone is multiple.

So, to go back to that question, who the hell was W. H.
Auden?

He was a poet, a dramatist, a librettist, a teacher, an amateur psychologist, a journalist, a reviewer, an anthologist, a critic, a Yorkshireman, an Englishman, an American.

That'll do, for starters.

NOT STANDING

So why is he sitting at the start of the poem?
   And how is he sitting?
   Is he on a chair? A stool? A bench?
   Is he perched on a stoop or a stairwell?

*

(And – my wife asks, appalled, having read the first draft of this
book, twenty-five years after I embarked upon it – are you really
going to spend all that time worrying over every single word in
the poem?)

   Many poets have some idiosyncrasy or tic of style which
   can madden the reader if he finds their work basically
   unsympathetic, but which, if he likes it, becomes
   endearing like the foibles of an old friend.
                                    (Auden, 'Walter de la Mare')

Of course I'm not going to worry over every single word in the
poem. That would be ludicrous – unfeasible, and unhealthy.

*

(Really unhealthy. Fatal. In a lecture on 'The Art of Literature and Commonsense', collected in his *Lectures on Literature*, Nabokov remarks that 'In a sense, we are all crashing to our death from the top story of our birth [...] and wondering with an immortal Alice in Wonderland at the patterns of the passing wall. This capacity to wonder at trifles – no matter the imminent peril – these asides of the spirit [...] are the highest forms of consciousness.' Twenty-five years of falling to my death, gazing around, wondering at trifles.)

*

Let me reassure you: we may have started out on the scenic route, but I promise there are going to be short-cuts. There's just a lot of heavy lifting to get through at the start. Think of all this as backstory. Think of these early chapters as foundation stones, as building blocks, as ... bricks.

(In Joe Brainard's cult classic *I Remember* he writes, 'I remember a back-drop of a brick wall I painted for a play. I painted each red brick in by hand. Afterwards it occurred to me that I could have just painted the whole thing red and put in the white lines.' I'm not going to be painting each red brick by hand: after a while, I'll be sketching in white lines.)

Civilization is a precarious balance between what
Professor Whitehead has called barbaric vagueness and
trivial order.

(Auden, 'The Greeks and Us')

(I have been reading – I have been teaching – Erich Auerbach's essay 'Odysseus' Scar', the first chapter of his book *Mimesis: The Representation of Reality in Western Literature*, published in 1946. It is surely one of the last great, readable works of literary criticism, in which Auerbach distinguishes between Hellenistic and Hebraic modes of storytelling:

> It would be difficult, then, to imagine styles more
> contrasted than those of these two equally ancient
> and equally epic texts. On the one hand, externalized,
> uniformly illuminated phenomena, at a definite time and
> in a definite place, connected together without lacunae in
> a perpetual foreground; thoughts and feeling completely
> expressed; events taking place in leisurely fashion and
> with very little of suspense. On the other hand, the
> externalization of only so much of the phenomena as
> is necessary for the purpose of the narrative, all else left
> in obscurity; the decisive points of the narrative alone
> are emphasized, what lies between is nonexistent; time
> and place are undefined and call for interpretation;
> thoughts and feeling remain unexpressed, are only
> suggested by the silence and the fragmentary speeches;
> the whole, permeated with the most unrelieved suspense
> and directed toward a single goal (and to that extent far
> more of a unity), remains mysterious and 'fraught with
> background.'

It's like that old Lenny Bruce routine – Jewish or goyish? In Bruce's estimation, Count Basie is Jewish, Ray Charles is Jewish – but Eddie Cantor, Eddie Cantor is goyish. The joke being that Eddie Cantor was Jewish, but he was nothing more than a smooth, crowd-pleasing entertainer. 'If you live in New York or any other big city, you are Jewish. It doesn't matter even if you're Catholic; if you live in New York, you're Jewish. If you live in Butte, Montana, you're going to be goyish even if you're Jewish.' Auden was a High Church Anglican, but he's definitely Jewish, in the same way Count Basie and Ray Charles are Jewish: his best poems are Hebraic rather than Hellenistic. They are fraught with background.)

*

I imagine Auden sitting in a straight-backed chair, both feet flat on the floor, upright, sitting slightly forward, intent – like a sphinx, benevolent, ferocious, strong.

*

One of the most famous of the early photographs of Auden is the head-and-shoulders snap taken by Eric Bramall in 1928, showing Auden sitting with head bowed, lighting a cigarette. Or at least, I think he's sitting – I'm not entirely sure. It's not quite clear. The image has been reproduced numerous times on book covers and in feature articles and probably owes its enduring appeal to its ambiguity: the pose is simultaneously feminine and macho, coy and defiant; Bramall has captured a gesture of the kind that Roland Barthes describes, in *Camera Lucida* (1980), as 'apprehended at the point in its course where the normal eye cannot arrest it', providing a privileged glimpse that stimulates in the viewer a secret or erotic thrill. W. H. Auden is Humphrey Bogart. He is Marlene Dietrich. Joan Didion. Tom Waits. (The critic Cyril Connolly admitted to having been 'obsessed' with Auden's physical appearance, recalling a homoerotic dream in which Auden 'indicated two small firm breasts' and teased him with the words, 'Well, Cyril, how do you like my lemons?')

There's no denying it. Look at the photos.

Auden is sexy.

Seriously.

*

Anyway. How he is sitting is less important than the fact that he is sitting: at the outset of the poem, he is assuming a definite relationship with and towards the world and towards the reader. He is adopting a particular posture.

What he's not doing is standing.

*

After a decade of running around all over the place – travelling to Iceland and to China and to Spain, and also undertaking vast intellectual journeys, from Marx to Freud and on towards Kierkegaard – sitting was something that Auden now believed people should be doing: being rather than doing, thinking rather than acting. He began his Smith College Commencement Address in June 1940 with these words:

> On this quiet June morning the war is the dreadful
> background of the thoughts of us all, and it is difficult
> indeed to think of anything except the agony and death
> going on a few thousand miles to the east and west of
> this hall. While those whom we love are dying or in
> terrible danger, the overwhelming desire to do something
> this minute to stop it makes it hard to sit still and think.
> Nevertheless that is our particular duty in this place at
> this hour.

It is our particular duty in this place at this hour to sit with him.

*

(In the poems where Auden is most truly himself, he is either sitting or lying down: 'Out on the lawn I lie in bed'; 'Lay your sleeping head, my love'; the flirtatious male of 'In Praise of

Limestone' who 'lounges / Against a rock in the sunlight, never doubting / That for all his faults he is loved.')

*

And if he's not standing, he's certainly not walking.

*

(After all these years, I realise I have no idea how Auden might have walked. I know in his later life he was famous for shuffling around outside in his carpet slippers, but how exactly did he walk? What was his gait? The truth is, I know both too much about Auden – endless, useless facts about him – and absolutely nothing. I know a lot of useless facts about a lot of writers: about William Burroughs, I know how he injected his morphine and how he scored his Benzedrine inhalers; I know the precise details of his sexual relationship with Allen Ginsberg, including the size of his penis; I know all about Marianne Moore's tricorne hats, and Elizabeth Bishop's taste in home furnishings; I know about Jack London's sweet tooth; I have read Reiner Stach on Kafka; and Richard Ellmann and Michael Holroyd on everyone. All of these books, all of this endless information about writers – and for what? If Auden were in the distance now, walking away from me, I wouldn't be able to recognise him. After all these years, I couldn't spot him in a crowd. He remains a total stranger.)

> In grasping the character of a society, as in judging the
> character of an individual, no documents, statistics,
> 'objective' measurements can ever compete with the
> single intuitive glance.
>
> (Auden, 'The American Scene')

In his essay 'My First Acquaintance with Poets' (1823), William Hazlitt recalls one fine morning, in the middle of winter in 1798, going for a walk with Coleridge:

> I observed that he continually crossed me on the way by shifting from one side of the foot-path to the other. This struck me as an odd movement; but I did not at the time connect it with any instability of purpose or involuntary change of principle, as I have done since. He seemed unable to keep on in a straight line.

Coleridge's strange saunter was matched only by his curious conversation. 'In digressing,' writes Hazlitt, 'in dilating, in passing from subject to subject, he appeared to me to float in air, to slide on ice.'

I can't imagine Auden sliding, or indeed shimmering, like Jeeves. Striding, maybe? No. Slouching? A little. Sauntering? Strolling? Strutting? Slinking? Shambling? No. No. No. Schlepping? Maybe, a little.

Auden, I imagine, would have schlepped like a mensch.

*

(He loved this sort of thing himself, of course, categorising people according to some weird feature. In *The Orators*, for example:

> Three kinds of enemy walk – the grandiose stunt – the melancholic stagger – the paranoic sidle.

> Three kinds of enemy bearing – the condor stoop – the toad stupor – the robin's stance.

Three kinds of highly entertaining bullshit.)

*

Just because he's sitting, he's not necessarily immobile. He's not inactive. He is observing. He is concentrating. He is preparing himself for the poem, perhaps, gathering his energies. When we think of authors sitting, we imagine them sitting with single-mindedness and with purpose – don't we? – sitting still but getting somewhere, going inwards.

❧

Or maybe he's just posing. He's pouting. He's sitting for a portrait.

(There is no recent book-length study of the phenomenon of the poet as pin-up, as far as I know. The best I can find is David Piper's *The Image of the Poet*, which was published in 1982, long before our current crop of selfie-loving Insta poets. Auden would have made an excellent Insta poet: he loved the camera. He was arguably – at least, I shall argue here, now – the first poet of the technologised twentieth century, his career formed not just through books but through the media of film, photography, radio, television, mass-circulation newspapers and poetry readings. Not only was he enormously ambitious, he was endlessly inventive. He used all the tools available to him. He took a camera to Iceland in 1936, and the photographs were included in his and MacNeice's travelogue, *Letters from Iceland*. At his parties in the 1950s, long before Warhol's snapping and spooling at the Factory, he would go around photographing his guests. The critic Edmund Wilson describes a truly Warholian scene at Auden's birthday party in 1955: 'Hordes of people arrived; the room became crowded and smoke-filled and the conversation deafening. Wystan went around with a camera taking flashlights of his guests. When he came to the group in which I was, I hung a handkerchief over my face at the moment he was taking the picture.')

*

Or perhaps he's 'sitting in', in the way a jazz musician sits in on a session.

The songwriter and historian of American popular music Arnold Shaw explains what it means to 'sit in':

> A man who sits in plays music that is unrehearsed, improvised and spontaneous. But the difference is that he invades a place where a set group of musicians is in residence at union rates. He comes for the sheer love of playing, for the stimulus of exchanging ideas with others, for the pleasure of speaking and communicating through his instrument.
>
> 'Sitting in' implies a freedom of movement, a body of shared feelings and a camaraderie that tended to disappear with the rise of bop and with the stringent enforcement of union regulations against free play. It was also based on a rare community of interests between performer and audience that placed *communication* and *expression* on the same level as *entertainment*. When the adventure worked, all three phases were present at a peak of excitement.
>
> (Arnold Shaw, *52nd St: The Street of Jazz*)

Communication, expression, entertainment: as good a definition as any of what one might expect from a work of art.

*

Of course, the mere fact of sitting – whatever kind of sitting it is – says something. It says, 'I am here with you.' When we sit next to somebody we are sitting with them. We sit alongside them, or opposite them. We sit shiva. We sit and wait. We sit and eat.

> 'You must sit down', says Love, 'and taste my meat.'
>> So I did sit and eat.
>>> (George Herbert, 'Love: Love bade me welcome')

In *The American Journal of Nursing*, vol. 70, no. 5 (May 1970), there is a letter to the editor from Louise Ryssmann, R.N.:

> I would like to contribute this idea to other nurses. When I am talking with patients, I sit in a chair next to the bed, rather than standing. By sitting, I can establish a closer rapport with patients because the physical distance is less and I am talking directly across rather than down to the patient. Sitting also creates a more relaxed atmosphere and the patient feels the nurse is not rushed and has time to talk. And as an additional benefit, I am not nearly as tired at the end of an eight-hour shift.

At the beginning of the poem Auden settles down, establishes a close rapport and starts to talk. Like a nurse, or a priest, or a therapist.

Or a man in a bar.

A NOT INSIGNIFICANT
AMERICANISM

I want the poem to be completely American in language.
(Auden on *The Age of Anxiety*,
in *The Table Talk of W. H. Auden*)

*

So, the speaker of the poem is sitting in a dive, and a dive, according to the *OED*, is 'An illegal drinking-den, or other disreputable place of resort, often situated in a cellar, basement, or other half-concealed place, into which frequenters may "dive" without observation.'

A dive is not, therefore, just a place to be seen or to look, but a place to disappear.

Auden is using a half-concealed place as a site of contemplation.

*

'Dive', by the way, is an Americanism. It's worth pointing out. It is not insignificant.

*

In a poem for his old friend Louis MacNeice, Auden wrote of his own desire to become a 'minor Atlantic Goethe'.

Which is exactly what he became.

*

He took the oath of allegiance and became an American citizen on 20 May 1946. His *Collected Poetry* had been published in America by Random House a year previously and had gone into its fourth impression, having already sold over 14,000 copies. (That's a lot of copies for a book of poems. It's a lot of copies for a book of anything. I would love a book of mine to sell 14,000 copies – even a third of 14,000 copies would do, a quarter. A tenth. I'll be honest, I'd take a tenth.) On this evidence, the critic Edmund Wilson pronounced that Auden had achieved 'almost the circulation of an American family poet'. Auden had, in other words, made it in America.

*

Though for America, one should probably read New York.

> Who am I now?
> An American? No, a New Yorker,
> who opens his *Times* at the obit page.
>
> (Auden, 'Prologue at Sixty')

He had arrived in New York with Christopher Isherwood on 26 January 1939. The two men had already visited America in the summer of 1938, on their way back from China, but this time they were there to stay.

On arrival in New York, they found rooms in the George Washington Hotel on 23rd Street and Lexington Avenue, and by spring 1939 they had moved into an apartment together on East 81st Street. Auden began reviewing for magazines and started to undertake speaking and lecturing engagements. He was getting his feet under the table.

*

Their departure from England caused considerable controversy. During 1940, the pages of Cyril Connolly's magazine *Horizon* were given over to a long-long-running debate about the rights and wrongs of the two young men's decision to remain in America, and in June 1940 Sir Jocelyn Lucas MP asked in the House of Commons 'whether British citizens of military age, such as Mr. W. H. Auden and Mr. Christopher Isherwood [...] will be summoned back for registration and calling up, in view of the fact that they are seeking refuge abroad'. The whole fuss was satirised by Evelyn Waugh in his novel *Put Out More Flags* (1942), in which Auden and Isherwood are caricatured as Parsnip and Pimpernell: 'The name of the poet Parsnip, casually mentioned, re-opened the great Parsnip-Pimpernell controversy which was torturing Poppet Green and her friends.'

Poor little Poppet.

*

(It's easy to mock, but I too have taken Auden's move to America personally, as a kind of rebuke, just as I've done with friends who've moved to America over the years. I mean, it always makes one wonder, doesn't it? Shouldn't I? Couldn't I? What might have been, could have been? As I get older, it gets worse, the challenge seems all the greater. 'What have I done for you, / England, my England?' asks W. E. Henley in his much-maligned poem 'Pro Rege Nostro'. Not a lot, is the honest answer: paid my taxes, kept out of trouble, apologised unnecessarily as and when required, and suffered in silence as the country becomes slowly but surely despoiled and divided up among tax-shy corporations and the south-east super-rich. Why not go to America, Auden seems to be asking, if you're just going to sit around complaining and doing nothing?)

*

(I will confess: years ago, in an attempt to write this book, to reinvent myself, I went to New York, to follow in Auden's foot-steps, with nothing more to sustain me than a pacamac, a bar of Kendal mint cake and a pair of good stout shoes. I lasted about two weeks.)

*

There were many who felt that Auden's remaining in America during the war was both a personal let-down and a matter of serious consequence. Poets, naturally, expressed their disappointment in verse: Christopher Lee, in a poem titled 'Trahison des Clercs', wrote wistfully about 'the poets we took for leaders', 'these swift migrating birds'; and Alan Ross took up the plaintive chant in his poem 'A Lament for the "Thirties" Poets', bemoaning 'They who for us were', and drily observing 'Their world and their words subsiding like flat champagne'.

Some people had good reason to take umbrage at Auden's behaviour: John Lehmann, for example, in the second volume of his autobiography, *I Am My Brother* (1960), describes a visit from Auden in 1945 on his way to Germany to work with the US Strategic Bombing Survey, during which Auden boasted to Lehmann about America's contribution to the war: 'There was no word from Uncle Sam Auden about what we had endured, the various skills, the faith, the unremitting industrial and mili-tary effort without which the fortress of Western civilization could never have held.'

And there were others who simply never forgave Auden for leaving. I think I have already mentioned the novelist Anthony Powell: 'I'm *delighted* that *shit* has gone ... It should have happened years ago ... Scuttling off to America in 1939 with his boyfriend like a ... like a ...'

Like a … like a … like a … Like a what exactly, Anthony? Spit it out, man. Like a …? What *is* Auden?

I'll tell you what he is: he is neither/nor.

*

After his trip to America in 1909, Freud remarked to Ernest Jones, 'America is a mistake; a gigantic mistake, it is true, but none the less a mistake.' Auden's move to America has often been viewed in similar terms, both by his contemporaries and by the literary historians and anthologists whose attempts to accommodate the move have obscured his place in literary history. In 1950, T. S. Eliot expressed his delight that Auden's 'influence, on both sides of the Atlantic, has only increased year by year; he can now justly be called "a famous poet"'. In fact, Auden's transatlantic fame and influence had only been achieved at the cost of his being disowned by both sides, by both England and America.

*

In his introduction to the 1970 anthology *British Poetry Since 1945* – standard issue when I was at school – Edward Lucie-Smith announced that he had decided not to include work by Auden because his 'long residence in America seemed to make him an American rather than a British writer', a decision ratified by George Watson in his 1991 critical survey *British Literature since 1945* – standard issue when I started teaching – from which Auden is excluded, along with Isherwood and Robert Graves, for being an 'expatriate'.

(It is interesting to compare the disapprobation that attaches to the word 'expatriate' with the valorisation of the word 'exile' in the formation of a writer's reputation.)

Unfortunately for Auden, the official keepers of American poetry have long been happy enough without him. For the mighty Norton anthologies, for example, Auden's residence in America was simply not enough: he does not figure in *The Norton Anthology of American Literature*, but he is included in *The Norton Anthology of English Literature*, and is safely ensconced in *The Norton Anthology of Poetry*, 'a wide and deep sampling of the best poetry written in the English language, from early medieval times to the present day'.

A comparison with T. S. Eliot, who became a British subject in 1927, is perhaps instructive, not least because Eliot himself sanctioned such a comparison in his essay 'American Literature and the American Language' (1953), in which he defined his position in the national literatures in direct relation to Auden: 'I do not know whether Auden is to be considered as an English or as an American poet: his career has been useful to me in providing me with an answer to the same question when asked about myself, for I can say: "whichever Auden is, I suppose I must be the other."'

There is in fact no equivalence of the kind suggested here by Eliot: while Auden is usually considered neither/nor, Eliot is often assumed to be both/and: Norton, for example, hedge their bets and include Eliot in both their English and American anthologies.

In many ways, Auden is the odd man out.

*

(When and how exactly, one wonders, does a writer become an American writer? Was Nabokov, for example, ever really an American writer? He certainly liked to think of himself as one – 'I am as American as April in Arizona,' he told an interviewer in 1966. And again: 'I feel intellectually at home in America.' And again: 'I am an American, I feel American.' And again: 'America is the only country where I feel mentally and emotionally at home.'

Arriving in America in 1940, aged forty-one, with his wife Véra and their young son Dmitri, Nabokov lived in the USA for over twenty years, teaching at Wellesley and Cornell, and writing many of his greatest novels in and about and around America, not least *Lolita* (1955), which was scribbled on his beloved index cards in his equally beloved Oldsmobile while touring the country on his long summer butterfly-hunting expeditions. Among other things, *Lolita* – whether you like it or not – is a celebration and denunciation of what Humbert Humbert calls that 'lovely, trustful, dreamy, enormous country'. But could Nabokov – or Auden – ever really be regarded as an American writer in the same sense that, say, F. Scott Fitzgerald or Sinclair Lewis, or John Updike, or Lydia Davis and Toni Morrison, are American writers? Updike probably had it about right: Nabokov, he declared back in the 1960s, is 'the best writer of the English language presently holding American citizenship'. And Auden was the best poet.)

*

(Auden's odd example has been useful to me, I should say, in my own modest way: he has helped me understand my own peculiar position. I happen to have lived on the island of Ireland for most of my adult life, but I'm clearly not an Irish writer, nor ever will be. I was born in England and live here in the north, in Northern Ireland, which is a double disqualification for Irishry, yet which also puts me at a far distance from the English and from English concerns. Like a lot of other people, I'm not a both/and: I'm a neither/nor.)

(Once, years ago, I was invited and then disinvited to a literary festival, when it was discovered that though I live on the island of Ireland, I am not in fact an *aboriginally* Irish writer: the festival organisers made it sound rather as though I had set out to deceive.)

*

Anyway, so, he's in a dive – and it's not an English dive.

(In William Empson's poem 'High Dive' (1955), a dive produces 'A cry, a greenish hollow undulation / Echoes slapping across the enclosed bathing-pool.' Empson's note to his poem is instructive. There are two ways down from a diving board, he writes: 'solid and airy, one of which the man must take'. In Louis MacNeice's poem 'The springboard' – dated June 1942 – a figure prepares to dive, 'spreadeagled above the town': 'He will dive like a bomber past the broken steeple, / One man wiping out his own original sin / And, like ten million others, dying for the people.' These are very different types of dive. Off the top of my head – and according to my notes, and without the assistance of Google, which is no good for this sort of thing anyway – they are the only other dives I can think of in English or Irish poetry. I'm sure there are many others. You'll let me know.)

*

Auden's dive is a place, not an action – though the more obvious English meaning of 'dive' puts a nice bit of tension, a little spring, into the line, from sitting to diving. (What might it mean to sit in a dive – to squat and to pause on the springboard?)

*

Imagining Auden's dive, one thinks perhaps of a Hopperesque sort of a place, a place of isolation, melancholy and alienation. So where is this dive?

It's in America, as we know.

But where exactly?

A ROLLING TOMATO
GATHERS NO
MAYONNAISE

It's on Fifty-Second Street.

*

So now we're getting somewhere.
    Aren't we?

*

In 1939, the Federal Writers' Project of the Works Progress
Administration – part of the great Roosevelt-funded programme
that provided employment for over six thousand writers, editors
and researchers to produce a series of state guides to America –
published their *Guide to New York City*, 'A Comprehensive Guide
to the Five Boroughs of the Metropolis'. The city of New York, the
Guide explained, 'is the largest in the Western Hemisphere', with a
population, in 1938, of exactly 7,505,068, in an area of just
332.83 square miles. The New York depicted in the pages of the
Guide is a city of vivid nightmares and astonishing dreams, a place
of cigar stores, rooming houses, hustlers and street hawkers, the
'Negro metropolis', 'the greatest city of the Jews', 'the most popu-
lous Italian city outside of Italy', and 'the world's third Irish city',
as strange and beautiful a place as anyone could possibly imagine.
    In his famous hymn to the city, *Here is New York*, published
in 1949, E. B. White described the place as 'without any doubt

the greatest human concentrate on earth, the poem whose magic is comprehensible to millions of permanent residents but whose full meaning will always remain elusive'.

For Auden, in 1939, New York was a puzzle waiting to be solved.

*

The Arts Project of the W.P.A. was, perhaps, one of the noblest and most absurd undertakings ever attempted by any state.

(Auden, 'Red Ribbon on a White Horse')

*

The WPA *Guide* works its way steadily from neighbourhood to neighbourhood, from street to street and building to building, offering commentary and insight (the old Custom House is 'somewhat ponderous in its neoclassic treatment', the Empire State Building is 'a great inland lighthouse', while 'the gaunt trestle-work of the els [elevated railways] brings twilight to miles of streets'). Fifty-Second Street, it notes, 'lying in the shadow of the Rockefeller Center between Fifth and Sixth Avenues', is renowned for its nightclubs and is therefore 'the source of much of the gossip of columnists and radio commentators'. At No. 72 there is the Little Club, and then at No. 66 the Famous Door, with its state-of-the-art glass-brick vestibule, and Leon and Eddie's (popular with out-of-towners), and the Twenty-one Club, Tony's, the Hickory House, and the black-and-white edifice of the Onyx – places known for their hot jazz and sizzlin' steaks. On any given night of the week you'd have been able to relax, glass of bourbon in hand, rib-eye set before you, and sit back and listen to Pee Wee Russell, Count Basie, Muggsy Spanier and Eddie Condon.

The *Guide* does not mention, however, the other kind of delights and temptations on offer in the area, including those available at the Dizzy Club, situated at 62 West 52nd Street. This gay bar, according to Harold Norse, in his *Memoirs of a Bastard Angel*, was a 'sex-addict's quick fix, packed to the rafters with college boys and working-class youths under twenty-five'.

And it was this particular 52nd Street dive – 'a writhing mass of tight boys in tighter pants', according to Norse – that Wystan Auden, the thirty-two-year-old English poet and new arrival in New York, preferred to frequent.

*

In his journal entry for 1 September, Auden writes, '10.30 Went to the Dizzy Club. A whiff of the old sad life. I want. I want. Je ne m'occupe plus de cela. Stopped to listen to the news coming out of an expensive limousine.'

It seems likely, then, that he was actually there: the *actual* Auden was in an *actual* dive on the *actual* September 1, 1939.

This is hardly news, and maybe it doesn't even matter.

*

(Does it matter? Does it matter, for example, if Marco Polo ever went to China? According to scholars, he probably didn't. Pierre Bayard, the French psychoanalyst and critic, and the author of *Comment parler des livres que l'on n'a pas lus?* (2007) and *Comment parler des lieux où l'on n'a pas été?* (2012), argues that what he calls the 'aberrant space' created by writers who imagine places is in fact a kind of comfort zone that resembles 'the universalized space of a collective mythology in which numerous readers can find themselves'. It's for this reason that we can all still recognise Wessex, say, or Laurie Lee's Cotswolds, or travel to Oz and Skull Island: these places are all true fictions, projections and idealisations of places, domains and realms of the imagination. Similarly, time in writing, just like space, according to Bayard, possesses an 'essential chronological mobility, a mobility that allows it to belong simultaneously to several periods, and whose transitory reunion writing illuminates and deepens'. A book's then is not really a then, then, any more than its here is exactly here. September 1, 1939, in this kind of a reading, is just the title of a poem, and Fifty-Second Street a place that occurs therein. Bayard proposes what he calls 'an atopic criticism' that would 'draw on all the consequences of the permeability of the boundaries between the space of the work and real space' – a proposal, in other words, to treat literature as literature and not as, say, geography, or history. Writing is not documentary. Poems are not necessarily statements of fact, even when they claim to be statements of fact.)

*

Does it matter?
Of course it matters.

*

We are forced to rest content with assumptions – if I want the door to turn, the hinges must stay put.
(Ludwig Wittgenstein, On Certainty)

*

Maybe it matters, but what's more important than whether or not the dive in the poem is indeed the Dizzy Club – motto, 'A rolling tomato gathers no mayonnaise', according to the historian Ellen NicKenzie Lawson in *Smugglers, Bootleggers, and Scofflaws: Prohibition and New York City* (2013), and which sported a sign behind the bar which read 'WYBMADIITY', and if a customer asked what it meant, the barman would reply, 'Will you buy me a drink if I tell you?' – is the fact that it is definitely on 52nd Street.

*

Known as Harlem Downtown, and also as Swing Street and Swing Alley, in Sammy Cahn's famous 1937 song, 52nd Street is described as 'the place where the swing cats meet'. (The other famous song, about 42nd Street, ten blocks to the south, from the 1933 Busby Berkeley musical *42nd Street*, claims that it's the place 'Where the underworld / Can meet the elite […] Naughty, bawdy / Gaudy, sporty / 42nd Street.') According to the *Variety* editor Abel Green, in the late 1930s 52nd Street was 'the nocturnal heart of America'. According to Arnold Shaw, in his book *52nd St.: The Street of Jazz* (1977): 'If you flagged a taxi in NYC and asked to be taken to The Street, you would be driven, without giving a number or avenue, to 52nd between Fifth and Sixth avenues.' 52nd Street was The Street: a midtown Manhattan block of five-storey brownstones, 'in whose drab and cramped street-level interiors – once known as English basements – there were more clubs, bars, bistros and boîtes than crates in an overstocked warehouse'.

*

52nd Street was at the centre of things – literally. (It was midtown, which was 'the new center of life in Manhattan' – according to Ric Burns and James Sanders, in *New York: An Illustrated History* (1999) – 'an intricate, ultramodern nexus of office buildings, department stores, apartment houses, and hotels', which had sprung up around Grand Central Terminal to service the modern new industries of advertising, communications, PR and mass-market entertainment. Midtown was where whatever was it was at.)

For years, between the mid-1930s and the 1950s, the clubs on 52nd Street – the Onyx, the Famous Door, the Three Deuces, Leon and Eddie's, Hickory House, Kelly's Stable, Club 18, Downbeat, Tillie's Chicken Shack, the Troc – were where you went to hear Art Tatum, Coleman Hawkins, Teddy Wilson, Lester Young, Dizzy Gillespie, Charlie Parker, Benny Goodman, Artie Shaw, Jack Teagarden, Buddy Rich … ('Fifty-Second Street was a mother,' according to Dizzy Gillespie. 'I say mother – and I don't mean motherfucker, though it was that, too.' Many of the clubs on the street had once been speakeasies. Several had been owned by Owney Madden, and Jack 'Legs' Diamond, and other notorious mobsters.)

It was seedy, it was splendid: it was central.

*

(It's interesting, isn't it: Auden had left England, where he was the centre of attention; and here on 52nd Street he quickly found himself at the centre of the action. He seemed to have a knack, a knack I've never possessed. I've never been anywhere near the centre of things. I've always lived on the fringes, at the edge: the end of the Central Line when I was growing up, literally and metaphorically; and now again, the end of an actual line in a small town on an island off an island off the mainland of Europe. I'm undoubtedly attracted to Auden's centrality because I am so entirely marginal. Auden was gay: I am straight. Auden a poet: I write prose. Central: marginal. Major: minor. Serious: less so. Opposites, etc.)

*

So what is Auden – or whoever the hell it is – doing sitting in this dive on 52nd Street, in the heart of Manhattan?

He is drinking, probably.

But you don't go to a dive just to drink: you can drink in any old bar.

You might go to listen to the music.

But you can listen to music elsewhere: at home, on the radio, at the concert hall.

You might go to meet other people.

But you can meet other people elsewhere: at work, at church, anywhere.

We should remember, lest we forget, as the poem really gets going, as it soars into the mystic and the ethereal, that a dive – or at least Auden's dive, the Dizzy Club – is a very particular place of encounter.

It's a pick-up joint.

A voice was heard from a bottle of hock,
saying:
I am the ghost of W. H. Auden's cock!
(Gavin Ewart, 'The Short Blake-Style
Gnomic Epigram')

'Never write from your head,' Auden advised John Pudney, 'write from your cock.' Auden was a writer who was more than willing and able to – excuse the expression – write from his cock. I am not, however – you will be delighted to hear – going to be writing about Auden's cock. Or indeed more generally about Auden and sex. It is not my area of expertise. Plenty of people have written about Auden and sex. Writing about writers and sex is boring. Unless it's not boring, in which case it's just weird. (All that discussion about Proust's reputation as the 'rat man', for example, with scholars and critics trying to identify exactly how he liked to achieve orgasm. By having caged rats set upon each other, apparently, in case you're interested, which I'm sure you're not. It was the kind of thing you could get people to do for you in Parisian brothels if you were in receipt, as Proust was, of the equivalent of about £10,000 private income per month. There was also his fetish for photographs, of course; and his obsession with cleanliness; and so on and so forth. If Proust was odd, which he certainly was, then his critics and biographers are surely even more perverse.)

*

(It's not just me who thinks sex is boring, by the way. Don't take my word for it. In an interview in Herbert Dreyfus and Paul Rabinow's *Michel Foucault: Beyond Structuralism and Hermeneutics* (1982), none other than Foucault himself remarks, 'I must confess that I am more interested in problems about techniques of the self and things like that rather than sex ... sex is boring.')

> Both in conversation and in books, people today are
> only too ready to take their clothes off in front of total
> strangers.
>
> (Auden, *Secondary Worlds*)

(But, just for the record, because it is no doubt fascinating – in his fascinating book *A Mind of Its Own: A Cultural History of the Penis*, the historian David Friedman points out that, in ancient Rome, a boy was often given something called a bulla, 'a locket containing a replica of an erect penis', to wear around his neck, which was known as a 'fascinum' and was said to signify his status and power, which is why 'today, fifteen hundred years after the fall of Imperial Rome, anything as powerful or intriguing as an erection is said to be "fascinating"' – just for the record, Auden's most famous erotic work is titled 'The Platonic Blow', thought to have been written in 1948, and published in 1965 in an issue of *Fuck You: A Magazine of the Arts*. It is also known as the 'Gobble Poem'. I'm not going to discuss it here. You can look it up online. In his 1939 journal, Auden criticises 'the American habit of washing one's hands after pissing, as if the penis were an object, too filthy for any decent person to touch'. I am not going to fiddle with this any further.)

*

What is perhaps relevant to this poem though, at this point, is to remember that Auden has only recently acquired a young lover, Chester Kallman, who was a student, eighteen years old when they met in April 1939, fourteen years Auden's junior, and that they had fallen in love, and that Auden believed that his new life had now properly begun. (He wrote to his brother in May 1939: 'Just a line to tell you that it's really happened at last after all these years. Mr Right has come into my life. He is a Roumanian-Latvian-American Jew called Chester Kallman.')

Maybe *this* is why he's uncertain and afraid. Maybe he's nervous. For all his adventurousness, he was English, after all. He's got a serious boyfriend, the love of his life, he's just back from honeymoon, and here he is, no longer as young as he used to be, sitting in a gay bar, alone – or maybe not alone.

Maybe it's making him anxious – the whiff of the old sad life.

Or maybe it's because of something else.

CLEVER-CLEVER

It is not enough to show how clever we are by showing
how obscure everything is.

(J. L. Austin, 'A Plea for Excuses')

A lot of clever things have been written by a lot of clever people
about the exact meaning of the 'clever hopes' of Auden's 'low
dishonest decade', but it's probably worth remarking that 'clever'
in the context of this poem is a bad thing.

(Indeed, in many poems, and in British English generally,
'clever' is a bad thing: it usually implies 'clever-clever', a clever
dick, a clever clogs, a clever boots, a clever shins, a cleverkins. The
closest American equivalent to a clever dick is probably a smart
ass, but smart ass implies street smarts while a clever dick is
likely to have their nose in the air and their head in the clouds.
In Browning's poem 'Bishop Blougram's Apology' (1855),
Blougram accuses the journalist Gigadibs of being 'clever to a
fault / The rough and ready man who write apace, / Read some-
what seldomer, think perhaps even less.' The English are suspi-
cious of 'clever': 'To be clever in the afternoon argues that one is
dining nowhere in the evening,' remarks Saki in one of his short
stories.)

*

If in later life Auden was often accused of being pompous, whimsical and clumsy, in his early life he was often dismissed as being merely 'clever'. A reviewer in the *Times Literary Supplement*, for example, writing about Auden's early book *The Orators*, remarked that 'On the lowest level it is very clever': clever clearly being only entry-level for serious consideration by a reviewer in the *TLS*. (Flann O'Brien's novel *At Swim-Two-Birds* was described in the same paper – which is essentially a paper for clever clogs, by clever clogs about clever clogs – as being 'as clever as paint', which is a backhanded compliment, paint being only clever insofar as it covers a multitude of sins.)

*

(And clever, note, is not scholarship: a review of Auden's *Nineteenth Century Minor Poets* splutters, 'Neither in Mr Auden's introduction, nor in the notes […] is there a word about textual sources' – *Times Literary Supplement*, 27 July 1967, p. 670. Disgraceful!)

*

Auden's clever hopes, then, are really clever-clever hopes – too-clever-by-half hopes, not-as-clever-as-they-think-they-are hopes, hopes that are destined to disappoint. The clever hopes he's presumably referring to include the Treaty of Versailles, the Covenant of the League of Nations, the Dawes Plan, the Locarno Treaties, the Young Plan, the Conference for the Reduction and Limitation of Armaments, the Tanggu Truce, the Pact of Friendship, Neutrality and Nonaggression between Italy and the Soviet Union, the German–Polish Non-Aggression Pact, the Soviet–Czechoslovakia Treaty of Mutual Assistance, the Franco-Soviet Treaty of Mutual Assistance, the Anglo-German Naval Agreement, the Anti-Comintern Pact, the Munich Agreement, the Molotov–Ribbentrop Pact … and every other pact, treaty and agreement after the First World War, all of which we now think of as leading directly to the Second World War, but which at the time were largely intended to avoid any such thing.

*

And what exactly – in brief – was 'low' about the 'low dishonest decade'? The definitive account can be found in the historian Piers Brendon's book *The Dark Valley: A Panorama of the 1930s* (2000) – a 700-page masterpiece – which enumerates the many ways in which 'During the ten years after 1929 […] America, Germany, Italy, France, Britain, Japan and Russia […] traversed a dark valley inhabited by the giants of unemployment, hardship, strife and fear.'

I shan't traverse that dark valley so many before me have trod – or indeed attempt a climb I cannot hope to achieve.

> Who in his daydreams does not prefer to see himself as
> a leader rather than a follower, an explorer rather than
> a cultivator and a settler? Unfortunately, the possibility
> of realizing such a dream is limited, not only by talent
> but also by time, and even a superior gift cannot cancel
> historical priority; he who today climbs the Matterhorn,
> though he be the greatest climber who ever lived, must
> tread in Whymper's footsteps.
>
> (Auden, foreword to Adrienne Rich's
> *A Change of World*, 1951)

But I shall venture to suggest, if I may, that Auden has descended here, at a startlingly early point in his poem, to the kind of grand gesturing that will eventually rather spoil and overwhelm 'September 1, 1939'.

If you're summing up a decade, after all, why not a century or an epoch? And why not start issuing edicts and instructions? Why not start telling your readers how they think, and what to think, and how they behave, and how to behave? Which is exactly what Auden goes on to do in the poem – 'low dishonest decade' is therefore, one might argue, the exact moment when the rot sets in.

(Great writers, alas, and poets in particular, are often tempted to write about the human condition with a capital H and a capital C: it's the price we pay for their wisdom and their fancy phrases; every genius, it seems, is more than capable of writing guff about the Human Condition and the State of the World. Personally, I always get a little queasy when writers start to pronounce on these matters, though of course I like nothing better than to pronounce on them myself.)

*

In a letter to his friend E. R. Dodds, Auden once claimed that a poet should have 'direct knowledge' of the major political events of his time. He certainly did have direct knowledge of the political events of his time, of the clever hopes of the low dishonest decade: he'd been in Spain during the civil war; and he'd been in China with Isherwood, where they wrote *Journey to a War* (1939), their reflections on the Sino-Japanese War. Perhaps he felt that this first-hand knowledge gave him the right to make his great oracular pronouncements, although as he grew older he rather changed his mind. In his T. S. Eliot Memorial lectures in 1967, he remarks:

In our age we are familiar with the case of a man, by nature a novelist or poet, who has to decide whether he will devote himself to his art alone or become politically engagé. On this issue his conscience is genuinely divided. One voice tells him, quite correctly, that politics is a dirty business, and if he meddles with it he will have to compromise his artistic integrity. Another voice tells him, equally correctly, that the voice of social justice is more important than the cause of art. And as a rule, backing the second voice, is a motive of which he's not conscious – the ambition of every man to shine in a field which is not his natural one: in the case of the artist, to come out of his cave and play a public role.

For better or for worse, 'a low dishonest decade' sees Auden emerging from his cave to play a public role.

One thing's for sure: once you start bandying about such grand phrases, there is trouble ahead.

VARIOUS COSMIC
THINGUMMYS

And so the trouble comes, in the very next line of the poem, with 'Waves of anger and fear'.

*

(And yes, yes, this is still the first stanza of the poem, but we're nearly there: the foundations are almost laid. At least, I hope the foundations are almost laid. I remember I was putting in some foundations for a small retaining wall in our front garden a few years ago, and I rang my dad for some advice and told him the dimensions of the wall and he suggested the depth of the footing required, the amount of concrete I might need and the number of blocks, but in the end I couldn't be bothered to go to all that trouble, so instead I just cut down the height and dimensions of the wall and went for shallow footings and a dry concrete mix for the base. 'It's a rustic look,' I said to my sister when she came to survey the wobbly, uneven construction, a wall so low it looks more like a path. It could almost be the remains of a Bronze Age hut found in an archaeological dig. Civilisation needs proper foundations.)

*

They're radio waves, as it turns out, the 'Waves of anger and fear', rather than ocean waves, although we don't learn that until the next line – and no matter how many times I read the poem I can't quite get away from thinking that there is a hint of moisture in this first stanza (the dives, the waves), just as there's fire (the points of light, the affirming flame) in the last stanza, and earth and air in between (the neutral air, the haunted wood).

*

(This is doubtless wilful, wild and whimsical misreading on my part – John Berryman begins one of his *Dream Songs* 'Misunderstanding. Misunderstanding, misunderstanding', and I hear you, John – but it's also because I'm coming at the poem with certain expectations. I am conditioned to expect waterworks in Auden's work.)

*

In his juvenilia and at the early stages of his career, Auden could barely begin a poem without recourse to water imagery of some kind: 'The twinkling lamps stream up the hill'; 'The sprinkler on the lawn'; 'Who stands, the crux left of the watershed'; 'Doom is dark and deeper than any sea-dingle'; 'Fish in the unruffled lakes'. Auden was obsessed with water as an element which the poet must in some way regulate and control: images of water provide a way of dramatising moments of crisis in his work, of inviting and overcoming threats and challenges, and, finally, they provide a way for him to imagine much-longed-for rest and bliss. In the poem 'Lullaby', from his last volume, *Thank You, Fog* (1974), the speaker yearns for oceanic oblivion:

Now you have licence to lie,
naked, curled like a shrimplet,
jacent in bed, and enjoy
its cosy micro-climate:
Sing, Big Baby, sing lullay.

(According to several sources, Auden believed his greatest success was to have been quoted by a prostitute in prison complaining about the infrequency of showers with a line from his poem 'First Things First': 'Thousands have lived without love, not one without water'.)

*

I am conscious of having opened a floodgate here, but let's follow this little tributary for a moment. It may get us somewhere.

*

While teaching at the Larchfield Academy in 1931, Auden wrote to his friend Gabriel Carritt:

The school gathers mildew. Numbers down, the
headmaster partially blind, his wife growing gradually
mad in a canvas shelter in the garden. I spend most of my
time adjusting the flow of water to the lavatories.

Humphrey Carpenter dismisses this account, claiming that it contains a 'certain amount of fantasy', but the critic Tom Paulin has made the valuable point that 'Auden the amateur plumber is a witty version of his view of the poet as a responsible maker, a kind of social engineer.' Paulin is correct: poet as plumber is indeed a domesticated version of a dominant trope in Auden's early poetry, which figures the writer as stowaway, sailor, even as a ship, the *Wystan Auden Esquire*, battling against the sea.

*

In a review in 1933 he wrote:

> What is a highbrow? Someone who is not passive to his experience but who tries to organise, explain and alter it, someone in fact, who tries to influence his history: a man struggling for life in the water is for the time being a highbrow.

Waves and water always provoke excitement and anxiety in Auden; his poetry exhibits what, in the work of Freud's great follower Sandor Ferenczi, is called a 'thalassal regressive' tendency, associating water with the water of the womb and with man's prehuman development, what Ferenczi, in *Thalassa: A Theory of Genitality* (1938), called a 'striving towards the aquatic mode of existence abandoned in primeval times'. In his poetry written in early adulthood Auden often imagines the sea as a hostile force, 'ungovernable' and transgressive, and resorts naturally to the sea as an image of crisis: 'the dangerous flood of history' in his poem 'August for the people', and 'Time's toppling wave' in 'Fish in the unruffled lakes'. In an intense love lyric first published in 1934 and later retitled as 'Through the Looking-Glass', he compares life and love to a seafaring journey and describes 'My sea' as 'empty' and its waves as 'rough'.

*

I could go on. But I don't need to: Auden usefully gathered together his thoughts about waves and oceans in a series of tour-de-force lectures at the University of Virginia in 1949, published as *The Enchafèd Flood* in 1950, in which he describes the sea as 'that state of barbaric vagueness and disorder out of which civilisation has emerged and into which, unless saved by the effort of gods and men, it is always liable to relapse'.

*

(The poet Ivor Gurney wrote of Walt Whitman,'he has taken me like a flood'.)

*

The waves in 'September 1, 1939' turn out to be radio waves, but no less dangerous than the waves of encroaching oceans.

Radio waves really were circulating over the bright and darkened lands from New York in 1939: the new national radio networks were based in midtown, NBC having made its inaugural broadcast in 1926 from the Waldorf-Astoria Hotel at 34th Street and Fifth Avenue, and CBS having set up its studio at 52nd Street and Madison Avenue in 1929. (The old RKO symbol showed a radio mast set atop the globe, beaming out to the hemispheres.)

Radio waves were everywhere during the 1930s: in America, these were the pioneering years of radio soaps and comedy hours, of radio jingles, and of FDR's fireside chats. The waves brought news, and entertainment, and reports and dramatisations of horror, mystery and crime. They were also a useful means of announcing states of emergency, both real and imagined: Orson Welles had broadcast his dramatisation of *The War of the Worlds* on CBS a year previously, at 8 p.m. on Sunday, 30 October 1938. (Recent research suggests that the story of mass panic excited by the programme is in fact a myth, a sort of hoax around a hoax: it seems that more people were listening to a popular Sunday-night comedy variety show, hosted by the ventriloquist Edgar Bergen, which was airing on NBC at the same time, than were listening to Orson Welles ventriloquising H. G. Wells.)

*

In *Understanding Media: The Extensions of Man* (1964), Marshall McLuhan describes radio as a tribal medium – which is nicely put. Demagogues and lunatics in every age are always looking for the means to influence the language of the tribe: radio, TV, Facebook, Twitter. In 1937, a film called *The Girl From Scotland Yard* featured a villain who fired 'radio thunderbolts' down from his plane, like Zeus, or some poet, or a president spraying out their words, obsessing our private lives.

*

In his comedy of manners *Private Lives* (1930), Noël Coward has Amanda say, 'I think very few people are completely normal really, deep down in their private lives. It all depends on a combination of circumstances. If all the various cosmic thing-ummys fuse at the same moment, and the right spark is struck, there's no knowing what one mightn't do.'

The fusing of cosmic thingummys is now about to happen – unexpectedly, entirely unbeknown to Auden – in this poem, in the very final lines of the very first stanza. But before the final lines, I should probably say something about the stanza as a whole. It is an important technical matter.

*

Remember Auden's two questions?

Speaking for myself, the questions which interest me
most when reading a poem are two. The first is technical:
'Here is a verbal contraption. How does it work?' The
second is, in the broadest sense, moral: 'What kind of a
guy inhabits this poem? What is his notion of the good
life or the good place? His notion of the Evil One? What
does he conceal from the reader? What does he conceal
even from himself?'

And remember, in a sense, that the first question is easy to
answer? 'September 1, 1939' consists of 99 lines, written in trim-
eters, divided into nine eleven-line stanzas with a shifting rhyme
scheme, each stanza being composed of just one sentence, so
that – as the poet Joseph Brodsky has usefully pointed out – the
thought unit corresponds exactly to the stanzaic unit, which
corresponds also to the syntactic and grammatical unit ...
    Pause.
    Note: *each stanza is composed of just one sentence.*
    So, that means that 'September 1, 1939' is a poem that
consists of just nine sentences. Nine. Nine! The grammarian and
the linguist may speak of clauses and phrases and parts of speech,
but for most of us, for everyday purposes, the standard unit of
meaning and of style is the sentence. We might think of the
sentence, therefore, not merely as the foundations, and the
bricks, and the planks, the pantiles and the timber frame of a
work of art, but also as the pelmets, the architraves, the knick-
knacks and the soft furnishings. Without the sentence, not only
would there be no house; there would be no home. It is by the
sentence that the writer stands or falls. Or, indeed, crawls, or
wanders, or runs. And Auden uses just nine sentences in this
poem, to build and furnish the whole thing. There are nine
sentences in this stupid paragraph alone; I know, I've counted.

*

('First I write one sentence: then I write another. That's how I write. And so I go on. But I have a feeling writing ought to be like running through a field.' Lytton Strachey, quoted by Virginia Woolf in *A Writer's Diary*, 1 November 1938.)

*

A sentence can fizz, or swish, or gabble. It can be solemn. It can be heroic. It may be hollow. When we admire a writer, what we are admiring are their sentences. And a beautiful sentence will be as different as are all beautiful things. It may be graceful, or gorgeous, or comely. It may – in the parlance of the property developer and the estate agent – be 'stunning'.

And I think that a lot of the time, with his sentences in this poem, Auden is attempting to dazzle: he wants to be *stunning*.

*

And why not? Why shouldn't he? George Saunders has an essay, 'The Perfect Gerbil', about the short-story writer Donald Barthelme, in his book *The Braindead Megaphone* (2007), in which he explains that a part of the appeal of Barthelme's work 'involves the simple pleasure of watching someone be audacious'. Saunders claims that 'the real work' of a story 'is to give the reader a series of pleasure-bursts'.

If nothing else, in 'September 1, 1939', in the very shape and structure of 'September 1, 1939', Auden is being audacious. Each stanza a sentence, no more, no less: let's be honest, it's showing off. It's a game.

*

And the metre! Ah, the metre: roughly, trimeters throughout, just three metrical feet per line, a cramped little space compared to the standard stretch of pentameter. Trimeters: a verse form

more suited to love songs and ballads than big discursive state-
ments about the state of the world. Again, Auden is setting
himself a challenge. (Yeats uses the same metre in 'Easter 1916',
so it's like, if he can do it, I can do it. 'Perhaps giving oneself a
tight structure, making limitations for oneself, squeezes out new
substance where you least expect it,' writes Doris Lessing, in her
preface to my old Flamingo paperback of *The Golden Notebook*,
1972.)

> The impulse toward the metrical organization of
> assertions seems to partake of the more inclusive human
> impulse toward order. Meter is what results when the
> natural rhythmical movements of colloquial speech are
> heightened, organized, and regulated so that pattern
> – which means repetition – emerges from the relative
> phonetic haphazard of ordinary utterance.
>
> (Paul Fussell, *Poetic Meter and Poetic Form*)

We know that Auden believed metrical order, regularity, to be a
primary defence against disorder, a method of preventing the
great flood of ideas and language overwhelming him.

Writing in his essay 'Tennyson' (1944), he wondered about

> the relation between the strictness and musicality of a
> poet's form and his own anxiety. It may well be, I think,
> that the more he is conscious of an inner disorder and
> dread, the more value he will place on tidiness in the
> work as a defense, as if he hoped that through his control
> of the means of expressing his emotions, the emotions
> themselves, which he cannot master directly, might be
> brought to order.

Musicality, strictness, tidiness – Auden adopted these themes as principles in his own practice and also as the criteria for judging his readers. 'Every poet has his dream reader: mine keeps a look-out for curious prosodic fauna like bacchics and choriambs.'

I am not, by any means, Auden's dream reader – I can barely tell my bacchics from my choriambs – but I think I can safely say that the showy, stunning, extraordinary prosodic and structural features of this poem are not insignificant.

OFFENSIVE SMELLS

Anyway, finally – finally! – we are at the end of the first stanza, with the 'unmentionable odour of death', and this is where things start to get really uncanny and unpleasant.

> Personally I have no bone to pick with graveyards, I
> take the air there willingly, perhaps more willingly than
> elsewhere, when take the air I must. The smell of corpses,
> distinctly perceptible under those of grass and humus
> mingled, I do not find unpleasant, a trifle on the sweet
> side perhaps, a trifle heady, but how infinitely preferable
> to what the living emit, their feet, teeth, armpits, arses,
> sticky foreskins and frustrated ovules. And when my
> father's remains join in, however modestly, I can almost
> shed a tear.
>
> (Samuel Beckett, 'First Love')

(One of my grandfathers, my other grandfather, my mother's father, was at Belsen. He was with the Royal Engineers. He was a digger driver. He died when I was quite young, but I remember this about him: he barely ate anything at all; dry toast and boiled eggs. He could not bear the smell of food, which reminded him, no doubt, of the unmentionable odour of death.)

*

There is an article to be written, if it hasn't already been written, on the scentscape, the scentsibilities of Auden's poems, and their peculiar human qualities. In Part III of Book I of *The Orators*, 'Statement' has a list of human types: 'One charms by thickness of wrist; one by variety of positions; one has a beautiful skin, one a fascinating smell. One has prominent eyes, is bold at accosting. One has water sense; he can dive like a swallow without using his hands.'

The smellscape of Auden's work: tracing the references to smells *in* the work. But then there's the smell *of* the work: the dried prunish note of the books, rotting and mulching on my shelves for twenty-five years; my own long exposure to the physical, biological fact of the work; our olfactory reception of books.

*

As for the odour in this poem, it could be that Auden remarks upon it because he was struck by the strange, disorientating smell of New York, of America, of the New World, the stink, the stench and the reek of it, compared to Olde England, that strange smell of a different place, a different city, with all the little 'infra-human' smells, the fragrance of men and women raised on all-American diets. The smell of sex, the whiff of the sad old life: the funk of the dive. Or it could be memories of China, of Spain: the actual unmentionable odour of death.

> In any modern city, a great deal of our energy has to
> be expended in not seeing, not hearing, not smelling.
> An inhabitant of New York who possessed the sensory
> acuteness of an African Bushman would very soon go
> mad.
>
> (Auden, 'The Justice of Dame Kind')

Whatever it is, this strong-smelling phrase is an important part of the lingering effect of the poem, and precisely because – alas – it 'Offends the September night'.

*

(When we think of a phrase beginning 'the odour of' we might usually think of the proverbial phrase 'the odour of sanctity' – and the poem undoubtedly reeks of that too. What does it smell like? 'Dr. George Dumas, of Paris, some time ago made a critical investigation of a number of cases in which mention is made of the odour of sanctity in the lives of certain saints, and he supplies physical explanations of them. The odour varies, being compared to the smell of the lily, the rose, the violet, the pineapple, and so forth. Subject to special modifications, Dumas gives the following general formula for the odour of sanctity: $C_6 H_{12} O_2$' – 'The Odour of Sanctity', *British Medical Journal*, 2:2706, 9 November 1912.)

*

In *Here is New York*, published in 1949, E. B. White remarked that:

> All dwellers in cities must live with the stubborn fact of annihilation; in New York the fact is somewhat more concentrated because of the concentration of the city itself, and because, of all targets, New York has a certain clear priority. In the mind of whatever perverted dreamer might loose the lightning, New York must hold a steady, irresistible charm.

The lightning was eventually loosed on 11 September 2001, in a series of coordinated attacks on New York by the terrorist group al-Qaeda.

*

Of the 2,749 murder victims of the terrorist attacks on the World Trade Center in 2001, only 292 'whole' bodies were ever recovered: the New York City Medical Examiner's Office defines 'whole' as 75 per cent or more of the body. According to Chip Colwell-Chanthaphonh, an adviser to a number of 9/11 family advocacy groups, 'thousands of fragments of human bodies descended with the grey ash of the World Trade Center that rained over the city. The human detritus ended up on rooftops and in sewers and intermixed with the steel and concrete of the skyscrapers.' That grey ash contained also burning rubber, plastic, metal, man-made fibres, silica, pulverised glass, concrete dust, lead, mercury and all sorts of other heavy metals, and led to the creation of a choking dust cloud over Ground Zero – which we now know has caused high levels of cancer among those working and living in the area at the time, including the thousands of men and women involved in rescue, recovery and reconstruction. (Christine Todd Whitman, who was head of the Environmental Protection Agency, the EPA, under George W. Bush at the time of the 9/11 attacks, and who told the public the air was safe to breathe, has since admitted that she was wrong.)

The unending unmentionable odour of death.

*

After 9/11, Auden's poem immediately struck a chord.

Last Wednesday I e-mailed W. H. Auden's poem
'September 1, 1939' to members of my family. Two days
later a friend e-mailed it to me, having received it from
another friend who was circulating it. On Saturday my
mother told me that Scott Simon had read portions of it
on NPR. And on Monday my wife, a prep school teacher,
saw it lying on the faculty photocopy machine.

(Eric McHenry, 'Auden on Bin Laden',
Slate, 20 September 2001)

Newspapers published the poem on their editorial pages. It was
discussed and circulated everywhere.

*

This terrible, incredible moment in the poem's afterlife has been
exhaustively researched and discussed by Stephen Burt, in
'"September 1, 1939" Revisited: Or, Poetry, Politics, and the Idea
of the Public', an essay published in *American Literary History*
(2003). It's a good essay. It's a great essay. Crucially, Burt asks the
central important question, which is why this poem should have
been the one that was adopted by readers at a time of national
crisis.

There are lots of reasons for the poem's continuing appeal –
this book is about some of them – but it's important to acknowl-
edge the simple fact that 'September 1, 1939' found a new
audience at *that* particular moment in American and world
history because it just so happens to be a poem that mentions
September, and New York, and circulating fears, and the unmen-
tionable odour of death, all in the first stanza. It was the right
poem, in the right place, for a wrong time.

*

(In October 2001, the poet Lawrence Ferlinghetti claimed that henceforth poetry would be dated as 'B.S. and A.S. – Before and After September 11'. Auden's poem is unique in that it spans, and seems to speak directly to, two eras and two centuries.)

*

Whatever the reasons, the horror of 9/11 reminded readers of Auden. 'In the past year, Auden has been everywhere, by the sheer force of popular will,' wrote Adam Gopnik in a piece in the *New Yorker* on the first anniversary of 9/11. 'Even fashion models, and not just fashion models, now name their sons Auden, as they might ten years ago have called them Dylan, and pose with them on the cover of *Vogue*.'

*

So, at the end of the first stanza, we have some unnamed individual, sitting in a dive in New York, speaking of their fears and concerns.

(You get the feeling that they're lonely – don't you? – this 'I'. Keith Douglas's great unfinished poem 'Bête Noire' contains the lines 'The trumpet man to take it away / blows a hot break in a beautiful way / ought to snap my fingers and tap my toes / but I sit at my table and nobody knows / I've got a beast on my back.')

And this is surely one of the things that draws us towards Auden's poem, again and again: that lonely frightened figure, surveying the world outside.

(Perhaps all great poems represent or contain such a figure, and express such a fear? The Psalms? Shakespeare? Milton? Wordsworth?)

*

'The attractiveness of America to a writer', Auden told an interviewer for the *Saturday Review of Literature* in 1940, 'is its openness and lack of tradition. In a way it's frightening. You are forced to live here as everyone will be forced to live. There is no past. No tradition. No roots – that is, in the European sense.'

Welcome, everyone.

This is the modern world.

2

Accurate scholarship can
Unearth the whole offence
From Luther until now
That has driven a culture mad,
Find what occurred at Linz,
What huge imago made
A psychopathic god:
I and the public know
What all schoolchildren learn,
Those to whom evil is done
Do evil in return.

A LITTLE SPANK-SPANK

Stanza 2.
    Accurate scholarship.
    Oh dear.

                        *

There was nothing remotely accurate about Auden's own schol-
arship. It wasn't accurate scholarship at all: it was wide reading.
There is a difference. I should know.

   Writers, on the whole, are just *not* scholars. (Cynthia Ozick, in
her essay 'Toward a New Yiddish': 'To be a writer is to be an
autodidact, with all the limitations, gaps, and gaucheries typical
of the autodidact, who belabors clichés as though they were
sacral revelation.')

   This is a book, it goes without saying – a phrase no scholar
would ever use ('Why say it goes without saying if it goes without
saying?') – built on nothing but limitations, gaps and
gaucheries.

                        *

(For me, writing has been not so much about finding out who I
am and what I can do – who cares? – but rather discovering who
I'm not and what I can't do, a kind of hazard prevention, and it
became clear to me many years ago that one of the things I was

not was a scholar, and that one of the things I could not do was traditional scholarship. I was simply never able to talk the talk. I am at best an example of what the Fowler brothers, H. W. and F. G. – of dictionary and usage fame – would have called 'a half-educated Englishman of literary proclivities'. What has encouraged and determined these proclivities is my indiscriminate appetite, which seems only to grow by eating. 'That inescapable animal walks with me, / Has followed me since the black womb held, / Moves where I move, distorting my gesture, / A caricature, a swollen shadow,' writes Delmore Schwartz in his poem 'The Heavy Bear Who Goes With Me'. '[…] The scrimmage of appetite everywhere.' I have been feeding wildly on books my entire life, like Gaffer Hexam, who in *Our Mutual Friend* gets his 'meat and drink' from the bodies he finds in the Thames. You will doubtless recall that scene in chapter 3 of Dickens's novel, when Gaffer shows Mortimer Lightwood and Eugene Wrayburn the handbills of the missing persons that he has pasted all over his wall. 'He waved the light over the whole, as if to typify the light of his scholarly intelligence.' Welcome to my 'umble abode.)

*

In this regard at least, I think I slightly – very, very slightly – resemble Auden, who was perhaps more magpie than mudlark, picking things up from anywhere and everywhere. Isherwood, in his early autobiographical novel, *Lions and Shadows* (1938), describes Auden seeking out 'oddments of scientific, medical and psycho-analytical jargon: his magpie brain was a hoard of curious and suggestive phrases from Jung, Rivers, Kretschmer and Freud.' Elizabeth Bishop, writing in tribute to Auden after his death, in the *Harvard Advocate*, reflected that '[he] gave us the feeling that here was someone who knew – about psychology, geology, birds, love, the evils of capitalism'.

Auden knew *a lot*.
He was also a bit of a bluffer.

A serious scholar has great merits. But a serious scholar
who is also a good man knows not only his subject but
the proper place of his subject in the whole of his life.

(Iris Murdoch, *The Sovereignty of Good*)

There have been hundreds of articles and books published about
Auden's work during the time I have been trying to write this
book, the kind of articles and books I should have been writing
but just can't, or won't, or simply couldn't, books written in a
style and a mode which I can vaguely approximate yet never
quite achieve. Serious books. Accurate scholarship. There have
also been complete editions of Auden's poetry, the plays, and the
libretti, and the prose, published by Princeton University Press:
again, volume after volume after wearying volume. Peter Edgerly
Firchow, in *W. H. Auden: Contexts for Poetry* (2002) – which is
exactly the kind of book this could have been and should have
been – remarks that all these additional new resources and
insights make it easier to think and write about Auden and his
work.

Easier?

He was no good in discussion, not because any amount
of argument could shake his faith, but because the mere
fact of hearing another voice disconcerted him painfully,
confusing his thoughts at once – these thoughts that for
so many years, in a mental solitude more barren than
a waterless desert, no living voice had ever combatted,
commented, or approved.

(Joseph Conrad, *The Secret Agent*)

In the Berg Collection in New York Public Library – a great repository of Auden archives – there's a letter that Auden wrote to Stephen Spender on 12 July 1963, chastising him for having apparently misread one of his poems, 'A Change of Air': 'You're a naughty girl,' writes Auden, 'and in her reply your Mother, sweet old lady we all know her to be, has had to give you a little spank-spank.'

No one wants a little spank-spank.

Actually, I suppose some people do.

But I certainly do not.

(I think part of the reason why I have been trying and failing to write a book about Auden for twenty-five years is that I'm scared: I fear the reprisals. Writing as a novelist, you're just making things up. But here, now, I'm making claims, truth claims, claims that are subject to refutation, and I know that a lot of what I'm saying is going to be proved downright *wrong*. There will be no second edition of the book, but to correct any mistakes, do please write, c/o my publisher. It's Ian – not C. J. – Sansom. S for Sierra, A for Alfa, N for November, S for Sierra, O for Oscar, M for Mike.)

*

Of the many books about Auden published during the past twenty-five years, there are perhaps two really important works, two works of not just accurate but astonishing scholarship – John Fuller's *W. H. Auden: A Commentary* (1998) and Edward Mendelson's *Later Auden* (1999) – works so accurate, so painfully accurate, as to have rendered all other commentary, including this, pretty much superfluous. The only honest way to deal with this brutal fact, it seems to me, is to give the books their full whack.

*

The dust jacket of Mendelson's book shows a sepia-coloured full-length photograph of Auden, circa 1947, his legs set firmly apart, broad-shouldered, hands in pockets – a boxer's or a writer's stance – looking sideways, away from the camera. His tie is too short – schoolboyish, or professorial. He looks purposeful, but slightly mad.

Fuller's fine dust jacket also shows a sepia-coloured photograph, probably also 1940s, but this is a head-and-shoulders shot, showing Auden up close, frowning, looking directly at the camera. He wears an open-necked shirt; you can see his throat; you can almost count the hairs on his head. And there is a menace and depth about the eyes.

From the dust jackets alone you can tell that they are serious books – different sorts of books, but serious books.

*

(John Fuller, I should say, was my PhD supervisor, many years ago. And he was a very decent chap. I met him perhaps half a dozen times during the three years I was studying. I always had the slight impression that he found me rather lacking in seriousness. Which, in fairness, I was, and am – but back then I was worse. I hadn't yet earned my frivolity.)

*

Fuller's *W. H. Auden: A Commentary* is a terrifying, stomach-churning sort of a book, in much the same way as, say, Richard Ellmann's biography of James Joyce is terrifying, or Christopher Ricks's edition of Tennyson is terrifying, or the Ralph W. Franklin three-volume edition of the poems of Emily Dickinson is terrifying. How, one wonders, did they do that – and why?

*

Fuller works his way steadily through Auden's oeuvre, volume by volume, poem by poem, from the privately printed 1928 *Poems* to the posthumously published *Thank You, Fog*, with five separate chapters on uncollected poems, 1925–30, 1930–36, 1937–39, 1940–48, 1949–73, another on 'Poems first published in the *Collected Poetry* (1945)', and two indexes. More than 600 pages.

If you really want to learn about Auden, this is where to start, although 'This book', cautions Fuller in his foreword, 'is not for reading in the normal way.' I'm not entirely sure what counts as reading in the normal way. Carelessly, or carefully? I have a horrible feeling – I've always had the feeling – that I've been doing it wrong.

*

Mendelson's book is another 600-pager, give or take, and is equally amazing, though it is scholarship of an entirely different kind.

Here is Fuller writing about the second part of Auden's early sequence 'The Megalopsych':

> This part, in a tone of hectic disgust, elaborates Aristotle's definition of the magnanimous man in the *Nichomachean Ethics*, 4.iii.15, as someone who is not a coward, and it confesses, in a style somewhat like an English translation of Catullus ('puella defututa' is from Carmen xli), that the homosexual's confidence is assisted by alcohol and cruising – 'the tirade is about a joy-boy' as he puts it to Isherwood.

Just one – rich, thick, stunning sentence – which manages to cover matters of tone, allusion, style and content in the time it would take me to make some sly remark or equivocation.

And here is Mendelson, on 'In Memory of W. B. Yeats':

> When all collective action seemed doomed to futility or injustice, Auden argued to himself that the only just acts open to him were private ones of teaching and praise. In his elegy for Yeats he portrayed these acts as the work of an exceptional individual who braved the realm of death and transformed the irrational powers; they were acts achieved through the mysterious power of a poet's gift, and were unconstraining acts that might teach a justice they would never impose.

Summary, speculation, argument and explication all at once.

While Mendelson announces from on high, Fuller works from the bottom up. Discussing the early, puzzling poem 'Who stands, the crux left of the watershed', for example, Fuller patiently provides a context ('Written in Harborne at his parental home'), a neat summary ('this poem is descriptive of Auden's sacred landscape'), a useful guide to grammar and syntax ('Auden begins the poem with a compound relative'), a brief outline of influences and sources ('If Hardy presides over the visionary distance of this poem, it is Eliot who has contributed to its diction'), and a polite acknowledgement of alternative commentaries and interpretations ('Reminders that Auden had driven for the TUC during the General Strike of the previous year may be salutary'). To manage this once, one might say, is mere criticism; to pull it off again and again, hundreds of times, is truly painstaking – it is accurate scholarship.

*

And painstaking indeed: Fuller's is a work of anatomy, while Mendelson's is more like a very long session on the psychiatrist's couch.

(Which makes *this* what? Some sort of sideshow perhaps? A comic interlude?)

*

Mendelson seems to believe that poems are made from big ideas, while Fuller works on the assumption that poetry is made up of many little parts (often from other poems). There is truth in both, but the different truths have their consequences. If a poem is made up of ideas, then it may be paraphrased. If a poem is made of parts, as the human body is made of parts, then it might more usefully be dissected and described.

So, Fuller dissects. (His first detailed forensic tests on Auden were carried out while the poet was still alive: his *A Reader's Guide to W. H. Auden*, published in 1970, was written, Fuller reveals in the preface to the updated *Commentary*, in a mere eighteen months, a piece of work as judicious as it was concise; his careful fingering of the allusions to anal intercourse in Auden's 'Letter to a Wound', for example – '"offal" is waste, "snig" an eel, "the hardware shop at the front" the erecting genitals' – can only now decently be published. The *Commentary* is a series of sharp, fresh cuts into the Auden corpus.)

*

(Fuller is also a poet, by the way – and the son of a poet, incidentally, Roy Fuller, who, like Auden, became Oxford Professor of Poetry – and there is no doubt, with the notable exception of Mendelson, that the best books and articles about Auden have all been written by fellow poets, who are at one and the same time the most and least qualified to judge him. In his book *The*

Hidden Law, published in 1993, the American poet Anthony
Hecht presented a picture of Auden as a poet profoundly trou-
bled by questions of morality and religion; a poet a lot like
Anthony Hecht. An American poet of an older generation,
Randall Jarrell, wrote about Auden's work as a sad process of
steady decline: a decline mirrored, one might argue, in the work
of Jarrell himself. Fuller, in turn, presents Auden as a poet of
great erudition and technical mastery: no surprise to find Fuller's
own poetry displaying the same extraordinary qualities.)

*

In 1972, the year before his death, Auden appointed Mendelson
as his literary executor, Mendelson being then a mere twenty-
five-year-old member of the English department at Yale. It may
have looked foolhardy at the time, but Auden was being very
shrewd: 'Wystan says that he has just met a young man', recalled
Chester Kallman, 'who knows more about him than he knows
himself.' Now, after a lifetime spent editing Auden's poetry and
prose and trawling through letters and drafts and diaries in New
York and London and Oxford and all over America, this is clearly
more true than ever, and Mendelson's uniquely intimate knowl-
edge takes many forms.

There are the little titbits of information, for example, which
he scatters and sprinkles over his prose like a dusting of icing
sugar, like hundreds-and-thousands: Auden's writing to his
publishers to find out exactly when Yeats died, to ensure the
accuracy of his line in 'In Memory of W. B. Yeats', about 'his last
afternoon as himself'; Auden's enthusiasm for the theories of
management guru Peter F. Drucker; his considering converting
to Judaism; his contacting the British embassy in Washington at
the outbreak of the Second World War to report that he was
'willing to do anything when and if the Government ask me';

and his brave response to T. S. Eliot, on receiving a copy of *After Strange Gods*, published in 1933, with its vile claim that 'reasons of race and religion combine to make any large number of free-thinking Jews undesirable', a response which is surely enough to make anyone shout hooray for W. H. Auden. (It reads, 'Some of the general remarks, if you will forgive my saying so, rather shocked me, because if they are put into practice, and it seems to me quite likely, would produce a world in which neither I nor you I think would like to live.')

And then there are the much larger patterns beneath this sweet top-dusting, the rich primary material that Mendelson kneads and teases and shapes into his various narrative threads and theories. There is the clever way in which he twists together poetry and biography, for example, and makes connections: how, on arriving in the USA, according to Mendelson, Auden abandoned the oratorical voice, adopted 'a lonely existentialist Protestantism' and began experimenting with different forms. Then in 1948, when he and Chester Kallman began holidaying on Ischia, how his poetry 'almost immediately found a new conversational tone of voice', and 'his beliefs turned in the direction of a shared, corporate Catholicism'. How, in 1958, he moved to his summer house in Kirchstetten, where he 'celebrated his privacy' and his poems 'explored the bleakly modern religion he found expressed in the letters written by Dietrich Bonhoeffer'. How in 1972, after his move to Oxford, 'His poems now increasingly addressed the dead instead of the living, and his religion took the form of timeless rituals in a dead language.'

Mendelson really knows how to tell a story.

*

(I have tried on numerous occasions to interest film and TV production companies in producing some kind of Auden biopic. It's an incredible story, the Auden Story – not just the work, the life. The closest I ever came, after months, years, was when I managed to set up a meeting with some magnates of moviedom and in the meeting they asked, 'And who do you have on board as the writer?' 'Me?' I said. Blank looks all round. I never heard from them again. The last thing I recall is the sound of their heels clicking away into the distance.)

*

The enormous strengths of the two books, then, and their many differences, are obvious. (Fuller is characteristically English, smuggling in the occasional light-hearted, donnish quip and tease, while Mendelson has chutzpah: he portrays an heroic Auden, a poet in the grip of constant mental tightenings and slackenings, a poet constantly clenching and unclenching his philosophical muscles, and the resulting poetry as a series of rippling, flexing renunciations and reversals and self-criticisms and rereadings. If Fuller is at times cautious, Mendelson is more often prepared to take a punt: he poses; he queries; he asserts; and in imitation of Auden he attempts to write his own memorable speech: 'This transformation of abandonment into love now became the central plot of Auden's poems'; '"New Year Letter" is Auden's Faust.' After quoting Auden's haiku 'He has never seen God, / but, once or twice, he believes / he has heard Him', the final sentence of Later Auden swells to hurrah and grandiloquence: 'With these words, he gave thanks for the last gift of vision, and his work was done.' Fuller, in contrast, winds up his book with a discussion of the poem 'Minnelied' and, comparing it with another, ends in diminuendo: 'The reader may be interested to compare these poems.' Indeed.)

*

Basically, everything Fuller and Mendelson can do and have done, I cannot. If this book has an apologetic tone, then there is – as I hope you can now appreciate – a very good reason. Two very good reasons.

Writing about Auden after Fuller and Mendelson is like playing tennis after Federer and Nadal. (I would like to think that I might be an Andy Murray, but I am definitely not at the level of an Andy Murray. A Tim Henman, then? Alas, no, I'm not even a Tim Henman. An umpire, perhaps? An unseeded pro? Semi-pro? Amateur? Ball boy? A professional queuer in the Wimbledon queue?)

*

Anyway, if you want to know the meaning of Auden's 'Accurate scholarship', you can find the answers in Mendelson and Fuller. (It's to do with German reparations and various psychoanalytic subjects.)

STRANGEWAYS

Fine. I'll happily leave the scholarship to the experts.

But here's something I can perhaps talk about with a degree of insight and certainly with enthusiasm: the unearthing of the whole offence. Because who unearths offences?

Detectives.

*

Apart from Auden, the only thing I have read consistently over the past twenty-five years is detective fiction, or crime fiction, or whatever you want to call it: hard-boiled, French noir, domestic suspense, you name it, I've read it. Hammett, Chandler, Ross Macdonald, Ellery Queen, Margery Allingham, Rex Stout, Patricia Highsmith, Derek Raymond, Barbara Vine, Simenon, Frédéric Dard, Fred Vargas, Camilleri, Ian Rankin, Val McDermid … The big names, and the little names, or the names that once were big: Dorothy B. Hughes, Gerald Kersh, Harry Kemelman. 'Just reeling off their names is ever so comfy,' writes Auden (about lakes, actually, 'Moraine, pot, oxbow, glint, sink, crater, piedmont, dimple', but the point stands).

He was a fan himself, of course, Auden. He loved detective stories. They were for him 'an addiction like tobacco or alcohol' – and he was *seriously* addicted to tobacco and alcohol. 'I've often thought of doing a versified detective story,' he once remarked, though in a sense he *was* always writing versified detective stories.

> Behind the corpse in the reservoir, behind the ghost on
>   the links,
> Behind the lady who dances and the man who madly
>   drinks,
> Under the look of fatigue, the attack of migraine and the
>   sigh
> There is always another story, there is more than meets
>   the eye.
>
> (Auden, 'At last the secret is out')

The appeal of the early poetry has much to do with this mysterioso Agatha Christie tone, and his deployment of detective-fiction tropes and images.

*

(Also, I rather wonder – although no one else seems to have done so, so I may be barking up the wrong literary historical tree here – if Auden's love of detective fiction explains what one might think of as the curiously commercial edge to his work, certainly compared with some of his contemporaries. I'm thinking in particular of his peculiar grasp of structure. According to Mickey Spillane, 'Nobody reads a mystery to get to the middle. They read it to get to the end. If it's a letdown, they won't buy anymore. The first page sells that book. The last page sells your next book.' A lot of poetry is in the middle: Auden sells at the beginning, and at the end. There's also that weird combination in his work of mental toughness and piercing insights, and also a deep, sweet sentimentality. As a writer, Auden's a bit like Ernest Bramah's creation Max Carrados, the blind detective: cultured, ruthless but also rather calm, who shoots by aiming at the sound of a beating heart, and who can detect a false moustache from its 'five-yard aura of spirit gum'.)

*

In fact, it's hard not to imagine Auden as a sort of detective. Not a police detective, of course, that would be ridiculous – DI Auden? – but one of those professional amateurs beloved of crime writers, the consulting detective, the private eye. He's got the brilliance, he's got the wit and he's got the trademark eccentricities. He's Sam Spade, Columbo, Philip Marlowe and Sherlock Holmes all rolled into one: the weary eye, the cigarette forever smouldering in the ashtray, the tobacco in the toe-end of his Persian slipper. It's obvious, isn't it: if Auden didn't exist, you'd have to make him up.

*

Auden was first represented in fiction as a detective by Cecil Day Lewis, writing as Nicholas Blake, in the novel *A Question of Proof* (1935), in which he features as the appropriately named Nigel Strangeways – 'every inch W. H. Auden', according to Day Lewis's son Sean – a character described in the novel as a 'nordic type' who 'can't sleep unless he has an enormous weight on his bed'. (In her short story 'How W. H. Auden Spends the Night in a Friend's House', Lydia Davis describes, entirely accurately, how Auden liked to sleep with a great weight on his bed and so used to pull down curtains and paintings to smother himself.) There are more than a dozen books in the Nigel Strangeways series, all of them excellent, but Auden also crops up in crime fiction elsewhere. There's the satirical detective novel *The Death of the King's Canary*, for example – which is terrible – written by Dylan Thomas and John Davenport in 1940, but not published until the 1970s, in which Auden becomes Wyndham Nils Snowden, 'the leader of the younger poets'. And he's also the *éminence grise* of the Amanda Cross novel *Poetic Justice* (1970), a campus thriller in which Kate Fansler, who is an amateur sleuth and an English professor – the best kind of English professor – is constantly quoting Auden, and who finally solves her mystery after attending one of his poetry readings.

*

('The Fictional Auden' might make an interesting PhD, beginning with Stephen Spender's novel *The Temple*, partly written in 1929 – in which Auden figures both as a character called Simon Wilmot and as the character 'W' in a novel by another character in the book, William Bradshaw, who is based on Christopher Isherwood, who also featured a fictional Auden, as 'Weston', in his own actual novel, *Lions and Shadows* (1938) – and all the way through to Polly Clark's *Larchfield* (2017), which is based on Auden's time teaching at the Larchfield Academy in Scotland. 'The Fictional Auden' would include separate chapters on 'Auden on Film' and 'Auden on Stage', plus a big appendix, 'Auden in Alan Bennett', which one might eventually turn into a quirky little book, like *The Lady in the Van*.)

*

Picturing my own fictional Auden, I see him rather like Horace Rumpole, as played by Leo McKern, who huffed and puffed his way through the long-running Thames Television series of John Mortimer's *Rumpole of the Bailey* when I was young, quaffing Château Thames Embankment at Pommeroy's, consorting with Fig Newton and dining with the Erskine-Browns, before coming home on the Tube to She Who Must Be Obeyed. Or perhaps he's a bit like Orson Welles (who might also have played Rex Stout's detective Nero Wolfe, Montenegrin by birth, weighing a seventh of a ton, and living in a brownstone on West 35th Street in New York, with his own Swiss chef, Fritz Brenner, and breeding orchids in his conservatory). Or even like Myrna Loy, as Nora Charles, in *The Thin Man*, based on Hammett's novel, which begins with Nick Charles waiting for Nora, 'leaning against the bar in a speakeasy on Fifty-second Street'.

*

(I used to think – who didn't? – that the best person to play Auden in a biopic would be Stephen Fry, but now I'm not so sure, now I think maybe Joaquin Phoenix, who was so good at playing Johnny Cash in *Walk the Line*, with that bloat-prone, slightly lopsided look of pain, but also with a sort of courtly magnificence, the hooded eyes, and the suggestion of both deep earnest thought and the lifelong indulgence of fleshly appetites. Actually, if he'd lived any longer, I rather fear Auden might have ended up like Johnny Cash, a sad, lost, lonely figure, appearing on *The Muppet Show* and *Columbo*, until the arrival of a Rick Rubin figure to revive his flagging fortunes. Or like Welles, dragging himself around the talk shows, and flogging Paul Masson wines.)

*

He has a whole essay about detective fiction, of course, Auden – he has essays about everything. Everything. (Volume II alone of the collected prose in *The Complete Works*, which covers the period 1939–1948, is enough to make any aspiring writer wilt: essays on Yeats and Henry James, on Mozart, on Shakespeare, the Brothers Grimm, 'The Mythical Sex'.) 'The Guilty Vicarage', published in *Harper's Magazine* in 1948:

The most curious fact about the detective story is that
it makes its greatest appeal precisely to those classes
of people who are most immune to other forms of
daydream literature. The typical detective story addict is
a doctor or clergyman or scientist or artist. […] I suspect
that the typical reader of detective stories is, like myself, a
person who suffers from a sense of sin […] The phantasy,
then, which the detective story addict indulges is the
phantasy of being restored to the Garden of Eden, to a
state of innocence, where he may know love as love and
not as the law. The driving force behind this daydream
is the feeling of guilt, the cause of which is unknown to
the dreamer. The phantasy of escape is the same, whether
one explains the guilt in Christian, Freudian, or any other
terms. One's way of trying to face the reality, on the other
hand, will, of course, depend very much on one's creed.

For me, the real thrill in reading crime fiction is the pleasure in
witnessing an active human consciousness trying to figure things
out, attempting to solve what it means to be alive, or not alive:
it is the pleasure of watching someone unearthing the whole
offence.

Which is what exactly?

IS BERLIN VERY
WICKED?

The whole offence is something to do with Germany.

*

Shortly after coming down from Oxford in the summer of 1928, Auden published his first pamphlet of poems, titled simply *Poems*, just thirty-seven pages long, printed on a hand-operated press by his friend Stephen Spender, and finished off in a bright orange wrapper by the Holywell Press in Oxford. He distributed copies to his friends. He may not have succeeded in his exams – 'I didn't do a stroke of work,' he boasted – but his career as a writer had begun, he was feeling confident and he was ready for adventure. His father had promised to pay him an allowance until his twenty-third birthday, which was eighteen months away. He considered going to Paris, but then decided to go to Berlin. 'Is Berlin very wicked?' he asked a friend.

It certainly wasn't Oxford.

*

Staying initially with a middle-class family in Nikolassee, a suburb on the east bank of the Wannsee, and soon joined by his old friend Isherwood, Auden became a regular at a bar called the Cosy Corner, at Zossener Strasse 7, in the working-class area of Hallesches Tor. The Cosy Corner was a kind of German dive, a place where adolescent boys were willing to have uncomplicated – or indeed sometimes very complicated – sex in exchange for money. 'I can still make myself faintly feel the delicious nausea of initiation terror which Christopher felt as Wystan pushed back the heavy leather door-curtain of a boy-bar called the Cosy Corner and led the way inside,' recalls Isherwood in *Christopher and His Kind* (1977). The Cosy Corner introduced Auden and Isherwood to another world. 'Berlin is the buggers daydream,' Auden wrote to a friend back in England. 'I am a mass of bruises.' But he wasn't just busy picking up boys and bruises. He was also busy picking up German.

*

Until arriving in Berlin, Auden knew little of either the German language or German literature. In his 1937 essay 'Some Notes on Auden's Early Poetry', Isherwood claimed that it was typical of Auden's 'astonishing adaptability that, after two or three months in Berlin, he began to write poems in German'. A few of Auden's German poems have survived, and they reveal much about his interest and understanding of Germany and its culture. The poem 'Chorale' is typical:

> Der ist ein schöne Junge
> Er wohnt jezt in Berlin
> Wo ich in vier Monaten
> Soll wieder kehren hin.
> Er hat kein' schwere Trippe
> Er ist nie nep bei mir
> Er hat kein Englisch Onkel
> Er sagt 'Ick bläb bei Dir.'
> …
> O warte nur, mein Junge,

In England bin ich fromm
Blubber und Geld zu sparen
Bestimmt ich wieder komm.

(He is a lovely boy / He now lives in Berlin / Where I in four months / Am to go back again. / He's got no serious VD / He's never over-pricey with me / He has no English uncle / He says 'I'll stay with you' ... 'Just wait, my boy, / In England I'm well behaved / To save blubber and money / Certainly I'll come again'.)

*

So, Germany for Auden in his youth was a site of fantasy and fulfilment.

By 1939 it had become a nightmare.

*

The idea that the Germans, unique among the nations, are somehow predisposed towards barbarism and totalitarianism runs deep in English culture – the novelist Henry Green, in his autobiography *Pack My Bag* (1940), recalled, 'We hated Germans and at school we did believe they were so short of food they boiled the dead down to get the fats, that they crucified Australians, and that they were monsters different from us.' (Even in the 1970s, I grew up on a diet of *Warlord* and *Victor* comics and playground games in which we were endlessly restaging the great British victory over the Hun.)

This idea of monstrous German exceptionalism is sometimes called Vansittartism, after Sir Robert Vansittart, who was a permanent undersecretary at the Foreign Office from 1930 to 1938, and the author of *Black Record: Germans Past and Present* (1941), a pamphlet based on a series of BBC broadcasts, in which he suggested that there were certain 'features of German policy, character and action which for centuries have been a burden to humanity'. ('No feats of scholarship', wrote Vansittart, 'console us for bloodshed.') Vansittart's broadcasts and his pamphlet were not just anti-Nazi, they were positively Germanophobic.

*

Auden, of course, was a -phile rather than a -phobe: in America, many of his friends were Germans who had fled the Nazis, and he was indeed married to a German of Jewish heritage (having entered into a marriage of convenience with Erika Mann in 1935, with the sole purpose of providing her with a British passport when she was about to be stripped of her German citizenship).

And yet in 'September 1, 1939' he seems to give Vansittartism a bit of an airing.

*

This takes some explaining.

(It's like Noël Coward's song 'Don't Let's Be Beastly to the Germans' (1943), which sounds like a plea for tolerance and understanding –

For many years –
They've been in floods of tears
Because the poor little dears
Have been so wronged and only longed
To cheat the world
Deplete the world
And beat
The world to blazes.
This is the moment when we ought to sing their praises.

– whereas it was written, according to Coward, 'as a satire directed against a small minority of excessive humanitarians who, in my opinion, were taking a rather too tolerant view of our enemies'. The BBC failed to see the irony and removed the song from its playlist.)

So, allow me to paraphrase.

('If there is a more unrewarding task than explaining jokes and allegory, I do not know what it is,' wrote the great bearded John Berryman – or rather, the great-bearded great John Berryman – in his book *The Freedom of the Poet*. Berryman was right about a lot of things, but about this he was wrong, because there is a more unrewarding task than explaining jokes and allegory: paraphrasing poems.)

If one were attempting to untangle this stanza, one might say that Auden is suggesting that the offence that has 'driven a culture mad' *may* be explained by factors specific to Germany, but that in fact if you treat anyone badly they'll do bad things. Thus, in summary, the gist of it seems to be: the roots and causes of human barbarism are particular, but human barbarism itself is universal ('Those to whom evil is done / Do evil in return'). It would be a mistake, Auden is suggesting, to assume that ordinary Germans are any different from the rest of the world's population.

This is not adequate as a summary of the stanza, and leaves a lot out, but it's the best I can do.

*

(I am currently reading Philip Roth's novel *American Pastoral*: indeed, I am currently teaching Philip Roth's novel *American Pastoral*. Over the years, almost all of my reading has found its way into my teaching, so now I no longer know: do I read to teach, or do I teach to read? The students absolutely hate

American Pastoral: it's too long; it's too complicated; there are too many words; Roth is a misogynist, a misanthropist; he's an apologist for white privilege. If my students are anything to go by, Philip Roth has well and truly had his day. Will Auden last? Auden has already lasted. Anyway, in the novel, the protagonist's brother, a man called Jerry, decides to make a coat out of hamster skins. He's trying to impress a girl and he can't afford to buy her a fur coat. So he dries out some hamster skins, sews them together and finishes the thing off with a silk lining made from an old parachute. This is what Roth writes about the coat: 'He was going to send it to the girl in a Bamberger's coat box of his mother's, wrapped in lavender tissue paper and tied with velvet ribbon. But when the coat was finished, it was so stiff – because of the idiotic way he'd dried the skins, his father would later explain – that he couldn't get it to fold up in the box.' This is a book made of badly folded hamster skins.)

*

(T. E. Hulme, in his 'Lecture on Modern Poetry', delivered in 1908: 'I want to speak of verse in a plain way as I would of pigs: that is the only honest way.' It's not the only honest way, but it's a pretty compelling way. It's what I'm trying to do here. Then again, as well as reading T. E. Hulme and Philip Roth, I have just been reading *Charlotte's Web* with my daughter.

'Where's Papa going with that ax?' said Fern to her
mother as they were setting the table for breakfast.
'Out to the hoghouse,' replied Mrs Arable. 'Some pigs
were born last night.'
'I don't see why he needs an ax,' continued Fern, who
was only eight.
'Well,' said her mother, 'one of the pigs is a runt.

It's very small and weak, and it will never amount to
anything. So your father has decided to do away with it.'

'That's me!' I think. 'I'm Mr Arable, the critic, and the poor little
poem is the pig.' And then I realise: the poem is Mr Arable, and
I'm the little runt. Poems aren't pigs – but we are.)

*

In 1996, Daniel Goldhagen, a young Harvard academic, revived
the idea that the horrors of the Nazis could somehow be ascribed
to Germans and their Protestantism, in his book *Hitler's Willing
Executioners: Ordinary Germans and the Holocaust*. The book's
argument was largely based on the evidence of the testimony of
members of the police battalions who had taken part in the
extermination of Jewish communities on the eastern front,
which led Goldhagen to conclude that it was not 'economic
hardship, not the coercive means of a totalitarian state, not
social psychological pressure, not invariable psychological
propensities, but ideas about Jews that were pervasive in
Germany, and had been for decades, [that] induced ordinary
Germans to kill unarmed, defenseless Jewish men, women and
children by the thousands, systematically and without pity'.

The book was widely criticised for what many regarded as its
inaccurate scholarship, and for taking a few examples of German
behaviour *in extremis* and applying them to all Germans, when
it might be more proper to ascribe such behaviour to all humans,
as for example Christopher R. Browning does in his book
*Ordinary Men: Reserve Police Battalion 101 and the Final Solution in
Poland*, published a few years before the Goldhagen, in which
Browning concludes that:

In every modern society, the complexity of life and
the resulting bureaucratization and specialization
attenuate the sense of personal responsibility of those
implementing official policy. Within virtually every social
collective, the peer group exerts tremendous pressures
on behavior and sets moral norms. If the men of Reserve
Police Battalion 101 could become killers under such
circumstances, what group of men cannot?

Auden's poem, one might say, leans more towards the Browning
than the Goldhagen.

*

Which is not to say that it's necessarily correct.

*

Auden's oft-repeated locution about what 'all schoolchildren'
learn – which is a variant of the historian Thomas Macaulay's
phrase 'every schoolboy knows' – is used in his poem 'It was
Easter as I walked in the public gardens', and in 'Letter to Lord
Byron', as well as here in 'September 1, 1939'.

The problem with the phrase is that it is indeed childish to
suggest that the wrong of, say, invading Poland on 1 September
1939 is somehow justified by, say, the Treaty of Versailles, or that
Hitler's childhood traumas might usefully explain his adult
behaviour. The Third Reich and the Holocaust were not like a
shove in the playground, nor were they simple manifestations of
some poor individual's upsets.

This seems to me another low point in the poem.

*

Auden had a tendency throughout his career to reflect upon and attempt to solve and explain problems using the simplifying logic of the child.

> The Poet is not only the man who is made to solve the riddle of the Universe, but he is also the man who feels where it is not solved and which continually awakens his feelings [...] What is old and worn out, not in itself, but from the dimness of the intellectual eye brought on by worldly passions, he makes new; he pours upon it the dew that glistens, and blows round us the breeze which cooled us in childhood.
>
> (Coleridge, 'Lecture on Poetry', 12 December 1811)

It has to be said – to Coleridge and to Auden – that there are other ways of solving problems than sprinkling glistening dew. There are also other ways of thinking about evil.

> My contention is that evil is quite literally a virus parasite occupying a certain brain area which we may term the RIGHT center. The mark of the basic shit is that he has to be right.
>
> (William Burroughs, 'My Own Business', in *The Adding Machine: Collected Essays*)

Auden, I think, fine rightly knew that poems aren't answers to problems, and that any suggestion that they might be compulsory wisdom is entirely false. Hence his intense dislike of 'September 1, 1939', which is a poem that wants desperately to be right, and which occasionally gets things desperately wrong. Anyone who's ever tried to write a poem will perhaps be familiar with the problem: you feel that this is an opportunity to deliver yourself of some extraordinary insight and wisdom, and what happens is that you end up speaking half-truths and nonsense.

*

Also, we surely can't but be deeply troubled now, reading the poem and knowing what we know, that this stanza's simplistic conclusion confuses victims with perpetrators.

> I do not know, and it does not much interest me to
> know, whether in my depths there lurks a murderer, but
> I do know that I was a guiltless victim and I was not a
> murderer. I know that the murderers existed, not only
> in Germany, and still exist, retired or on active duty, and
> that to confuse them with their victims is a moral disease
> or an aesthetic affectation or a sinister sign of complicity;
> above all, it is a precious service rendered (intentionally
> or not) to the negators of truth.
>
> > (Primo Levi, *The Drowned and the Saved*,
> > trans. Raymond Rosenthal)

It is worth pointing out, though, that one might still admire a poem, and indeed might spend years studying a poem, that may be diseased, sinister or affected.

> One problem absorbs me above all others: it is what I
> will call the intermittency of genius. Why, more often
> than not, does a poet blossom out in his adolescence
> and early manhood, and then wither to pedantry and
> dullness.
>
> > (Herbert Read, *Form in Modern Poetry*)

What's really absorbing is when a poet's genius both blossoms and withers in the course of the same poem. Thank goodness that we don't need writers always to be right; there'd be no writers left to study.

*

In a series of lectures at the Lowell Institute in Boston in 1906, William James addressed himself to the question of pragmatism and in passing attempted to solve the problem of why a writer and thinker of such obvious insufficiencies as Herbert Spencer, with 'his preference for cheap makeshifts in argument' and vague ideas, remained so popular that 'half of England wants to bury him in Westminster Abbey'. It is because, James concluded, 'we feel his heart to be in the right place'.

Precisely.

Herbert Spencer, Philip Roth, W. H. Auden, whoever: they are not infallible.

They're just writers.

DO NOT TELL OTHER WRITERS TO F*** OFF

You're still with me?

('What you need is some beta-readers,' one of my students told me, some years ago. 'Beta-readers?' 'To test the book.' 'As in, like, readers?' I asked. 'Yeah, beta-readers.' They were kind enough to read the book, this student – an earlier version of this book. 'You lost me round about the Holocaust,' they said. 'That's where I gave up.')

Good.

As for 'what occurred at Linz' (European Capital of Culture 2009) – what occurred at Linz?

Well, Anton Bruckner was the organist at the cathedral in Linz, and Ludwig Wittgenstein went to school there, but what Auden is obviously referring to is Linz's dubious honour of being Adolf Hitler's home town. (He was born, actually, in nearby Braunau am Inn, on 20 April 1889, but he lived in Linz betwen 1898 and 1907 – and loved it. As Führer, he planned for Linz to become one of his five great 'Führer Cities', along with Berlin, Munich, Hamburg and Nuremberg, and to be home to a Führermuseum, and a Nibelungen Bridge across the Danube, and a luxury Hitler Hotel.)

So, mostly what occurred at Linz was Hitler's childhood and schooling. Both Wittgenstein and Hitler attended the Linz Realschule, though they were both together there only from

1903 to 1904, according to Wittgenstein's biographers, and there is no need to attend to the various claims in Kimberley Cornish's book *The Jew of Linz* (1998), including his extraordinary suggestion that it was Wittgenstein who made Hitler anti-Semitic.

*

The other thing that occurred at Linz is something to do with a 'huge imago'.

*

Ah. Now.

I'll be honest, when I read this sort of thing in Auden, or elsewhere, I feel a slight twinge of my inner Philistine, my inner Kingsley Amis, who has Jim Dixon, the hapless lecturer in his novel *Lucky Jim*, become enraged and overwhelmed with a desire to torture a colleague 'until he disclosed why, without being French himself, he'd given his sons French names'.

Imago, I want to say: what the hell's an imago when it's at home? (And how do you even say it? Im-ar-go? Im-may-go? Im-ah-go? I'm going with im-may-go.)

*

According to the accounts of accurate scholars, Auden seems likely to have come across the term 'imago' in Jung, in the B. M. Hinkle translation of *Wandlungen und Symbole der Libido*:

> Imago: Here I purposely give preference to the term
> 'Imago' rather than to the expression 'Complex,' in
> order [...] to invest this psychological condition, which
> I include under 'Imago,' with living independence in
> the psychical hierarchy [...] 'Imago' has a significance
> similar on the one hand to the psychologically conceived

146

creation in Spitteler's novel [...] and upon the other hand
to the ancient religious conception of 'imagines and
lares.'

(Jung, *Psychology of the Unconscious*,
B. M. Hinkle trans., 1916)

In plain English: the 'imago' seems to be the subjective image of
someone which has been formed in another's mind and which
influences that other's behaviour.

Fine. OK.

So why didn't you just f***ing say so in the first place?

*

(You can take the boy out of Essex, it seems, but you cannot take
the Essex out of the boy. I went up, as they say, from Essex to
Cambridge in 1986, a long time ago now – yet I never seem to
learn. All of the usual clichés applied back then: I was the first
person in my family to attend university; I came from a compre-
hensive school; I felt I didn't fit in; I became ill and overwrought,
and had to take time off to recover; I fell in love; I went travel-
ling, to find myself, and found I wasn't there; worse, I completely
lost my sense of humour. It was, I suppose, looking back on it,
like most things in life, completely unoriginal and stereotypical:
three years of confused and straining emotions, and intense,
overdramatised intellectual activity, accompanied by endless
instant coffee and Leonard Cohen. Now, more than thirty years
later, looking back at my student life, it all seems utterly ludi-
crous, like something from one of those melancholy foreign
films I used to go and see with my friend Nick at the Cambridge
Arts Cinema – more *Betty Blue* than Andrei Tarkovsky. It seems
unreal. And thinking about it, it even seemed unreal at the time
– a kind of fantasy. I remember arriving at the college and walk-

ing through the big carved wooden gates with my rucksack and my carrier bags and being amazed at the sight of all the trunks lined up outside the porter's lodge. I had no idea people actually owned trunks. I'd never seen an actual trunk before, a trunk in the flesh, as it were. You didn't get trunks where I was from: we had hold-alls. I thought trunks were just props in Sunday-night BBC costume dramas, like elephant-foot umbrella stands, and tiger-skin rugs. Trunks were from another, imaginary world. Going to university felt like going to New York: it felt as though I wasn't there, and yet as if I'd been there all my life. I'd gone to a place that existed in my head. I was taught by some brilliant people – great, famous scholars and writers, most of them now long dead – and what they taught me above all was the importance of the careful choice of words. That's what I understand it means to be a serious writer, that it's not enough merely to say what you think or whatever's on your mind. Yet even now that's exactly what I seem to do, and so my writing remains as wayward and impressionistic as it ever was, associative, undisciplined, ill-judged and ill-considered, and I have slowly come to realise that I do not possess the necessary skills to become a great writer, a serious writer, a writer, frankly, who does not tell other writers to f*** off.)

*

Auden was always susceptible to big explanatory ideas and psychological theories like this – Jung, Freud, Georg Groddeck, Homer Lane. For me, suffice it to say, this tendency is perhaps the least appealing aspect of his work, though the true scholars and critics seem to love it. I suppose this exposes my shallowness and superficiality.

Oh well.

*

What I do find interesting here, though, in a stanza that offers a number of possible answers to the question of who's to blame and who's responsible, is the way in which it wanders, 'From Luther until now', swerving wide, taking in history, current affairs, psychology and a dose of folk wisdom.

I like the swerve.

One might argue that the whole poem is a kind of swerve, or a series of swerves. At the end of the first stanza, a moment ago, we were on 52nd Street. Now the attention has shifted to Europe, and we're about to head to ancient Athens, and there's lots more to come.

Yes: this is what I love about Auden, the fact that his poetry is dynamic rather than static, that it looks at things from high dimensions and low dimensions and in multi-dimensions, that it is interested in interactions as much as it describes actions, that it … wanders.

(In the prefatory note to *Holzwege* (1950) – a collection of essays translated into English as *Off the Beaten Track* and in French as *Chemins qui ne mènent nulle part* ('Paths that lead nowhere') – Heidegger explained his title:

In the wood there are paths, mostly overgrown, that come to an abrupt stop where the wood is untrodden. They are called Holzwege. Each goes its separate way, though within the same forest. It often appears as if one is identical to another. But it only appears so. Woodcutters and forest keepers know these paths. They know what it means to be on a Holzweg.

(*Off the Beaten Track*, trans. Julian Young and Kenneth Haynes)

This book is doing its best to follow Auden on his Holzweg.)

Anyway, the poem has clearly moved here into a different mode. This is Auden's Sunday-high-tea-at-the-vicarage manner, that cup-and-saucer-tinkling, slightly vague sermonising manner. Everywhere throughout his work you get these little pronunciamentos, these sermonettes – which does mean he sometimes ends up sounding rather like Jesus addressing the multitude.

Or like a teacher.

3

Exiled Thucydides knew
All that a speech can say
About Democracy,
And what dictators do,
The elderly rubbish they talk
To an apathetic grave;
Analysed all in his book,
The enlightenment driven away,
The habit-forming pain,
Mismanagement and grief:
We must suffer them all again.

THE LATIN FOR
THE JUDGIN'

Looking back, I cannot think of a better preparation for
writing about Hitler and Stalin than the familiarity I
acquired at Oxford in the 1930s with Thucydides, Tacitus,
and those sections of Aristotle's Politics that deal with the
Greek experience of tyranny.

(Alan Bullock, *Hitler and Stalin*)

OK. Ready, class, for stanza 3?

I promise, the pace picks up from here. And no more bad
language.

*

The funeral oration spoken by Pericles at the end of the first year
of the Peloponnesian War is – or was – perhaps the best-known
passage in Thucydides, and therefore one of the best-known
passages in all of Classical literature.

Though not by me, I should say.

(Ben Jonson wrote that Shakespeare had 'small Latin, and less
Greek'; I have absolutely none of either. I went to what is some-
times referred to in England as a 'bog-standard comp', where we
trained not to be leaders of men but to be the followers, the
factory machinists and the foot soldiers, so I have had to struggle
through Thucydides in later life with a Loeb Classical Library

edition and various ancient and modern translations. Personally, I would recommend the Rex Warner translation, though the recent Jeremy Mynott is excellent, and the Richard Crawley is the standard, published in 1874.)

Whatever. Whenever, wherever and however you get to grips with it, *The History of the Peloponnesian War*, Thucydides' book, is tedious, difficult – and essential reading.

*

Rex Warner, by the way, in one of those inevitable coincidences, was a friend – or at least an acquaintance – of Auden's. They met at Oxford. The two got on, as undergraduates do: they both liked to wear cloaks and silly hats, and wrote poetry, and they both got Thirds. In his 1929 'Verse-letter to C. Day-Lewis', Auden wrote that Warner 'looked at much and much saw through'. After Oxford, like Auden, Warner taught at the obligatory prep schools and he went on to write more poetry, and novels, and literary criticism, history, and popular translations of Aeschylus, Thucydides, Euripides, Plutarch and Xenophon. He was the Director of the British Institute in Athens, a professor in America, and an Honorary Fellow of Wadham College, Oxford. He was married to a Rothschild. He died as recently as 1986, and most people have never heard of him.

I always think of Rex Warner as a sort of unlucky Auden.

*

(Though is it luck? Was Warner unlucky? Am I? I'm currently reading Oliver Sacks, another friend of Auden's – but of course. A very disturbing passage in his posthumously published book *The River of Consciousness*:

Why is it that of every hundred gifted young musicians who study at Juilliard or every hundred brilliant young scientists who go to work in major labs under illustrious mentors, only a handful will write memorable musical compositions or make scientific discoveries of major importance? Are the majority, despite their gifts, lacking in some further creative spark? Are they missing characteristics other than creativity that may be essential for creative achievement – such as boldness, confidence, independence of mind?

It takes a special energy, over and above one's creative potential, a special audacity or subversiveness, to strike out in a new direction once one is settled. It is a gamble as all creative projects must be, for the new direction may not turn out to be productive at all.

I have also been reading *The Letters of Samuel Beckett*, volume 4. 'Krapping away here to no little avail,' writes Beckett to the actor Patrick Magee in September 1969. Years and years of krapping away to no little, little and no avail.)

*

There's a Peter Cook sketch from *Beyond the Fringe* in which he plays a miner: 'I could have been a judge,' he says, 'but I never had the Latin for the judgin'. I never had it, so I'd had it, as far as being a judge was concerned.'

Maybe if I'd had the Greek, I could have been a poet.

*

(The poet Charles Olson once wrote of Herman Melville, 'He read to write', which is a profound tribute: it's certainly better than writing to be read. One of the reasons to read Auden is to

read what he's been reading, and his reading is always unpredict-
able, in much the same way, say, that Alistair Cooke delivering
his weekly *Letter from America* used to be unpredictable. Tuning
in to Radio 4 when I was young, you never knew whether you
were going to be hearing about golf, or Nixon, or Abraham
Lincoln. It was an important part of my education, precisely
because it was unpredictable and unexpected. Philip Larkin
dismissed Auden's later work as 'a rambling intellectual stew' –
but some of us are grateful for any source of nourishment, and
the more in the stew the better. What have I learnt from Auden?
I have learnt about Thucydides, obviously, and lots of other
things. Auden has acquainted me with my own vast, wide-rang-
ing ignorance.)

*

(This book is not, I realise, the biography of a poem: it is the
biography of a mind. But whose? 'Oh, why am I not smart like
Auden?' – Theodore Roethke, letter to Louise Bogan, 1939, in
Selected Letters of Theodore Roethke.)

*

Auden may have first come across Thucydides in his lessons at St
Edmund's preparatory school, where the headmaster, a Mr Cyril
Morgan-Brown, was a strict Classicist who believed that Latin
and Greek, plus a little mathematics and divinity, were all that
were required for training the minds of young gentlemen. The
adult Auden was inclined to agree. He was forever grateful for his
early training in Classics:

> Anybody who has spent many hours of his youth
> translating into and out of two languages so syntactically
> and rhetorically different from his own, learns something

about his mother tongue which I do not think can be learned so well in any other way. For instance, it inculcates the habit, whenever one uses a word, of automatically asking: 'What is its exact meaning?'

(Auden, *A Certain World*)

What's often striking in Auden is the combination of terminological exactitude with wild and woolly thinking: Boris Johnson's is perhaps a modern version of the manner. Public schoolboy cant.

*

Auden had been sent to St Edmund's, at Hindhead in Surrey, in the autumn of 1915. He was eight years old. 'For the first time I came into contact with adults outside the family circle', he recalled in 'The Prolific and the Devourer' (1939), 'and found them to be hairy monsters with terrifying voices and eccentric habits, completely irrational in their bouts of rage and good-humour, and, it seemed, with absolute power of life and death. Those who deep in the country at a safe distance from parents spend their lives teaching little boys, behave in a way which would get them locked up in ordinary society.' (These days, they do get locked up.)

Despite his misgivings about his teachers, Auden spent much of his life in the same profession.

*

After returning from Berlin in 1929 – where he sometimes traded impromptu English lessons for sexual favours – he worked first as a tutor in London, and then as a schoolmaster teaching English and French at the Larchfield Academy in Helensburgh, Scotland. He then moved on to the Downs School in Herefordshire for a number of years, until the summer of 1935. 'I teach English, Arithmetic, French, Gym and Biology,' he told his friend Naomi Mitchison (pupils recall his gym classes as being 'giggly'). Later, in America, he taught at a number of colleges and universities, before finally returning to Oxford as Professor of Poetry. He was, in other words, serious about teaching and about education. (As his biographer Humphrey Carpenter points out, there were family precedents: Auden's great-uncle, the Reverend Thomas Auden, had been headmaster of Wellingborough Grammar School, and another great-uncle had been tutor to King Edward VII when Prince of Wales.) In Kirchstetten, the Austrian town where Auden bought a house in 1957, within driving distance of Vienna for the opera, and where he spent much of his later life, he was known by the locals as 'Herr Professor'.

*

(Biographers and critics always take this fact – the honour paid the poet by the locals – entirely at face value, though I often wonder if the people of Kirchstetten were half-mocking or speaking in jest. I happen to have spent most of my adult life as a teacher, and the only people who ever refer to me as 'Professor' are always taking the proverbial. Mustafa, my barber, for example, always calls me 'The Professor', with ill-concealed contempt, and rightly so: he taught himself English in six months by reading Dickens and watching *Only Fools and Horses*; his favourite book is *Les Misérables*, which he read in French, he claims, in three days, twelve hours a day, using a dictionary; and he speaks Turkish, Arabic, English, German, some language I've never heard of, and some Spanish. 'I should have been a professor, like you,' he always likes to say, when he's tackling my nose hair and my eyebrows. 'Why didn't you become a professor?' I always reply. The answers vary. 'Because I am a black sheep,' I remember he said once, 'I am not a good person.' 'Why are you not a good person?' I asked. 'Because I drink and I smoke. I love women.' 'I know a lot of professors who drink and who smoke and love women,' I said. 'Not in my country,' said Mustafa. There is a difference between being a professor and being professorial. Auden was both.)

*

Though himself a practitioner of unorthodox teaching methods – he was renowned for insisting that his students memorise long passages of prose and poetry, including an entire canto of Dante's *Inferno*, in Italian – Auden claimed not to approve of newfangled and progressive educational ideas and theories. In 'Letter to Lord Byron' (1936), he says he has 'no use for all these new academies':

> Where readers of the better weeklies send
> The child they probably did not intend,
> To paint a lampshade, marry, or keep pigeons,
> Or make a study of the world religions.

Not surprisingly, then, when he set out a possible programme for poets, in the form of a curriculum for a 'daydream College for Bards' in his essay 'The Poet & The City' (1962), it focused largely on Classics, and gardening:

1. In addition to English, at least one ancient language, probably Greek or Hebrew, and two modern languages would be required.
2. Thousands of lines of poetry in these languages would be learned by heart.

3. The library would contain no books of literary criticism, and the only critical exercise required of students would be the writing of parodies.
4. Courses in prosody, rhetoric and comparative philology would be required of all students, and every student would have to select three courses out of courses in mathematics, natural history, geology, meteorology, archaeology, mythology, liturgics, cooking.
5. Every student would be required to look after a domestic animal and cultivate a garden plot.

Doubtless one of the passages Auden would have asked his students to memorise would have been Pericles' funeral oration.

*

Just to recap, for those of us without the benefit of Auden's Classical education: we know little about Thucydides, born c.460 BC, died c.400, except that he was an Athenian and a general, who was exiled from Athens in his late thirties for having failed in battle against the Spartans, at which point he wrote his history of the Peloponnesian War (which was named after the Peloponnesus peninsula), which lasted for twenty-seven years. It was Thucydides' hope that his *History* – in the words of the Crawley translation – would be 'a possession for all time', and so it has become. His account of the war has long been a favourite not just among Classical scholars, for its eyewitness accounts and its eye-wateringly complex rhetoric, but also among politicians and military leaders, for what it says about democracy and war.

*

Exactly what it says about democracy and war is complex and ambiguous. (What any writers say about democracy and war is often complex and ambiguous: Plato, Heidegger, Nietzsche, Rousseau. Yet these days we often expect thinkers and writers – poets and novelists in particular – all to be tender- and liberally minded. We certainly expect them to agree, say, about the value of democracy. This has not always been the case. In his book *The Intellectuals and the Masses*, John Carey made a persuasive claim that 'the principle around which modernist literature and culture fashioned themselves was the exclusion of the masses, the defeat of their power, the removal of their literacy, the denial of their humanity'. To take just one example, D. H. Lawrence, in his book *Fantasia of the Unconscious*, which we know Auden read 'avidly': 'I don't intend my books for the generality of readers. I count it a mistake of our mistaken democracy, that every man who can read print is allowed to believe that he can read all that is printed. I count it a misfortune that serious books are exposed in the public market, like slaves exposed naked for sale. But there we are, since we live in an age of mistaken democracy, we must go through with it.')

*

Anyway, this is Pericles, by Thucydides, making his speech about democracy, in the Rex Warner translation:

> Our form of government does not enter into rivalry with
> the institutions of others. Our government does not copy
> our neighbours', but is an example to them. It is true
> that we are called a democracy, for the administration is
> in the hands of the many and not of the few. But while
> there exists equal justice to all and alike in their private
> disputes, the claim of excellence is also recognised; and

when a citizen is in any way distinguished, he is preferred
to the public service, not as a matter of privilege, but as
the reward of merit. Neither is poverty an obstacle, but
a man may benefit his country whatever the obscurity
of his condition. There is no exclusiveness in our public
life, and in our private business we are not suspicious
of one another, nor angry with our neighbour if he
does what he likes; we do not put on sour looks at him
which, though harmless, are not pleasant. While we
are thus unconstrained in our private business, a spirit
of reverence pervades our public acts; we are prevented
from doing wrong by respect for the authorities and for
the laws, having a particular regard to those which are
ordained for the protection of the injured as well as those
unwritten laws which bring upon the transgressor of
them the reprobation of the general sentiment.

What we have here is a speech that, in the words of Tony Blair's
one-time chief speechwriter Philip Collins, contains 'democratic
multitudes': the importance of the many, not the few; the impor-
tance of equal justice; the idea of the meritocracy; private liberty;
public interest; respect for institutions.

Yet in both this speech and throughout the *History*, Thucydides
contradicts and undermines his own arguments: democracy is a
great thing, he seems to suggest, but it can also be dangerous; it
relies on the participation of the many, but is determined by the
few; leadership is essential, and misleading is inevitable; the
populace must judge rightly the evidence of speech-makers and
law-givers, but they will happily believe lies about the past and
about the future.

*

('The whole earth is the tomb of famous men,' proclaims Pericles, and, alas, it is the case. I have been writing this book for so long that I have seen the likes of Blair and Obama come and go, with their fine rhetoric about hope, and in their stead the rise of the populists, with their rhetoric of fear, and the language of speech-making and public discourse become malignant.)

*

Auden knew only too well 'All that a speech can say / About Democracy'. It can say everything and mean nothing, and amount to nothing. Or it can mean the opposite of what it appears, and have consequences that last for generations. If speech-making is essential to democracy, it can also be a lie. After giving a speech at a political meeting in March 1939, a dinner held to raise money for refugees from the war in Spain, Auden wrote to his friend Annie Dodds:

> I suddenly found I could really do it, that I could make a fighting demagogic speech and have the audience roaring [...] It is so exciting but so absolutely degrading; I felt just covered with dirt afterwards.

Auden may have felt like he was covered in dirt, but the whole world was about to become engulfed in filth.

> What was the most powerful Hitlerian propaganda tool? Was it the individual speeches of Hitler and Goebbels, their pronouncements on this or that theme, their rabble-rousing against the Jews, against Bolshevism? [...]
>   No, the most powerful influence was exerted neither by individual speeches nor by articles or flyers, posters

or flags; it was not achieved by things which one had to absorb by conscious thought or conscious emotions.

Instead Nazism permeated the flesh and blood of the people through single words, idioms and sentence structures which were imposed on them in a million repetitions and taken on board mechanically and unconsciously. […] Words can be like tiny doses of arsenic: they are swallowed unnoticed, appear to have no effect, and then after a little time the toxic reaction sets in after all. […] The Third Reich coined only a very small number of the words in its language, perhaps – indeed probably – none at all. […] But it changes the value of words and the frequency of their occurrence, it makes common property out of what was previously the preserve of an individual or a tiny group, it commandeers for the party that which was previously common property and in the process steeps words and groups of words and sentence structures in its poison. Making language the servant of its dreadful system, it procures it as its most powerful, most public and most surreptitious means of advertising.

(Victor Klemperer, *The Language of the Third Reich*)

In a review of Reinhold Niebuhr's book *The Nature and Destiny of Man* in 1941, Auden wrote that 'It has taken Hitler to show us that liberalism is not self-supporting.' And as he became disillusioned with the limits of liberalism, so he became disillusioned with politicians ('I think we should do very well without politicians,' he told an interviewer in 1972. 'Our leaders should be elected by lot') and suspicious of himself. In his 1962 essay 'The Poet & The City', he compared the poet with the authoritarian ruler:

A society which was really like a good poem, embodying
the aesthetic virtues of beauty, order, economy and
subordination of detail to the whole, would be a
nightmare of horror for, given the historical reality
of actual men, such a society could only come into
being through selective breeding, extermination of the
physically and mentally unfit, absolute obedience to
its Director, and a large slave class kept out of sight in
cellars.

A reported speech, from the *New York Times*, on 1 September
1939: 'Hitler Tells the Reichstag "Bomb Will Be Met by Bomb"':

Chancellor Adolf Hitler of Germany, in a world broadcast
this morning, opened 'a fight until the resolution of the
situation' against Poland, announcing that 'from now on
bomb will be met by bomb.'

   At the same time he announced, to face any
eventuality, that if anything 'happened' to him, Field
Marshal Hermann Goering was to be in charge; if to
Marshal Goering, Rudolph Hess; if to Herr Hess, the
Senate, which he proposes to appoint, will select a
successor. [...]

   In the early part of his address, Herr Hitler electrified
his audience with this declaration: 'We have all been
suffering under the tortures that the Versailles treaty has
been inflicting upon us.'

'We have all been suffering,' says Herr Hitler. 'We must suffer
them all again,' writes Auden.

*

Auden had some odd and interesting ideas about suffering, many of them picked up from Homer Lane, who was an eccentric American educationalist – 'a mountebank', according to Auden biographer Richard Davenport-Hines; Lane was deported from England in 1925, accused of being 'a dangerous charlatan and an adventurer, who, for the safety of the public, ought to be out of the country' – and from the German psychologist Georg Groddeck, who ran a water-therapy institute at Baden-Baden. Both Lane and Groddeck believed that people brought suffering upon themselves, an idea that Auden took seriously and literally. In 'Letter to Lord Byron', Auden asserts that 'No one thinks unless a trauma makes them' – really? – and in his poem 'Miss Gee' he imagines a Miss Gee who has so repressed her sexual longings and desires as to develop a tumour – again, really? In his notes to *New Year Letter*, Auden claimed that 'In the expression of suffering […] Wagner is perhaps the greatest genius who ever lived' – which, in fairness, may be correct – and when, in the body of the poem, he describes the activities of a Wagnerian 'mental hero' (Siegfried? Tristan?), they conform with this image of Wagner as the genius of suffering:

Loud Wagner, put it on the stage:
The mental hero who has swooned
With sensual pleasure at his wound,
His intellectual life fulfilled
In knowing that his doom is willed
Exists to suffer; borne along
Upon a timeless tide of song,
The huge doll roars for death or mother,
Synonymous with one another;
And Woman, passive as in dreams,
Redeems, redeems, redeems, redeems.

*

(Another final passing observation on technical matters, which I hope is not entirely irrelevant to the tone and purpose of the poem. As in this stanza, 'September 1, 1939' is studded throughout with semicolons. I know that Auden was casual with his punctuation, but I've just been reading *Armageddon in Retrospect*, a posthumously published collection of Kurt Vonnegut's prose. One of the last things Vonnegut ever wrote was a speech, in 2007, written shortly before his death aged eighty-four, in which he offers some sage advice about semicolons, advice which I know he had often offered before, but which is certainly worth repeating: 'My advice to writers just starting out? Don't use semicolons! They are transvestite hermaphrodites, representing exactly nothing. All they do is suggest you might have gone to college.' Vonnegut's semicolon warning identifies the characteristic pitch and tone of Auden's work: it is definitely poetry written by someone who went to college. One might imagine a parlour game in which all authors are reduced down to a representative punctuation mark, to their actual pointe, as it were, to the punctum: Emily Dickinson and Herman Melville to their em-dashes; Lewis Carroll to his exclamation marks; and Henry James and Auden stripped down to their semicolons.)

4

Into this neutral air
Where blind skyscrapers use
Their full height to proclaim
The strength of Collective Man,
Each language pours its vain
Competitive excuse:
But who can live for long
In an euphoric dream;
Out of the mirror they stare,
Imperialism's face
And the international wrong.

AERODYNAMICS

Stanza 4, almost halfway, and with tales of the ancient Greeks behind us, we're now back on the streets of New York: we've gone from looking back to looking up. We are hurtling through this poem now.

Auden's always moving around like this. He's a terrible fidget. It's what makes the poems entertaining, and infuriating.

(I remember when the children were young, some of my favourite books to read with them were Miroslav Šašek's *This is* … series: *This is London, This is Paris, This is Rome, This is Venice.* I picked up a set in an Oxfam shop. *This is New York* was published in 1960. Šašek's signature storytelling style is to glance around everywhere, like an overgrown child, or an excited visitor: it creates a sensation of being overwhelmed; it allows for that thrill of discovery. 'New York', he writes, 'is the largest city in the Western Hemisphere, and it is full of the Biggest Things.')

So, let's go and look around the city with Uncle Wystan, shall we? Let's look up. Let's look at the sky.

*

What on earth is neutral air?

*

Gerard Manley Hopkins writes of air 'that's fairly mixed / With, riddles, and is rife / In every least thing's life'. Air is everywhere, in other words, and it is everywhere in 'September 1, 1939': the radio waves, the windy militant trash. In a sense, air is the empty space through which a poem moves – like a plane sky-writing through big blue skies, or through silence, or margins, or prose. I suppose air might be considered neutral insofar as it's difficult to consider in and of itself.

(And even more difficult to consider when you do. Philosophical fashions come and go, but in recent years there's been a marked interest in what one might call the 'aerological', from the German philosopher Peter Sloterdijk's *Terror from the Air*, in which he claims that the deployment of chlorine gas in the First World War unleashed a new kind of 'atmo-terrorism', to Steven Connor's *The Matter of Air*, a tornado-strength tour de force on all things ethereal, and Tonino Griffero's atmospheric *Atmospheres: Aesthetics of Emotional Spaces* – but I have to admit that I have struggled to comprehend and contain all these ideas and theories, and am only still just catching the drift of Gaston Bachelard's *L'air et les songes*, published way back in 1943, in which he makes the case for air as providing a model for our understanding of dreamlike states and environments. Air, I will say, though – having had an intoxicating sniff of these notions, and so being emboldened to offer a little philosophical puff of my own – air seems to me to be neutral like ideology. It is invisible until you notice it, and then it's everywhere.)

> The air rippled like camouflage. Behind it something else seemed to carry on in secret. At any moment the illusion they stood on would dissolve and they would fall to earth.
>
> (Thomas Pynchon, *Gravity's Rainbow*)

The idea of neutral air also perhaps suggests America as a land of opportunity, a big blank space. The music journalist Greil Marcus – a writer who really achieved something, who almost single-handedly made rock criticism respectable – argues in his book *The Shape of Things to Come: Prophecy and the American Voice* (2006) that 'America is a place and a story, made up of exuberance and suspicion, crime and liberation, lynch mobs and escapes; its greatest testaments are made of portents and warnings, Biblical allusions that lose all their certainties in American air.' Auden, I think, would agree with Mr Marcus, that the invented and unscripted nature of America is what constitutes its appeal and its vulnerability. As the American story is retold and its dreams and promises fulfilled, betrayed and undermined, so the great drama continues.

Neutral air: endless opportunities.

> Above them, expensive and lovely as a rich child's toy,
> The aeroplanes fly in the new European air,
> On the edge of that air that makes England of minor
>   importance.
>
> (Auden, 'Dover')

Yet the neutral also suggests the suspension of all activity and meaning. Two years before his death at the age of sixty-four in 1980, Roland Barthes delivered a course, 'Le Neutre', 'The Neutral', at the Collège de France, in which he offered all sorts of ideas and versions of the neutral. 'I define the Neutral as that which outplays the paradigm, or rather I call Neutral everything that baffles the paradigm. For I am not trying to define a word; I am trying to name a thing: I gather under a name, which here is the Neutral.' (Uh-huh, you might say, if not French, 'Mr Barthes, would you mind just clarifying …'). 'The Neutral', Barthes goes on, means both violence and the suspension of violence, wherein lies 'the paradox of the desire for the Neutral'.

The neutral represents both violence and the suspension of violence: perplexing as it seems, this may be close to what Auden is thinking about in the poem.

*

Because, of course, what he's actually thinking about is an entirely obvious kind of neutrality.

In August 1935, the United States Congress passed the first of a series of Neutrality Acts, designed to limit American involvement in future wars. And, sure enough, when the future war did come to Europe, Roosevelt was quick to reassure his neutral nation:

At this moment there is being prepared a proclamation of American neutrality. This would have been done even if there had been no neutrality statute on the books, for this proclamation is in accordance with international law and in accordance with American policy. This will be followed by a proclamation required by the existing Neutrality Act. And I trust that in the days to come our neutrality can be made a true neutrality.

But he went on:

This nation will remain a neutral nation, but I cannot ask that every American remain neutral in thought as well. Even a neutral has a right to take account of facts. Even a neutral cannot be asked to close his mind or close his conscience.

(Roosevelt, 3 September 1939, *Fireside Chat* 14)

Examine your conscience, you neutrals, the poem says. Open your mind. Look around!

GET RID OF THE
(EXPLETIVE) BRAILLE

First, neutral air and now blind skyscrapers. Blind skyscrapers?

*

The *AIA Guide to New York City* is the standard guide to the architecture of the five boroughs of New York City, first published in 1967, with the most recent, the fifth edition, published in 2010.

The 2010 *AIA Guide* describes Trump Tower, at 721–725 Fifth Avenue, between 56th and 57th Streets, in midtown, a few blocks from 52nd Street, as 'flamboyant, exciting, and emblematic of the American Dream'.

*

Trump Tower has a sixty-foot waterfall in the lobby. The public spaces are clad in pink marble. There is a Trump Bar, a Trump Cafe and a Trump Grill, or 'Grille', filled with mirrors (and which, according to *Vanity Fair*, 'could be the worst restaurant in America'). President Donald Trump's wife, Melania, lives there with their son, Barron. President Trump himself likes to spend as much time as possible in Trump Tower, away from the White House in Washington, and at his Mar-a-Lago resort in Palm Beach, his 'winter White House'. Some New Yorkers like to refer to Trump Tower as 'the Black House'. Residents of Trump Tower have included Steven Spielberg, Sophia Loren, Jean-Claude

'Baby Doc' Duvalier, the former president of Haiti, Prince Mutaib bin Abdulaziz Al Saud, Bruce Willis, Andrew Lloyd Webber and Michael Jackson – who converted a room in his apartment into a mirrored dance studio.

In order to build the Tower, in 1980 Mr Trump demolished the art-deco Bonwit Teller department store, having promised the limestone reliefs on the building's facade to the Metropolitan Museum of Art, which wanted them for its sculpture collection: rather than removing the reliefs, though, he had them destroyed. According to Kent Barwick, the then chairman of the New York City Landmarks Preservation Commission, it was the building of Trump Tower that established Trump's reputation 'as a bad guy': 'Afterwards, rightly or wrongly, there was a question of trust.' Trump Tower has fifty-eight floors: Trump claims there are sixty-eight. The building is entirely clad in glass.

On 12 September 2018, Barbara Res, a former vice-president in charge of construction for the Trump Organization, wrote an op-ed piece for the New York *Daily News* in which she claimed that during the construction of Trump Tower, Mr Trump asked an architect to remove Braille from the elevators:

'What's this?' Trump asked. 'Braille,' the architect replied. Trump told the architect to take it off, get rid of it. 'We can't,' the architect said, 'It's the law.' 'Get rid of the (expletive) Braille. No blind people are going to live in Trump Tower. Just do it,' Trump yelled back, calling him weak.

Well. What can you say? Maybe there is a blind man living in Trump Tower. It's certainly a blind skyscraper.

*

According to the *Oxford English Dictionary* – which was a true skyscraper enterprise if ever there was one, compiled by the Scottish polymath lexicographer James Murray with the assistance of a team of researchers and volunteers, and a murderer locked up in Broadmoor, who would all send Murray instances of the usage of particular words, which Murray would then organise and arrange in a system of pigeonholes he had set up in a corrugated iron shed in the back garden of his house in Oxford, a house just around the corner from where I used to live, in fact and by the by, when I first started reading Auden, and a house which remained a landmark because the Post Office had agreed to erect a special postbox outside, since Murray sent and received so much mail as he worked on the dictionary for over thirty-five years, and the postbox was still there when I was there, though Murray of course was long gone, having died before the dictionary was completed, failing to see it to press – the great *Oxford English Dictionary* lists no fewer than six definitions for the word 'skyscraper'.

*

First there is the nautical meaning – 'a triangular sky-sail'. Then there are a number of colloquial meanings: 'a high-standing horse', derived from the name of a horse that won the Epsom Derby in 1789; 'a very tall man' ('I say, old sky-scraper, is it cold up there?'); 'a rider on one of the high cycles formerly in use'; and a form of 'exaggerated' story. And then, finally, the meaning with which we are now most familiar: 'a high building of many storeys, especially one of those characteristic of American cities'.

The earliest quoted citation for this usage – a high building characteristic of American cities – is from an article published in the *American Architect and Building News* on 30 June 1883. The article makes a passionate claim for squat, ugly public buildings to become tall, towering structures: 'This form of sky-scraper gives that peculiar refined, independent, self-contained, daring, bold, heaven-reaching, erratic, piratic, Quixotic, American thought ...' Refined, independent, self-contained, daring, bold, heaven-reaching, erratic, piratic, Quixotic, the skyscraper 'gives' American thought, it embodies a certain kind of economic and social activity and it defines the American city landscape, a landscape that, of course, changed for ever on 11 September 2001, with the destruction of the Twin Towers of the World Trade Center, which at the time of their completion were the tallest buildings in the world (1 World Trade Center was 1,368 feet, 2 World Trade Center was 1,362 feet).

*

(Not long after the attacks of 11 September 2001, discussions began about what, if anything, to build in place of the Twin Towers. Proposals for a replacement building or buildings included a cultural centre, various kinds of memorials and even an underground Twin Towers, mirroring the originals. In the end, the decision was made to build another, even bigger skyscraper. Construction of this new building – to be called Freedom Tower – began in 2006. In 2009, it was officially renamed One World Trade Center. When finally completed in 2014, the building, though taller than the original Twin Towers, was by no means the tallest in the world: times had changed. The top five tallest buildings in the world are now all in what Miroslav Šašek might call the eastern hemisphere: in Dubai, Shanghai, Shenzhen, Seoul and Mecca. The Burj Khalifa in Dubai tops out at 2,722 feet. The height of One World Trade Center is 1,776 feet – recalling the year of the American Declaration of Independence. Some buildings are built as symbols, but all buildings are symbolic.)

Manhattan has generated a shameless architecture that
has been loved in direct proportion to its defiant lack of
self-hatred, has been respected exactly to the degree that
it went too far.

(Rem Koolhaas, *Delirious New York*)

It's difficult to determine when the first American skyscraper was
actually built: was the fourteen-storey sugarhouse on Duane
Street near Broadway, constructed sometime around 1840, really
a skyscraper? It had no elevator. Perhaps it was Burnham and
Root's Montauk Building in Chicago, completed in 1882?
Elevators, but only ten storeys. In *Rise of the New York Skyscraper
1865–1913* (1996), Sarah Landau and Carl W. Condit explain
that the skyscraper – which might include not only tall office
buildings but also high-rise apartments and hotels, and, more
recently, in our own time, entertainment complexes and casinos
– is an ever-evolving idea of a building that designates neither a
specific style nor size and which takes particular forms in
particular places. Chinese skyscrapers probably represent the
future of the form, but there is no doubt that in the twentieth
century, in Auden's age, the skyscraper was distinctively and
recognisably American – indeed, in the words of the architec-
tural historian Roberta Moudry, in *The American Skyscraper:
Cultural Histories* (2005), it was 'the signal architectural and
spatial event of the modern American city'.

*

On 18 January 1939, Auden and Isherwood caught the boat-
train from Waterloo to Southampton, departing for New York
on the SS *Champlain* the next morning. 'Well,' said Isherwood,
'we're off again.' 'Goody,' said Auden. They arrived in New York
after a stormy journey on 26 January. Isherwood, recalling their

arrival, wrote of 'the Red Indian island with its appalling towers […] You could feel it vibrating with the tension of the nervous New World, aggressively flaunting its rude steel nudity.' (It was snowing: the city, he wrote, looked like a 'wedding-cake'.) Writing to a friend back in England in September 1939, having moved into an apartment in Brooklyn Heights, at 1 Montague Terrace, with a view across the East River, Auden described 'looking out over water at the towers of Manhattan. The skyscrapers with the exception of Radio City which is one of the architectural wonders of the world are ugly close to but lovely from a distance.' (Auden's skyscrapers in the poem are a reminder that, among other things, 'September 1, 1939' functions as a kind of postcard home. Look, I'm in New York!)

*

(Years ago, I planned to go on an Auden pilgrimage, visiting the places Auden had lived, starting at his birthplace, 54 Bootham, York, and taking in the various schools, then Oxford, Berlin, London, Manhattan, Brooklyn, Fire Island and Ischia, ending up in Kirchstetten and the hotel where he died, the Altenburger Hof, No. 5, Walfischgasse, Vienna. My wife suggested instead that we should go on a package tour to Fuerteventura, which we did. I didn't see a skyscraper until I visited New York in my late twenties. When I was young, London did not boast skyscrapers – now, of course, it boasts like everywhere – so in my youth my familiarity with skyscrapers was strictly limited to watching the opening credits of the TV series *Kojak*, and *Taxi*, and reruns of the films of Harold Lloyd on BBC2 at teatime, including *Look Out Below, High and Dizzy* and *Safety Last!*, in which the great silent-comedy star hangs from the hands of a large clock on the outside of a skyscraper, dangling above the traffic below, a star about to fall.)

*

Auden's skyscrapers, it is important to note, were not our own. Our skyscrapers are ludic, playful, transparent boxes which reflect the triumph of International Style modernism and self-referential postmodernism, with their vast curtain walls, blank spaces and ironic curves. Our skyscrapers, for better and for worse, are Trumpian. Auden's skyscrapers were serious stone, brick and terracotta echt American monuments: the Flatiron Building, the Metropolitan Life Insurance Company Tower, the Bankers Trust Company Building, the Woolworth Building. And, of course, the Empire State Building, which was just a five-minute walk from the Dizzy Club on West 52nd Street.

*

Auden, as Edward Mendelson points out, can often be found in his early work writing at 'high altitudes'. He can also be found late at night in upper rooms: the poem 'August for the people', for example, from *Look, Stranger!*, is written 'From the narrow window of my fourth-floor room', with the poet musing and smoking into the night; similarly with the poem 'Now from my window-sill I watch the night'. At this early stage of his career, Auden believed in privileged perspectives, viewing the world through the eyes of the airman, the hawk, the mountaineer and the spy – those with an insight or an overview. His early verse undoubtedly has what one might call a superior aspect.

*

But he spied the dangers of his superior vantage point almost from the moment he took it up, recognising the motive for high-flying as vanity and the usual result of lofty observation as casual indifference and solipsism. Throughout the 1930s and 1940s, he launched a spate of attacks on the idea of the artist's garret. As early as 1932, in 'I have a handsome profile', he mocked attic pretensions:

I'll hire a furnished attic
A room on the top floor
I'll spend my mornings writing
A book that would cause a furore
About a world that has had its day.

And at the Poet's Party in 'Letter to Lord Byron', he ridiculed the artist's arrogance:

How nice at first to watch the passers-by
    Out of the upper window, and to say
'How glad I am that though I have to die
    Like all those cattle, I'm less base than they!'

He broadened and conceptualised his discontent with high altitudes and high-handed attitudes in a passage in his essay 'Hic et Ille' (1956), which reads very much like a repudiation of the hawk's perspective:

From the height of 10,000 feet, the earth appears to the human eye as it appears to the eye of the camera; that is to say, all history is reduced to nature. This has the salutary effect of making historical evils, like national divisions and political hatreds, seem absurd. I look down from an airplane upon a stretch of land which is obviously continuous. That, across it, marked by a tiny ridge or river or even by no topographical sign whatever, there should run a frontier, and that the human beings living on one side should hate or refuse to trade with or be forbidden to visit those on the other side, is instantaneously revealed to me as ridiculous. Unfortunately, I cannot have this revelation without simultaneously having the illusion that there are no historical values either. From the same height I cannot distinguish between an outcrop of rock and a Gothic cathedral, or between a happy family playing in a backyard and a flock of sheep, so that I am unable to feel any difference between dropping a bomb upon one or the other.

The bigger the picture, the broader the perspective: the more you see, but the less you care.

*

So, anyway, the point is, despite the view, skyscrapers might well be described as 'blind'.

TOWER OF BABEL TIME

But hold on – hold on! – now the blind capitalist skyscrapers, centres and symbols of private enterprise, are proclaiming the 'strength of Collective Man'?

It's another classic Auden swerve, identifying American individualism with European collectivism, before swerving again into an allusion to the Tower of Babel, which prepares us for the 'euphoric dream', which turns out to be the horrible reality of international imperialism at the very end of the stanza ...

You really have to be very nimble to keep up with Auden at this point – you've got to be quick on your feet to follow his every move. It's the sort of fancy footwork that appeals to the young.

*

(William Carlos Williams on Auden: 'There is no modern poet so agile – so impressive in the use of the poetic means. He can do anything – except one thing.')

*

Auden always appealed to the young. Ill in hospital watching the 1985 Wimbledon tennis tournament, Philip Larkin expressed his delight that Boris Becker, the winner of the men's singles, looked 'just like the young Auden'. Larkin was dying of cancer and suffering from 'debility and depression', and his remarking on the similarity in appearance between the blond Becker and the famously tow-haired Auden is poignant and significant, not because of the striking resemblance between the two – I can't quite see it myself – but because the 'young Auden' was so much a feature of Larkin's own vanished youth. It is clear from the evidence of Larkin's posthumously published letters and from biographies that Auden was associated with all the sweet things of Larkin's adolescence and early adulthood, the holy trinity described in his unfinished poem 'The Dance': '"Drink, sex and jazz"'. Generations have felt the same. The Confessionals, the Beats, the New York School: in their youth they all looked up to Auden.

> Can Sixty make sense to Sixteen-Plus?
> What has my camp in common with theirs,
> with buttons and beards and Be-Ins?
>
> (Auden, 'Prologue at Sixty')

It's partly to do with the caps.

The strength of Collective Man comes in caps. Auden loved using capitals: his later work was, in the words of Randall Jarrell, 'An Elks' Convention of the Capital Letters', full of personified allegorical beings whose origins and activities become quite difficult to fathom and to follow. Auden's favourites were what he called the Censor and Dame Kind, though their names sometimes change and there are crowds of minions: the poems 'Homage to Clio' and 'Dame Kind', both in the collection *Homage to Clio* (1960), are a good introduction to the upper-case Auden pantheon. (He also sticks with the traditional pantheon: the poems throng with Zeus and Apollo, Hermes, Eros, Aphrodite et al.)

People love caps: they make an otherwise unremarkable phrase Sound Serious.

*

It's probably worth acknowledging here, at least in passing, that it is Collective Man that he refers to, as in mankind, which in our age of gender-neutral pronouns perhaps runs the risk of offending.

◉

There is a whole book to be written about Auden and woman-kind: that book is not going to be written by me, and in fact maybe shouldn't be written at all. ('Gynocritics begins at the point when we free ourselves from the linear absolutes of male literary history, stop trying to fit women between the lines of the male tradition, and focus instead on the newly visible world of female culture.' Elaine Showalter, 'Toward a Feminist Poetics', in *The New Feminist Criticism*.) But a few remarks, maybe, on his influence and relations with some women writers – would that not be appropriate?

> I want a form that's large enough to swim in,
>> And talk on any subject that I choose.
>>>> (Auden, 'Letter to Lord Byron')

In his foreword to Adrienne Rich's first collection of poems, *A Change of World* (1951) – chosen by him as part of the Yale Younger Poets series – Auden writes:

> Miss Rich, who is, I understand, twenty-one years old,
> displays a modesty not so common at that age, which
> disclaims any extraordinary vision, and a love for her

medium, a determination to ensure that whatever she
writes shall, at least, not be shoddily made. In a young
poet, as T. S. Eliot has observed, the most promising
sign is craftsmanship for it is evidence of a capacity for
detachment from the self and its emotions without which
no art is possible.

He resorts here to stereotypes on the one hand (Rich displays
'modesty' and 'disclaims any extraordinary vision'), but on the
other hand he praises her for the traditionally masculine virtues
of 'determination' and 'craftsmanship'. In a speech in 1971,
'When We Dead Awaken: Writing as Re-Vision', it was this latter
quality, the quality of craft, that Rich particularly scorned:
'Poems are like dreams,' she said; the formalism she had inher-
ited from male poets had prevented her for many years from
realising this and writing as a woman. In order to gain the
'perfection of order' and the approval of male poets, she had had
to suppress, omit and falsify her experiences as a woman. It is
unfortunate.

*

Elizabeth Bishop, on the other hand, believed that Auden's
'sexual courage' made him an ideal poetic model – and her own
great mentor, Marianne Moore, Bishop claimed, was so devoted
to Auden that 'the very cat he had patted [...] was produced for
me to admire and pat too'. Sylvia Plath, meanwhile, described
herself falling under Auden's spell in a letter to her brother in
March 1953, after Auden had visited Smith College:

The great W. H. Auden spoke in chapel this week, and
I saw him for the first time. He is my conception of the
perfect poet: tall, with a big leonine head and a sandy

mane of hair, and a lyrically gigantic stride. Needless to
say he has a wonderfully textured British accent, and I
adore him with a big Hero Worship. I would someday
like to touch the Hem of his Garment and say in a very
small adoring voice: Mr Auden, I haveapomeforyou [sic]:
'I found my God in Auden.'

He is Wonderful and
Very Brilliant, and
Very Lyric and Most
Extremely Witty.

(This description of the 'perfect poet' haunts Plath's description
of Ted Hughes some three years later: she tells her mother that
Hughes is a 'brilliant poet' but also 'large, hulking' and a 'lion'.
Auden was a model in more ways than one.)

*

Auden's Collective Man, anyway, is intended as inclusive, since
all of us are guilty, which is the ultimate point of the stanza.

'Normality! What murders are committed in thy name!'
(Auden, *Letters from Iceland*)

Throughout Auden's early work, in poems such as 'Gare du Midi'
and 'Certainly our city', there's an air of menace – the critic Terry
Eagleton calls it 'an atmosphere of evil too widespread for anal-
ysis, too self-generating for control'. It's still there lurking at the
beginning of *New Year Letter*:

As on the verge of happening
There crouched the presence of The Thing.
All formulas were tried to still
The scratching on the window-sill,
All bolts of custom made secure
Against the pressure on the door,
But up the staircase of events
Carrying his special instruments,
To every bedside all the same
The dreadful figure swiftly came.

In fact, this isn't just menace, it's like something out of a horror film. In *New Year Letter*, he goes on to describe the 'crooked claws / Emerging into view and groping / For handholds on the low round coping, / As Horror clambers from the well', while in *For the Time Being* he describes how 'Outside the civil garden / Of every day of love there / Crouches a wild passion / To destroy and be destroyed.'

Evil in Auden is often outside, around, underneath and encroaching, 'the abyss / That always lies just underneath / Our jolly picnic on the heath' in *New Year Letter*, the 'faint tang of irretrievable disaster' in *The Orators*. Violence and pain are just within earshot:

Who, thinking of the last ten years,
Does not hear howling in his ears
The Asiatic cry of pain,
The shots of executing Spain,
See stumbling through his outraged mind,
The Abyssinian, blistered, blind.

(Auden, *New Year Letter*)

But worst of all is when it turns out that the evil is not outside but inside, and it's you.

> Evil is unspectacular and always human,
> And shares our bed and eats at our own table.
>
> (Auden, 'Herman Melville')

The true horror: we're the horror.

5

Faces along the bar
Cling to their average day:
The lights must never go out,
The music must always play,
All the conventions conspire
To make this fort assume
The furniture of home;
Lest we should see where we are,
Lost in a haunted wood,
Children afraid of the night
Who have never been happy or good.

THE LIQUID MENU

Stanza 5, and frankly we all deserve a drink.

So, to the bar. But there are bars, and there are bars.

(And this is definitely a bar, not a dive. We've maybe moved on from 52nd Street: this bar's more like a bar in some *New Yorker* cartoon.)

You know the old joke. Two men are in a bar, old friends, drinking silently. After a couple of hours, one of the men raises his glass to the other and says, 'Cheers.' To which his friend responds, 'Did we come here to talk or to drink?'

*

Auden is definitely here to talk. And to drink. His capacity for both was extraordinary.

*

Robert Craft, in his book *Stravinsky: Chronicle of a Friendship*, writes of a typical evening in January 1964, 'Auden for dinner. He drinks a jug of Gibsons before, a bottle of champagne during, a bottle (sic) of Cherry Heering (did he think it was Chianti?) after dinner [...] Despite this liquid menu, he not only is unblurred, but also performs mental pirouettes for us [...] the only sign of tipsiness is an initial lurch at departure, after which a gyroscope seems to take over.'

Let's lurch a little, before the gyroscope takes over.

ALAN ANSEN: I should think you might almost be ready to
   issue a volume of collected prose.
AUDEN: I don't think so. Criticism should be a casual
   conversation.

(Alan Ansen, *The Table Talk of W. H. Auden*)

In his 1946 essay 'The Moon Under Water', George Orwell described his perfect pub: 'only two minutes from a bus stop ... on a side-street ... its whole architecture and fittings ... uncompromisingly Victorian ... The grained woodwork, the ornamental mirrors behind the bar, the cast-iron fireplaces, the florid ceiling stained dark yellow by tobacco-smoke, the stuffed bull's head over the mantelpiece – everything has the solid, comfortable ugliness of the nineteenth century.'

Orwell's Victorian fun palace boasted a public bar, a saloon bar, a ladies' bar and a dining room. Creamy stout was served in pewter mugs, there were matronly barmaids, liver-sausage sandwiches and mussels for bar snacks, with a good lunch also available – 'a cut off the joint, two vegetables and boiled jam roll – for about three shillings'. Outside there was a large garden with plane trees, with swings for the children.

The only problem with the Moon Under Water, as Orwell acknowledged at the end of his essay, was that it did not exist. He was describing a fantasy. Nonetheless, the Moon Under Water is what one might regard as the quintessentially – or Platonically – English pub.

There are some important differences between English pubs and American bars. And indeed, I might add, between English pubs, American bars and Irish pubs and bars, certainly from the perspective of where I'm sitting, which is not in fact a bar or a pub, but which will be soon, and which bears little resemblance to either Orwell's or Auden's, but is not far from Louis MacNeice's:

> In the road is another smile on the face of day.
> We stop at random for a morning drink
> In a thatched inn; to find, as at a play,
>
> The bar already loud with chatter and clink
> Of glasses …
>
> … in sheer
>
> Rebuttal of the silence and the cold
> Attached to death.
>
> (Louis MacNeice, *Autumn Sequel*, Canto XX)

The most famous New York bar in American literary history is probably Charles Pfaff's beer cellar, on Broadway near Bleecker (recently re-established at 643 Broadway). In the mid-nineteenth century, Pfaff's became a popular meeting place for writers and artists. Rumours abounded of its bohemian clientele. Walt Whitman has an unfinished poem in praise of Pfaff's ('The vault at Pfaffs where the drinkers and laughers meet to eat and drink and carouse / While on the walk immediately overhead, pass the myriad feet of Broadway'), and on 2 August 1862, the *New York Illustrated News* described it thus:

> As so much has been said in the papers, from time to time, about Pfaff's it may be well to state that the name is descriptive, simply, of a restaurant and lager bier saloon, kept at No. 647 Broadway, by a Teuton of that name, and

which, partly from its central position, and partly from
the excellence of its fare, has been such a favorite resort,
for several years, for artists, litterateurs, actors, managers,
editors, critics, politicians, and other public characters,
as to have become quite famous. It is not, as has been
often reported, the rendezvous of a particular clique or
club of Bohemians (whatever they may be), but simply
a general and convenient meeting-place for cultivated
men, and one where, almost any evening, you may meet
representatives of nearly every branch of literature and
art, assembled, not by appointment, nor from habit even,
but met by chance, the usual way.

In Pfaff's they may have assembled by chance, but in England the
litterateurs liked to gather by appointment. During the 1930s,
for example, the Eagle and Child, opposite St John's College on
St Giles' in Oxford, played host to the so-called Inklings – J. R. R.
Tolkien, C. S. Lewis, you know the lads – who would get together
on Monday lunchtimes to drink half pints of warm beer and
discuss literature, theology and their various works in progress.

*

Auden was not one to discuss with chums his work in progress,
nor was he much of a half-pint man: he tended to hold forth in
ex cathedra fashion, and his favourite tipple was a Martini.

*

The Martinis are sending a clear signal:

The Martini sends seven Simple Messages. I call these
messages simple because they are binary in form (the
Martini is x, it is not y, the opposite of x). They are:

MESSAGE ONE: The Martini is American – it is not
European, Asian, or African
MESSAGE TWO: The Martini is urban and urbane – it is not
rural or rustic
MESSAGE THREE: The Martini is a high-status, not a
low-status, drink
MESSAGE FOUR: The Martini is a man's, not a woman's,
drink
MESSAGE FIVE: The Martini is optimistic, not pessimistic
MESSAGE SIX: The Martini is the drink of adults, not of
children
MESSAGE SEVEN: The Martini belongs to the past, not to
the present

[…] The fact remains that the binary oppositions
on which the Simple Messages are based include a
potentially disturbing hierarchical ranking. The first term
is good or superior, the second bad or inferior:

AMERICAN: European, Asian, African
URBAN, URBANE: rural, rustic
UPPER-CLASS: lower-class
MALE: female
OPTIMISTIC: pessimistic
ADULT: immature
PAST: present

The net result for the Martini is politically incorrect, to
say the least.

(Lowell Edmunds, *Martini, Straight Up*)

Auden was omnibibulous, but he was also a superior drinker.

*

Interviewing Auden in 1972, for the *Paris Review*, Michael Newman noted that Auden 'drank Smirnoff martinis, red wine, and cognac' – during the interview, though? it's not entirely clear – 'shunned pot, and confessed to having, under a doctor's supervision, tried LSD: "Nothing much happened, but I did get the distinct impression that some birds were trying to communicate with me."' At poetry readings later in his life he occasionally turned up drunk, and famously celebrated his daily 'Martini-time' – 6 p.m. – in a poem ('The Garrison'), his preferred preparation being one part vermouth, Noilly Prat, to three parts vodka, with both the vodka and the glasses being first cooled in the refrigerator. As he grew older, he liked to take a bottle of wine – a Valpolicella, preferably – to bed, as well as a glass of vodka, which, according to Humphrey Carpenter, 'he would swallow as a soporific after his trip to the lavatory'.

> In some poems you're taking the risk of sentiment brimming over into sentimentality.
> Am I? I don't understand the word sentimentality. It reminds me of Dylan Thomas's definition of an alcoholic: 'A man you don't like who drinks as much as you do.' I think sentimentality is someone you don't like feeling as much as you do. But you can't win, can you?
> (John Haffenden, interview with Philip Larkin, *Viewpoints: Poets in Conversation*)

You can't win.

These days, the way he carried on, Auden might be counted by many as a slovenly, drink- and drug-addicted boor – and indeed he probably was. But by the standards of old? I don't know. In all sorts of ways, what we now regard as unacceptable, our parents and grandparents would have regarded as normal, just as what we now accept as everyday and average, they would have regarded as abnormal, irregular, extreme and outrageous. When he was at work, my father would go to the pub at lunch-time before operating heavy machinery: at least Auden was only using a pen. The American poet Howard Nemerov has a poem called 'Life Cycle of Common Man', published in 1960, well within living memory, in which the common man, an 'average consumer of the middle class', is said to get through, in a life-time, 'Just under half a million cigarettes / Four thousand fifths of gin and about / A quarter as much vermouth.' Nemerov's account of the average American consumer now seems about as strange and outlandish as a Victorian explorer's account of the lives of primitive tribespeople in some distant land. Half a million cigarettes? Four thousand fifths of gin? A quarter as much vermouth? It's like watching *Mad Men*, season 1. Presumably we watch historical drama on TV, or old footage of our parents and grandparents caught on cine film, because the past really is another country: they really did do things differ-ently there. No one swings a scythe like that any more. No one wears a suit like that. And no one now drinks and smokes like Auden. (When his friend James Stern commented to Auden about his constantly chain-smoking Lucky Strikes, which Stern reckoned worked out at about 15,000 cigarettes a year, Auden responded, 'Ah, but I don't inhale!')

*

I imagine Auden at the bar rather as he's recalled in this poem by Bertolt Brecht:

Lunching me, a kindly act
In an alehouse, still intact
He sat looming like a cloud
Over the beer-sodden crowd.

>   (Bertolt Brecht, *Poems 1913–1956*)

(The two men met on numerous occasions and worked together
on Brecht's adaptation of *The Duchess of Malfi* for the Broadway
stage, which turned out to be a disaster. Auden thought Brecht
an 'odious' person, while Brecht thought Auden filthy.)

*

My point is, Auden was convivial – intellectually, I mean, as well
as socially. In 'Making, Knowing and Judging', for example, he
turns T. S. Eliot's 'Tradition and the Individual Talent' inside out
and upside down, with the imperial heights of Eliot's 'Theory of
Impersonal Poetry' refigured as a 'Mad Hatter's Tea-Party':

> Could he look into a memory, the literary historian
> would find many members of that species which he calls
> books, but they are curiously changed from the books
> he finds in his library. The dates are all different. *In
> Memoriam* is written before *The Dunciad*, the thirteenth
> century comes after the sixteenth […] *Piers Ploughman
> III* is going about with Kierkegaard's *Journals, Piers
> Ploughman IV* with *The Making of the English Landscape*.
> Most puzzling of all, instead of only associating with
> members of their own kind, in this extraordinary
> democracy every species of being knows every other
> and the closest friend of a book is rarely another book.
> *Gulliver's Travels* walks arm in arm with a love affair, a
> canto of *Il Paradiso* sits with a singularly good dinner.

Auden's idea of a canon is an eccentric one, appealing to personal experience as its judge, with the final criterion for judgement being the quality of the experience being shared by persons, or between persons and poems as what he called 'pseudo-persons'. Indeed, he seems to have understood personal relations as the paradigm and basis for all literary production, which explains many of the seemingly disconnected elements in his work: the insistent forms of address, the tendency towards argument and explanation, the confusion of personified hosts who inform his poetics, and, might I say, the exemplary idiosyncrasies of his criticism and reviews, the effect of which can be shocking, even now, as when he begins an essay on Thomas Hardy with the words 'I cannot write objectively about Thomas Hardy because I was once in love with him.'

(We don't expect such explicitness from critics. We do get it now occasionally, with the likes of, say, Maggie Nelson, and those working under the influence of affect theorists like Rita Felski, but at one time William Empson was one of the few who, like Auden, was prepared to own up to the effects of his affections on his work. Empson wrote of Eliot that 'I do not propose here to try to judge or define the achievement of Eliot; indeed I feel, like most other verse writers of my generation, that I do not know for certain how much of my own mind he invented.' Writing about Auden, Empson on several occasions calls him 'wonderful', and the epithet is not trivial nor its object single-minded; its meaning connects Empson's excitement with Auden's own.)

*

As for the other faces along the bar with Auden? I imagine perhaps Elizabeth Bishop (I'm thinking of her poem 'A Drunkard', with its lines 'I had begun / to drink, & drink – I can't get enough'); Jane Bowles (who lived with Auden in Brooklyn and used to get up at 6 a.m. after a hard night's drinking to do his typing for him); the American poet Richard Wilbur (who in an interview in the indispensable *Auden Society Newsletter*, recalled that 'Auden had ordered a martini and I had ordered a martini, and we talked about martinis, and we discussed the fact that if you are devoted to martinis, it's very hard to get a good one away from home'); Joseph Brodsky (who in his cups would sob and confess that he loved Auden: 'When I am on the road, I am thinking of Wystan – of Wystan all the time – as if he was a girl, wohhl [...] You think I am sick?'); and maybe Bernard Kops (who in his poem 'On a Brief Meeting with Auden' recalls him 'Leaning against the bar / as if receiving extreme unction [...] Pissed out of his mind in total elation, / beautiful boys surrounding him in / absolute adulation').

BELOW AVERAGE

Can't you just see them all there, drinking together? Auden and Elizabeth Bishop and Jane Bowles? Maybe? Not? That's because they're all drinking in the VIP lounge.

If 'September 1, 1939' is a deeply troubled poem, which it certainly is, it's partly because it is haunted by the lurking figure of the average man – 'I and the public know', the 'Collective Man', 'our' crude wish, the 'dense commuters', the 'sensual man-in-the-street' – who now looms fully into view and who is not, I think, entirely welcome.

The average man is Auden's audience, his compatriots – and the enemy.

The average man is … well, me.

In order that everything should be reduced to the same level, it is first of all necessary to procure a phantom, its spirit, a monstrous abstraction, an all-embracing something which is nothing, a mirage – and that phantom is the public […]

A public is neither a nation, nor a generation, nor a community, nor a society, nor these particular men, for all these are only what they are through the concrete; no single person who belongs to the public makes a real commitment […]

> A public is everything and nothing, the most
> dangerous of all powers and the most insignificant: one
> can speak to a whole nation in the name of the public,
> and still the public will be less than a single real man,
> however unimportant.
>
> (Søren Kierkegaard, *The Present Age*)

Auden himself was anything but average. Prep school, public school, Oxford, all of that – and he was an out-and-proud gay man when it wasn't easy to be an out-and-proud gay man, and he was a poet. He was definitely not average, but most of us are. Most of us are utterly ordinary. We can't all be exceptional. In Philip Roth's novel *Everyman* (2006), the grim Everyman figure of the book's title, Roth's protagonist, is granted the unusual gift of being able to observe his family grieving at his own graveside. To his horror, he realises that, for all his achievements, his life was nothing but average: 'Up and down the state that day, there'd been five hundred funerals like his, routine, ordinary [...] no more or less interesting than any of the others.'

*

According to the *OED* – which is itself a triumph of the art of averaging, a dictionary of the everyday usage as well of the historical development of words, a dictionary of the central tendencies of meaning in the English language – 'Few words have received more etymological investigation' than the word 'average'. It is a word that has suffered a long, slow decline in meaning, from its ancient sense of being some kind of service due by tenants to their feudal lords, to the point at which it is now considered to be merely the opposite of 'awesome'. 'Averageness', according to the *OED*, is 'mediocrity'. Average has somehow become below average.

*

(For forty years Garrison Keillor would end his weekly mono-
logue about his home town, Lake Wobegon, on the *Prairie Home
Companion* radio show – which American friends would send
me, on cassette, and which I would play in the car while driving
– with the words 'That's the news from Lake Wobegon, where all
the women are strong, all the men are good-looking, and all the
children are above average.' Lake Wobegon does not exist. It is
an imaginary place – and a statistical impossibility.)

*

Some words become sullied by association over time, others fall
into misuse and others fall out of use entirely. The word 'average'
has simply sunk in our estimation. *Average is Over* proclaims the
title of one recent bestselling book about economics. *Start:
Punch Fear in the Face, Escape Average, and Do Work That Matters*
suggests the title of another. *Conquering Average. Mastering
Average. Overcoming Average.* This is the mantra of our age.

(Or rather it *was* the mantra: while I've been writing this
book, things have changed. Trump, Brexit, the *gilets jaunes*, the
rise of the right-wing populists: one might interpret all these
phenomena as the return or the revenge of the average. Even the
Occupy movement, that great protest against social and
economic inequality that swept through America and many
other parts of the world a few years ago, and whose slogan was
'We Are the 99%', was premised on the idea that for the *average*
person the economy, the 'system', wasn't really working any
more, that the fundamental promise offered by the governments
and economies of the West – work hard, play by the rules and
you will succeed – has been broken by the actions of govern-
ments, giant corporations and the global banking system, who
represent the 1%. 'We Are the 99%' sounds a lot better – and is
much more statistically compelling – than 'We Are the Average',

but it amounts to the same thing. We have been excluded, we are overlooked and we're angry. We're deplorable.)

*

Of course, things could be even worse for the 'average'. A recent paper published in the *Journal of Positive Psychology* analysing the appearance and frequency of words related to moral excellence and virtue in American books published between 1901 and 2000 found a decline in the use of general moral terms such as 'virtue' and 'conscience'. (This doesn't necessarily mean that we no longer have a shared moral framework, but it may mean that we're beginning to lack the vocabulary to describe it.)

Our changing understanding of what it might mean to be 'average' perhaps indicates a crisis in how we think and talk about the social contract, about how we think and talk about each other – what makes us similar, what binds us together, and what constitutes a culture, a democracy and a commonweal.

And that crisis, I think, is already apparent in Auden's use of 'average'.

> It is both the glory and the shame of poetry that its
> medium is not its private property, that a poet cannot
> invent his words and that words are products, not of
> nature, but of a human society which uses them for a
> thousand different purposes.
>
> (Auden, 'Writing')

(Now, I am perfectly aware that all this might sound like just so much hogwash and hooey, an example of what the late great Gilbert Adair liked to refer to as 'the Tardis doctrine of criticism', the ludicrous idea that 'within a single detail, a detail as humble and as measurable as a telephone booth, there may be contained a whole world', but I suppose I am a bit of a critical Whovian and I happen to think that 'average' is one of those telephone booth-type words, or a trapdoor, or a portal; I think it leads to all sorts of strange and dark places.)

*

There's a sequence of sonnets in his book *New Year Letter* in which Auden sets out to investigate the meaning of what he called 'true happiness or authenticity of being', and in one sonnet – titled, guess what, 'The Average' – he examines the sad case of a typical young man who has been encouraged by his well-meaning parents to think of himself as exceptional:

His peasant parents killed themselves with toil
To let their darling leave a stingy soil
For any of those smart professions which
Encourage shallow breathing, and grow rich.

The pressure of their fond ambition made
Their shy and country-loving child afraid
No sensible career was good enough,
Only a hero could deserve such love.

So here he was without maps or supplies,
A hundred miles from any decent town;
The desert glared into his blood-shot eyes;

The silence roared displeasure: looking down,
He saw the shadow of an Average Man
Attempting the Exceptional, and ran.

Auden seems in sympathy with the young man's plight, but there's also a hint of danger: the Average Man as bogeyman.

*

Here comes the bogeyman.

*

Ezra Pound was an above-average poet with famously strong feelings about those he felt did not come up to the mark. 'A miracle of ebulliency, gusto, and help', James Joyce called him – but it rather depended on whether you were worth helping, or beyond saving. Pound has a poem, 'Portrait d'une Femme', published in 1912, long before his great notoriety as a propagandist for fascism, in which he imagines an adventuress who prefers her own life to 'the usual thing', 'One dull man, dulling and uxorious, / One average mind – with one thought less, each year.' It is but a short step from contempt for the average to disgust with the Untermensch – a step that Pound was more than willing to take. Objecting to some of his idiotic anti-Semitic ravings, Pound's fellow poet Basil Bunting wrote to him, 'Either you know men to be men, and not something less, or you make yourself an enemy of mankind.'

*

The enemies of mankind tend to despise the average – for what is mankind but an average, and what is the average man but an Everyman?

Auden, thank goodness, doesn't go there, but is there perhaps just a hint of distaste in Auden's bar, for the non-Martini-swilling masses?

*

And does it – in Auden's case – have something to do with class? I hesitate even to mention it: I am conscious that it makes me look bad. R. H. Tawney, in *Equality* (1931): 'The word "class" is fraught with unpleasing associations, so that to linger upon it is apt to be interpreted as the symptom of a perverted mind and a jaundiced spirit.'

On the other hand:

It is fatal to repress doubt; it turns the doubter into a humorless bigot.

(Auden, *A Certain World*)

(I'm just finishing rewriting this chapter during the ongoing, seemingly never-ending Labour Party anti-Semitism crisis. 'Whatever you do,' says my wife, 'don't write about the Labour Party anti-Semitism crisis.' I have promised I will not write about the Labour Party anti-Semitism crisis. There are some things you can't say, or shouldn't say.)

SOFT FURNISHINGS

Auden saves himself here in the poem from accusations of elitism, classism and snobbery – as so often – with his very useful 'we'.

'Lest *we* should see where *we* are.'

So it's fine, it turns out he's *one of us*, he's on our side, the average. Which is great, fine, and totally fine – but a dangerous card to play.

(I am writing this during the 2016 US presidential campaign, and Hillary Clinton keeps insisting that she's 'just a grandmother'. A former First Lady, former United States Secretary of State, former Congressional legal counsel, graduate of Yale Law School, and the former Senator representing New York, Hillary Clinton is a lot of things, but she is certainly not 'just a grandmother'. Her grandmother gambit is a version of her husband Bill 'Bubba' Clinton's good-ol'-boy routine and the kind of gimmick played by Tony 'Pretty Straight Sort of Guy' Blair and David 'Call Me Dave' Cameron, who during the 2015 election campaign here in the UK liked nothing better than to slip off his Savile Row suit jacket, flatten his Eton drawl and pretend to love football and getting 'pumped up' by the thought of people "avin' a go' and 'takin' a punt'. How anyone could possibly be taken in by these blatant attempts by politicians to make themselves appear ordinary and average when they are clearly and necessarily anything but is astonishing, though then again, according to the journalist, satirist and out-and-out bigot H. L. Mencken, 'No one in this world, as far as I know, has ever lost money by under-estimating the intelligence of the great masses of the plain people' – those whom he liked to refer to as the 'booboisie'. As it turned out, 2016 saw the revolt of the booboisie, with the average finding their champion in an unapologetic billionaire.)

> What is a hero? The exceptional individual. How is he recognised, whether in life or in books? By the degree of interest he arouses in the spectator or the reader. A comparative study, therefore, of the kinds of individuals which writers in various periods have chosen for their heroes often provides a useful clue to the attitudes and preoccupations of each age, for a man's interest always centres, consciously or unconsciously, round what seems to him the most important and still unsolved problem. The hero and his story are simultaneously a stating and a solving of the problem.
>
> (Auden, *The Enchafèd Flood*)

Anyway, back in the bar, and we are making 'this fort assume / The furniture of home'. And he's right, of course, we all do it: put up some curtains; arrange a few knick-knacks; throw around some throw cushions. Home. It is inevitable and unavoidable: our nesting instinct. In *Civilization and its Discontents* (1930), Freud claims that 'the dwelling-house' is 'a substitute for the mother's womb, the first lodging, for which in all likelihood man still longs, and in which he was safe and felt at ease': we spend our lives creating fortresses and refuges. And then they become places from which we can't escape.

214

In E. L. Doctorow's novel *Ragtime*, Houdini – a man who could get out of any set of handcuffs – feels irked by his own upholstery. 'He felt trapped by the heavy square furnishings, the drapes and dark rugs, the Oriental silk cushions, the green glass lampshades.' It's hard to escape from one's own soft furnishings. Even in time of war.

> Important progress in the furniture industry will be revealed during Wycombe Month, 'shop window' display of the furniture town, which opens at High Wycombe to-morrow.
> Wycombe Month, which was inaugurated in 1932 by High Wycombe Furniture Manufacturers' Federation, provides manufacturers in High Wycombe's 200 or more furniture factories an opportunity of displaying for the benefit of thousands of buyers from all parts of the country their latest styles of furniture.
> The international crisis has not deterred manufacturers from arranging elaborate showroom displays. New models which will be shown during Wycombe Month, which continues throughout September, will reveal that the 'straight line' furniture of somewhat stereotyped design which was expected a year or two ago to maintain popularity as ultra modern is being discarded, to be succeeded by more homely styles of a type formerly associated with the antique.
>
> ('More Homely Styles of Furniture: Displays at "Wycombe Month"', *The Times*, Friday, 1 September 1939)

*

Even in America.

Auden left England in part to avoid becoming a domesticated pet of the Left. In America he became a sort of household god.

(In October 1940, he moved to a big brownstone at 7 Middagh Street, a house whose other inhabitants included the novelist Carson McCullers, George Davis the fiction editor at *Harper's Bazaar*, Paul Bowles and his wife Jane, Oliver Smith the theatre designer, Thomas Mann's son Golo (in the attic) and the striptease artist Gypsy Rose Lee. Visitors to this artistic outpost in Brooklyn – now long since demolished to make way for the Brooklyn–Queens Expressway – included Aaron Copland, Salvador Dalí and Leonard Bernstein. Auden triumphantly ruled the roost. James Stern recalled 'George naked at the piano with a cigarette in his mouth, Carson on the ground with half a gallon of sherry, and then Wystan bursting in like a headmaster, announcing: "Now then, dinner!"' Peter Pears and Benjamin Britten managed to cope with living there for a while, Pears later describing the whole set-up as 'sordid beyond belief'. One man's sordid is another man's home sweet home.)

*

Some of Auden's finest later poems – 'Thanksgiving for a Habitat', from *About the House* (1965), 'The Garrison', 'Thank You, Fog' – are celebrations of house and home. In his early poems, he's often in search:

A home, the centre where the three or four things
That happen to a man do happen?

(Auden, 'Detective Story')

Happy only to find home, a place
Where no tax is levied for being there.

(Auden, 'Order to stewards and the study of time')

The only house he ever owned was his cottage in Kirchstetten –
bought in 1957 on the proceeds of his being awarded the Italian
Feltrinelli Prize. 'I am enchanted and so is Chester with our
Austrian house,' he told a friend. 'It's just like Beatrix Potter.'

*

And so Peter Rabbit has to face his Mr McGregor, because
suddenly we're in the woods and the home has become
unheimlich.

It's no use turning nasty
It's no use turning good
You're what you are and nothing you do
Will get you out of the wood
Out of a world that has had its day.

(Auden, 'I have a handsome profile')

(I am reading *Great Expectations*. I am teaching *Great Expectations*.
If I could, I would always be reading and teaching *Great
Expectations*. And Dante. *The Odyssey*, and Marianne Moore.
Maybe Chaucer, George Eliot. Virginia Woolf. Then I'd be happy.
I had forgotten about Pip's fear of being devoured: '"You young
dog," said the man, licking his lips, "what fat cheeks you ha' got.
[…] Darn Me if I couldn't eat 'em," said the man, with a threat-
ening shake of his head, "and if I han't half a mind to't! […] You
fail, or you go from my words in any partickler, no matter how
small it is, and your heart and your liver shall be tore out, roasted
and ate."' That threat of being devoured by others – by Miss

Havisham, who we are told 'wanders about in the night, and then lays hands on such food as she takes'.)

Auden's wood is, of course, a fairy-tale wood – Hansel and Gretel? – but it's also the forest of the mind.

*

(My grandmother had a saying – it was her only one – that to know the mind of another was like wandering in a dark Russian forest, lost, alone, and at night.)

*

The contemplation of the self in Auden's poetry involves a great deal of what we might now call psychic geography, the transposition of inner and outer worlds. In his later work, these transpositions tended to involve a graphic exploration of the provinces of his own body – as Edward Mendelson and lots of other critics have pointed out, Auden's landscapes increasingly became his own microcosmos. In an emotional tribute to Auden, the neurologist Oliver Sacks claimed that Auden could have been 'one of our greatest physicians' because he knew 'what was going on in people, physically and spiritually'. (Auden's advice to Sacks when he was working on his book *Awakenings* was 'to go beyond the clinical', to 'be metaphorical, be mystical, be whatever you need'.) In 'Talking to Myself', a poem dedicated to Sacks, Auden writes of his body as if he were a foreigner trying to understand an exotic island, perplexed by its odd customs and rules:

I'm always amazed at how little I know You.
Your coasts and outgates I know, for I govern there,
but what goes on inland, the rites, the social codes,
Your torrents, salt and sunless, remain enigmas:
what I believe is on doctors' hearsay only.

And in 'A New Year Greeting', he addresses his body's 'Yeasts, / Bacteria, Viruses / Aerobics and Anaerobics'.

If Auden devoted an increasing amount of attention in later life to his own internal organs and to figuring out the meaning of the cellular and microscopic activities of his body, in his earlier poetry the mind and soul remain the site of his interest, and the site of the battle – psychological, cosmic, philosophical – between the forces of good and evil.

But this is starting to sound like pub talk.

It's getting late.

Let's move on.

6

The windiest militant trash
Important Persons shout
Is not so crude as our wish:
What mad Nijinsky wrote
About Diaghilev
Is true of the normal heart;
For the error bred in the bone
Of each woman and each man
Craves what it cannot have,
Not universal love
But to be loved alone.

TALKING TRASH

One useful way of thinking about Auden's massive oeuvre – or at least, one useful way I have of thinking about Auden's massive oeuvre – is to imagine it as a kind of depository fed by his extraordinary brush-equipped pick-up belt of a brain, which managed to load and deliver material for recycling over a sustained period of more than forty years. As one might expect of a major processing plant – Auden Inc., established 1930, HQ NYC, with branch offices throughout Europe – most of the output during that period is of an excellent quality. But some of it is merely satisfactory. And some of it is rubbish. (Randall Jarrell described the late Auden manner as the work of someone who had 'turned into a rhetoric mill grinding away at the bottom of Limbo'.)

*

This is a stanza that concerns itself with various kinds of rubbish: trash, excess, unmet needs and bad ideas.

*

(I have been reading Walter Benjamin – thirty, forty, fifty years after everyone else, having been thoroughly put off when I was a student. I remember once I mentioned his name in a seminar and was corrected in my pronunciation by our polyglot tutor: it was just one of those things, absolutely nothing, but one of those significant nothings. I'd like to say that Benjamin's example is a model for this work, but his is a model I cannot possibly hope to follow; this book not so much an *Arcades Project* as an Auden minimart or corner shop. But I do know that no book on a serious subject is complete without a quote from my old friend Valthar Binhyameen:

> 'Here we have a man whose job it is to gather the
> day's refuse in the capital. Everything that the big city
> has thrown away, everything it has lost, everything
> it has scorned, everything it has crushed underfoot
> he catalogues and collects. He collates the annals of
> intemperance, the capharnaum of waste. He sorts things
> out and selects judiciously; he collects, like a miser
> guarding a treasure, refuse which will assume the shape
> of useful or gratifying objects between the jaws of the
> goddess of Industry.' This description is one extended
> metaphor for the poetic method, as Baudelaire practised
> it. Ragpicker and poet: both are concerned with refuse.
>   (Walter Benjamin, *Selected Writings*)

Auden is not a ragpicker, but he does talk trash.)

*

According to William Rathje and Cullen Murphy, garbage archaeologists with the University of Arizona's Garbage Project, 'garbage' refers 'technically to "wet" discards – food remains, yard waste, and offal' – 'trash' refers, strictly speaking, to the 'dry' stuff – 'newspapers, boxes, cans, and so on' – while 'refuse' covers both, and 'rubbish' refers 'to all refuse plus construction and demolition debris'.

*

Why is it 'windy' militant trash? Auden might be talking about Party pamphlets, I suppose, stuff that blows away in the wind, but also about speeches and statements that are themselves full of wind – rhetorical puff. Or perhaps it's ideas that cause wind – matter that is hard to swallow, to digest and to stomach. Whatever it is, there is no doubt that Auden is partly addressing himself here: he could be windy and waffly at the best of times. (For Wystan at his windiest, see 'A Communist to Others', which is another of those poems that he revised and altered, before eventually excising it from his canon altogether, scribbling 'O God what rubbish' in the margins of one copy. He wasn't alone, of course: lots of poets in the 1930s were writing poetry which they later came to regard as rubbish, particularly those in Auden's crowd, who spent the decade slumming it and then regretting it. In their attempts to identify with the workers' cause, they were driven towards what they felt was self-treachery. As Spender put it in *The God That Failed* – a book of confessions by ex-communists – 'I was driven on by a sense of social and personal guilt which made me feel firstly that I must take sides, secondly that I could purge myself of an abnormal individuality by co-operating with the workers' movement.' Spender might have learnt from Lenin: purges never work.)

*

Following his self-important windy years, Auden became insistent, going to the opposite extreme in his ideas about the social utility of art:

Art is impotent. The utmost an artist can hope to do
for his contemporary readers is, as Dr Johnson said, to
enable them a little better to enjoy life or a little better to
endure it.

(Auden, Secondary Worlds)

Art is not life and cannot be
A midwife to society,
For art is a *fait accompli*.

(Auden, New Year Letter)

By all means let a poet, if he wants to, write engagé
poems, protesting against this or that political evil or
social injustice. But let him remember this. The only
person who will benefit from them is himself; they will
enhance his literary reputation among those who feel as
he does. The evil or injustice, however, will remain exactly
what it would have been if he had kept his mouth shut.

(Auden, A Certain World)

When disowning his work, Auden invariably referred to it as
'trash': the word registers his self-disgust. But I think it also regis-
ters something else, something rather slippery and disturbing.

*

Freud had some notorious ideas about faeces and defecation
and their role in the development of character, ideas most clearly
expressed in his short paper 'Character and Anal Eroticism'
(1908), and in 'Dreams in Folklore' (1911), in which he sets out
his belief that 'all the interest which the child has had in faeces
is transferred in the adult on to another material which he learns
in life to set above almost everything else – gold'. The connection

between the child's esteem of faeces and the adult obsession with some other precious material perhaps tells us something about writers' tendencies towards both self-disgust and self-esteem: Montaigne described his essays, for example, as 'the excrements of an ageing mind'; Kafka in his diaries remarks that 'writers speak a stench'; and Freud himself, writing to Wilhelm Fliess in 1899 about *The Interpretation of Dreams*, claimed that 'no other work of mine has been so completely my own, my own dung heap'. Here, look at this amazing, disgusting thing!

*

It's certainly one of the more remarkable and endearing aspects of Auden's work that he was prepared to consider his own great dung heap. In his foreword to his *Collected Shorter Poems* (1966), he notes that 'some poems which I wrote and, unfortunately, published, I have thrown out because they were dishonest, or bad-mannered, or boring'. (If only Eliot had said the same about some of the infamous lines in 'Gerontion' and 'Burbank with a Baedeker: Bleistein with a Cigar'.) It makes him sound honest to admit to being dishonest, but it also signifies strength, and self-discipline – not so much self-abnegation as self-assertion. It's reminiscent perhaps of Eliot's description of the poet's role as being to purify the language of the tribe, or of W. V. O. Quine's description of the philosopher's role – in *Word and Object* (1960) – as 'exposing and resolving paradoxes, smoothing kinks, lopping off vestigial growths, clearing ontological slums'. (I'll tell you what: you wouldn't want to have got on the wrong side of W. V. O. Quine.)

Genius often has this ferocious aspect: to proceed to the furthermost extremities of one's art or one's activities seems to require it.

*

(I have known a few people in my life who I regard as actual geniuses, and there is no doubt that there is something ruthless about them all, something in them that's prepared to discard and abandon whatever needs to be discarded and abandoned – people, things, ideas – and to allow others to suffer the consequences. It's a quality I rather admire. Two of them are novelists, incidentally, the geniuses. Auden thought all novelists were sadists – and he may be right. William Trevor has a couple of sad, put-upon characters, Keith and Dawne, in a short story, 'A Trinity', from his collection *Family Sins* (1990), who are described as being 'familiar with defeat', and it could be argued that the purpose of all great literature is to familiarise characters with defeat. That's what authors do: think Ahab, Madame Bovary, Heathcliff, Othello, Macbeth. Trevor's characters are particularly interesting because of the way in which they slowly drift towards crisis and then into decline: they tell each other pointless lies; they misunderstand each other; their hopes fail; their marriages collapse; they suffer petty humiliations and embarrassments; their conversations stumble. William Trevor is prepared not just to sacrifice his characters, but to rubbish them, and to have them rubbish each other.)

> Only a minor talent can be a perfect gentleman; a
> major talent is always more than a bit of a cad. Hence
> the importance of minor writers – as teachers of good
> manners.
>
> (Auden, 'Writing')

And just to go back to Freud and faeces for a moment: in describing his work as trash, isn't Auden implicitly making a claim that it matters? A poem might be memorable and durable, it might be pointless and forgettable, but if it's trash, doesn't that rather imply that it had value at some time? (Derek Mahon has a poem, 'Roman Script', in which he translates a phrase from Pasolini, 'Nei rifiuti del mondo nasce un nuovo mondo': 'in the refuse of the world a new world is born'.)

Trash isn't valueless: its value is simply exhausted, depleted, soiled, disputed or hidden.

> One of the most striking features of rubbish is that we all instantly recognise it when we see it, hear it, read it, smell it or, horror of horrors, touch it. The pleonasmic vehemence of the typical response, 'That is complete and utter rubbish', would appear to confirm the all-or-nothing quality of rubbish. Just as dogs are undoubtedly dogs, so rubbish is undoubtedly rubbish. There are no questions of degree. An animal is either a dog or it is not a dog, and something is either rubbish or it is not rubbish. Yet in the one case there is (apparently) complete unanimity concerning which animals are dogs and which are not, whilst in the other case there is often complete disagreement as to what is rubbish and what is not.
>
> (Michael Thompson, *Rubbish Theory: The Creation and Destruction of Value*)

A poem is not a dog. (Nor, for that matter, is dessert. The Stravinskys went to dinner once with Auden and Kallman in New York. In the bathroom, Vera Stravinsky found a bowl of brown fluid, which she emptied into the sink – only to discover that she had flushed away Chester's pudding. The boundary between what's waste and what's not can sometimes be difficult to discern.)

*

You might say that after the 1930s and 1940s, Auden treated all his old poems like dogs – or like sheep and goats. Saved or damned, yes or no, good or bad. Which may or may not be a bad thing to do; it may even be the right thing to do. The philosopher Alain Finkielkraut, in his book *La Défaite de la pensée* (1987), argues that our culture has ended up in its sorry state precisely because we have been unwilling to distinguish between art and non-art, between rubbish and non-rubbish. We have become victims, he argues, of 'la non-pensée' – non-thinking. At least Auden was thinking.

*

On the other hand, maybe he was able to view his work as trash because for him it was all just too easy. His facility was so great – his ability to turn his hand to anything, or his face from anything – it's disturbing. Randall Jarrell, in his essay 'Changes of Attitude and Rhetoric in Auden's Poetry', which really remains *the* essay on Auden, just twenty-three pages long, published in the autumn issue of the *Southern Review* (1941), in case you want to look it up, an essay which took Jarrell six years to write – if I was as good as Randall Jarrell, if I was as diligent, working at his pace, this book would have taken not twenty-five but sixty years to write – declares that 'Auden was like someone who keeps showing how well he can hold his liquor until he becomes a drunkard [...] he is like a man who will drink canned heat, rubbing alcohol, anything.'

Virtuosity can be dangerous. It can make you careless.

It can make you say things you don't mean.

*

(One reason this book has taken me so long to write is that I have tried only to say things that I mean and to mean the things that I say. This has proved much more difficult than I thought.)

YOU CAN'T SAY
'MAD' NIJINSKY

Auden borrowed some of the most famous lines of his poem from 'mad' Vaslav Nijinsky, the great Russian ballet dancer whose diary had been published to some acclaim in England and America in 1936. (Apparently, Auden picked up the diary on the day war was declared and started reading it at random. Poems often rely on such chance operations: you don't have to be a surrealist to write here, but it helps.)

*

('You can't say "mad" Nijinsky,' says my daughter. 'But Auden says "mad" Nijinsky in the poem,' I say. 'Everyone used to call everyone mad,' I explain, 'if they were mad. Bonkers, nutty, barmy, crackers, loopy, loony.' 'That doesn't make it right,' she says. 'Well, what would you say?' I ask, knowing full well what she would say. 'Nijinsky, who was suffering from mental-health problems.' Times change, mostly for the better.)

*

Nijinsky had been the star of the Ballets Russes. In his heyday he was famous not just for his physical strength and skill – he was known for his incredible jumps – but also for his beauty. Parisians called him *le dieu de la danse*. (Proust, obviously, adored him.) The Ballets Russes had been established by the impresario Sergei Diaghilev and he and Nijinsky became lovers, though Nijinsky eventually married and there was a falling-out. Nijinsky composed his strange, tormented diary while living in Switzerland after having being interned during the First World War. Though he lived for another thirty years or more, his career was effectively over, and the diary, written over a period of just six and a half weeks, is an account of someone descending into a state of madness.

(Over the years, of all the books I've read while reading about Auden – and there have been hundreds and thousands – the Nijinsky, in the new unexpurgated edition translated into English by Kyril FitzLyon, is by far the most shocking and memorable. It predates by many years the kind of work being produced now by writers like Sarah Manguso and Maggie Nelson. So, Auden took from me twenty-five years, but in return he gave me Nijinsky. And the theologian Reinhold Niebuhr. And the Swiss cultural theorist Denis de Rougemont. And many others too numerous to mention, books and authors I would never otherwise have encountered. A good poem is often built with cellars and storerooms, accessed directly or by trapdoors and back doors, and if you follow those secret passages and entranceways, it's amazing what you can find. A poem is not an object, it's an actant, or rather it's not a single object, it's part of a vast network: poems are like a vast fungal growth.)

> His guardian-angel
> has always told him
> What and Whom to read next.
>
> (Auden, 'Profile')

'Some politicians are hypocrites like Diaghilev,' writes Nijinsky in his diary, 'who does not want universal love, but to be loved alone. I want universal love.'

Auden, I suppose, wanted both – he was Diaghilev *and* Nijinsky, both dancer and impresario – though in the end he settled for one, or 'The One', as he often referred to him, his partner Chester Kallman.

*

Son of a Manhattan dentist and a mother who had died young, Chester Kallman was louche, long-haired, wide-mouthed and an aspiring poet. His face, according to Auden, expressed 'pure pride'. They first met on 6 April 1939, when Auden and Isherwood gave a talk at the League of American Writers, under the title 'Modern Trends in English Poetry and Prose'. The student Kallman attended with his friend Harold Norse and they asked the famous Englishmen for an interview for the Brooklyn College literary magazine. When Kallman then duly turned up to conduct the interview, Auden apparently told Isherwood that he was the 'wrong blond'. And so began what Auden called 'l'affaire C'.

*

Auden was in his early thirties when he came to live in New York – no longer really young. He had published five volumes of poetry, and plays, essays, reviews, and was the editor of two anthologies, *The Poet's Tongue* (1935) and *The Oxford Book of Light Verse* (1938). He was an Important Person. But he was single. Not for long: 'This time, my dear,' he wrote to his brother about Kallman, 'I really believe it's a marriage.' And he wrote to Kallman, 'You are to me, emotionally a mother, physically a father, and intellectually a son […] With my body, I worship yours.' Unfaithful and unpredictable, Kallman nonetheless stayed with Auden for the rest of Auden's life and they were like any other married couple, though Kallman is often portrayed as a rather bad influence on Auden. I don't know why. I think he saved him from a much worse fate: not to be loved alone, but universal love.

*

(Sometimes I try and imagine what might have happened to Auden had he gone west with Isherwood, say – because we know exactly what happened to Isherwood, living out in Santa Monica, the archetypal expat Brit about town. His published diaries recount endless parties and dinners and soirées: out one night with the King Vidors, and then another night out with Nehru; Marlon Brando; Danny Kaye. He pops round to Kenneth Tynan's to watch Tynan's new TV show, does a quick bit of pall-bearing at David Selznick's funeral, has drinks with Freddy Ashton and enjoys an afternoon on a 'famed fag beach' with Wayne Sleep. Given his hectic social schedule, it's difficult to see how he ever did any work at all. And a lot of the time he didn't – too pissed, too tired, and then too much time in the gym. 'Drinking, idling, wasting time with people I didn't really want to see; and getting nearly nothing done on the novel,' he complains in November 1960. Isherwood's idea of a good night in: 'Everybody got high, and Ginsberg recorded our conversation and chanted Hindu chants, and Orlovsky [...] kept asking me if I had ever raped anyone, and the boy Stephen unrolled a picture scroll he had made, under the influence of something or other, to illustrate the Bardo Thodol.' He also devoted himself to Hindu philosophy and became casually anti-Semitic. Reading Paul Goodman's *Making Do*, in July 1965, for example, he remarks that Goodman 'redeems single-handed the drivel of the other Jews'. In November

1966, he doesn't go to see the play of *Cabaret* because 'it sounds Jewish beyond all belief'. In 1961, when some representatives from UCLA come to see him to ask him to give some lectures, he is appalled when they try to negotiate with him over the fee. 'Whatever anyone says, this kind of thing nauseates me; it is Jewy and vile and utterly shameful, coming from the representative of a serious institution of learning instead of an old clothes dealer.')

*

Kallman saved Auden from all that. He also introduced him to opera.

*

(I'm not going to discuss Auden and opera, though I would love to discuss Auden and opera. There are a number of reasons why I'm not going to discuss Auden and opera, not the least that a friend borrowed my copy of Auden's *Libretti* five or six years ago and never gave it back. But the big question, obviously, is why?

*

Seriously, why? Why do they all do it? Why do some of the world's greatest writers humble themselves so, as Schikaneder to Mozart, subjecting themselves to the drudgery of writing libretti, which no one really listens to, whose stories are often derivative and ludicrous, whose poetry is more often ridiculous than sublime, which are enjoyed more often than not by a posing dinner-jacketed elite, and are usually better when old, tried-and-tested and sung in Italian? Alone and with Kallman, Auden wrote five new libretti – *The Rake's Progress, Elegy for Young Lovers, The Bassarids* and *Love's Labour's Lost* – as well as producing translations of *The Magic Flute, Don Giovanni, The Seven Deadly Sins, Mahagonny* and *Arcifanfano*. Which is a lot of libretti. But even

Samuel Beckett managed the eighty-five words of *Neither*, 'Written for the composer Morton Feldman, 1962'; Brecht, who famously said he despised the 'culinary' form, nonetheless happily cooked some up for children and for adults with Weil; Jean Cocteau collaborated with Stravinsky and Poulenc; an initially reluctant E. M. Forster worked with the assistance of Eric Crozier on Britten's *Billy Budd*; and Gertrude Stein did extraordinary things with Virgil Thomson, producing the abstract *Four Saints in Three Acts*, and *The Mother of Us All*, about the pioneering American feminist Susan B. Anthony. (And this is not even to mention the likes of Pirandello, Racine, Boileau, La Fontaine, Diderot, Zola, Colette, Goethe, Dryden, Lope de Vega and Turgenev. And Chekhov, who suggested one to Tchaikovsky. More recently, Anthony Burgess redid Weber's *Oberon*; Craig Raine's *The Electrification of the Soviet Union* was set to music by Nigel Osborne; Blake Morrison wrote *Dr Ox's Experiment* with Gavin Bryars; David Harsent produced *Gawain* for Harrison Birtwistle, who also, incidentally, worked with Tony Harrison on *Bow Down* and *Yan Tan Tethera*. Ted Hughes worked on something called *The Story of Vasco*, which features crows, for Gordon Crosse. Even Kurt Vonnegut – Kurt Vonnegut! – got round to providing a new libretto for Stravinsky's *L'Histoire du soldat* a few years ago, basing his update of Charles-Ferdinand Ramuz's folk tale on the true story of the soldier Eddie Slovik, who was executed by firing squad for deserting his infantry unit in France in 1945. The first words uttered by the soldier/Slovik, in true Vonnegut style, are 'A sack of shit. I quit. I quit.')

Again, why?

*

For the poet, an opera is a poem with a practical purpose: it enables them to do and say things they might not otherwise be able to do; Auden claimed that opera was 'the last refuge of the High Style'. And for the novelist it's maybe a chance to tell a completely different kind of story: 'No good opera plot can be sensible', according to Auden, 'for people do not sing when they are feeling sensible.'

*

But I also have my own little theory: I think writers turn to opera because opera is about love.

*

And Auden's great subject is love: it's a cliché even to say it, let alone to try and explain it, as so many others have done, and because it involves lots of talk of Agape and Eros, and visions of Dame Kind and Christian brotherhood and the doctrine of the Trinity. To put it at its simplest: Auden's idea of love is all-encompassing and all-embracing. 'The mere fact that A prefers girls and B boys is unimportant,' he wrote in a review in *The Criterion* in January 1933. (Unimportant, perhaps, but not uninteresting. When he was young, Auden was engaged to a nurse, according to biographers, but broke it off before the wedding; and then he married Thomas Mann's daughter in 1935; and he had numerous affairs, for example, with an Austrian landlady, apparently, and with someone called Rhoda Jaffe; and he proposed to Hannah Arendt, whom he met in 1958, and also to Thekla Clark, who claimed he also had crushes on Ursula Niebuhr and Nancy Spender, his friend Stephen's brother's widow; and then there were all the male lovers; and the long-lasting friendships; and Chester.) In his memorial address for Auden, Stephen Spender recalled that 'The last time we met in America I asked him how a reading which he had given in Milwaukee had gone. His face lit up with a smile that altered its lines, and he said: "They loved me!"'

*

They did.
  We do.
  I do.

*

(There seems to me, by the way, to be something a bit medical in Auden's manner here at the end of this stanza, as if he were not so much writing as dispensing, as from a black bag, or ministering from a sick-call set, prescribing lozenges – or offering wafers. In the next stanza he goes from quasi-medical to full pontifical.)

*

I just wish he didn't speak of 'our wish'. It's presumptuous. I don't know what it's like inside you. And you don't know what it's like inside me. Indeed, I don't really know what it's like inside me.

My crude wish may not be your crude wish. Although I suppose some of our basic questions might be similar:

The great question now is, what would give one pleasure?
Ought one to write poetry, or fuck?
                              (Auden, *The Table Talk of W. H. Auden*)

When I started writing this book I could just about manage one; now I can barely do either.

7

From the conservative dark
Into the ethical life
The dense commuters come,
Repeating their morning vow,
'I *will* be true to the wife,
I'll concentrate more on my work',
And helpless governors wake
To resume their compulsory game:
Who can release them now,
Who can reach the deaf,
Who can speak for the dumb?

HOMO FABER

Stanza 7: the end is in sight.
   If we can only make it through the crowds.

*

In 1926, Thomas Edison suggested that if New York kept on permitting the building of skyscrapers, 'disaster must overtake us':

> When all the people in those skyscrapers start to flow
> out into the street at approximately the same moment or
> within a half-hour or an hour, try to get to the entrances
> of those buildings so that they may begin the day's
> business, there must be such overcrowding of the streets
> near those skyscrapers as must stop traffic.

There were just too many people working in Manhattan. When the IRT (Interborough Rapid Transit Company) opened the first New York City subway line in October 1904, more than 100,000 people took a ride on the very first day, arriving at their destinations from their subterranean travels blinking into the light.

   Auden's 'conservative dark' is both literal and metaphoric, his 'dense commuters' likewise. During the 1930s, New York's subway lines had been extended, creating an even larger, sprawling metropolitan area from which to draw its vast workforce, far removed in their homes and in their personal lives from the heart of the city, with its skyscrapers, its dives and its liberal writers and intellectuals with their fancy-schmancy ideas about life and work.

*

Having spent the past twenty-five years as a commuter – a 'dense' commuter, indeed, part of that great weight and volume of people flooding into the cities from our ticky-tacky houses in the suburbs, the great undifferentiated and undistinguished, just like the commuters in Eliot's *The Waste Land*, who 'flowed over London Bridge, so many, / I had not thought death had undone so many. / Sighs, short and infrequent, were exhaled, / And each man fixed his eyes before his feet' – let me speak up on our behalf.

*

I know that for Auden, 'work' was an important legitimating term in both his poetry and his career as a poet.

I know that throughout his life he was drawn towards the idea of 'work' as a form of salvation ('he who works shall find our Fatherhood,' he writes in 'Christmas 1940'; 'Only his verses / Perhaps could stop them: He must go on working,' states 'Voltaire at Ferney').

I know also that in 1939, Auden's friends and defenders found it useful to appeal to the idea of his 'working' abroad, rather than fleeing from England. The poet Louis MacNeice wrote that 'Auden … working eight hours a day in New York, is getting somewhere.'

But *where* he was getting exactly – and *what* he was getting at – is another matter.

An artist is not a doer of deeds but a maker of things, a
worker.

(Auden, 'Genius and Apostle')

I must admit, I do find it a little aggravating, writers going on
about workers and working, because when one reads the biog-
raphies and the autobiographies, what surely strikes anyone
with an actual job is that even the hardest-working authors are,
frankly, lightweights and part-timers: Trollope, renowned for his
determined working habits, and often held up as an exemplar
with his little charts and his writing slope and his 1000 words
per page, or whatever it was, used to put in just a couple of hours
a day, which is less time than my grandfather used to put in on
his vegetable patch. But Trollope also worked at the Post Office,
people say – well, so did my granddad. Writing, it seems to me,
is a business full of boasters and shirkers who talk a lot of
nonsense about craft and technique, for example, but the truth
is, in order to publish anything, you have to be prepared to
bodge and to skimp; you have to accept that this, in the end, will
just have to do. If you don't, you're Harold Brodkey. Writing is a
form of work, but it is not the same as working: it's nothing like
being a wage-slave or a commuter. If you still believe that writers
work hard – poets in particular – go and live with one for a
week, and the next time they're whining about their sad and
difficult lives pushing back the frontiers of human knowledge
while having another coffee-break and trying to decide which
notebook size really suits, dash the cup from their lips and offer
to swap their life of ease for your own twelve-hour days at the
chalk-face/coal-face/screen-face under cheap fluorescent lighting
and machine coffee, working with shifty, scheming and very
probably psychopathic colleagues, and cry out to them,
'Whatsoever thy hand findeth to do, do it with thy might; for

there is no work, nor device, nor knowledge, nor wisdom, in the grave, whither thou goest' (Ecclesiastes 9:10), or something similar. That might get their attention, although it probably won't: most writers, in my experience, are so wrapped up in their own dawdlings that it'd take a smack in the face with a piece of two-by-four to get them to sit up and take notice of the world outside.

(Clearly, I have issues, which is neither here nor there, but what's perhaps interesting is how, during the course of writing this book, the idea of the 'conservative dark' has crept up on us and found its voice and expression: the emergence of the so-called 'intellectual dark web', the Brexit vote in the UK, the rise of Trump. The long shadow of the average man: excluded, derided, put upon, 'dense'.)

*

By the time he was putting in his hours in New York, Auden had passed through his crude Marxian stage of thinking about work ('"Work" is action forced on us by the will of another'), and he eventually developed an understanding of the idea of work derived from the finessing theories of Hannah Arendt in her book *The Human Condition* (1958), in which she differentiates between work and labour as the activities of 'homo faber' and 'animal laborans', with labour prescribed by our biological make-up and work distinguished as 'the activity which corresponds to the unnaturalness of human existence, which is not embedded in, and whose mortality is not compensated by, the species' ever-recurring life cycle'.

> Man working and fabricating and building a world
> inhabited only by himself would still be a fabricator,
> though not homo faber: he would have lost his

specifically human quality and, rather, be a god – not,
to be sure, the Creator, but a divine demiurge as Plato
described him in one of his myths.

(Hannah Arendt, *The Human Condition*)

Arendt's definitions provided both a philosophical justification
for Auden's view of himself as a worker and a philosophic
language for him better to describe his notion of the poet as
'homo faber': in his 1932 essay 'Writing', he wrote, figuratively,
'People write books because they enjoy it, as a carpenter enjoys
making a cupboard'; in his 1967 T. S. Eliot Memorial lectures, he
made the same point conceptually, echoing Arendt: 'The artist is
not a man of action but a maker, a fabricator of objects. To
believe in the value of art is to believe that it is possible to make
an object, be it an epic or a two-line epigram, which will remain
permanently on hand in the world.'

*

As far as I know, Sigmund Freud never actually said whatever it
was he was supposed to have said about the importance in
people's lives of love and work (*lieben und arbeiten*), but they are
important, obviously, and they were important to Auden: work
is a central feature of his work. Which marks him out not only
among his contemporaries but even now. With a few notable
exceptions, most writers don't make a habit of writing about
what's at the centre of most people's lives – which is work. (Not
sex. Not God. They're peripheral.)

No other technique for the conduct of life attaches
the individual so firmly to reality as laying emphasis
on work; for his work at least gives him a secure place
in a portion of reality, in the human community. […]

> Professional activity is a source of special satisfaction
> if it is a freely chosen one – if, that is to say, by means
> of sublimation, it makes possible the use of existing
> inclinations, of persisting or constitutionally reinforced
> instinctual impulses.
>
> (Freud, *Civilization and its Discontents*)

(One of the most famous poems in the English language about work is Philip Larkin's 'Toads' – 'Why should I let the toad work / Squat on my life?' etc. – and I have occasionally wondered if Larkin's working toad comes from Auden, who introduced an unpleasant early-morning toad in a passage in *New Year Letter*: 'the heart / As Zola said, must always start / The day by swallowing its toad / Of failure and disgust.' Auden's toad in fact comes not from Zola but from Chamfort – the quotation is correctly attributed in Auden's *Book of Aphorisms*: 'A man must swallow a toad every morning if he wishes to be sure of finding nothing still more disgusting before the day is over.' Chamfort – Auden – Larkin. The toad as a metaphoric tool handed down through generations. It's a nice idea, but I'll leave that to the scholars.)

*

Anyway, in New York, for all his theorising, Auden was also learning the hard way how to make a living: lectures, teaching, reviewing.

(One of the pieces of work he undertook in 1939 was writing the libretto for an operetta by Benjamin Britten. Britten and Auden had worked together in England on documentary films, radio scripts and cabaret songs, but this was a much bigger project and it was Auden who settled on the subject matter: the story of an American folk hero, the lumberjack Paul Bunyan. The project gave Auden the opportunity to address what he called the 'matter of America': the conquering and taming of a continent. *Paul Bunyan* may be a minor work in Auden's oeuvre, but it tells us much about how he conceived of his own activities: as a latter-day Bunyan or John Henry, hammer in hand. If you're interested in *Paul Bunyan*, might I refer you to my learned essay on the subject in the programme notes to the Royal Opera House production in 1997: the closest I have ever come to writing an opera being, of course, writing about Auden's opera.)

'We're pretty busy,' he wrote to Mrs Dodds in March 1939. He was so busy, one might almost think of him as a martyr to his craft.

*

Which doesn't mean he was a saint. (Donald Attwater, who revised Alban Butler's standard eighteenth-century collection of *The Lives of the Saints* and who also translated Hippolyte Delehaye's *Legends of the Saints*, helpfully points out that 'The according of public veneration to a certain category of Christian men and women, and the giving to each of them of the appellation Saint, originated in the reverence given to martyrs.')

What I mean is, Auden was self-sacrificing, in a very particular way.

> The nineteenth century created the myth of the Artist as
> Hero, the man who sacrifices his health and happiness to
> his art and in compensation claims exemption from all
> social responsibilities and norms of behaviour.
> (Auden, 'Calm Even in the Catastrophe')

Auden did not claim exemption from all social responsibilities and norms of behaviour – some, maybe. There is a compelling account of Auden's many acts as a citizen in an article by Edward

Mendelson, 'The Secret Auden', in which he lists some of the ways in which Auden made 'unobtrusive gifts of time, money, and sympathy'. The list includes:

- sleeping outside the apartment building of someone who was suffering from night terrors
- sponsoring war orphans
- donating manuscripts to pay for medical bills
- corresponding with a prisoner
- refusing to accept the National Medal for Literature in 1967 at Lyndon Johnson's White House during the Vietnam War and arranging for the ceremony to take place instead at the Smithsonian.

Basically, Auden did good: he did the right thing. (Also, you have to respect him for the respect he paid to others in their work. He was certainly no Studs Terkel – his poetry is not filled with the voices of working men and women – but when he had the opportunity to acknowledge his fellow workers, he did. 'Let me take this opportunity', he wrote in a piece for the *New York Times* on 18 March 1972, bidding farewell to New York, 'to thank in particular Abe and his co-workers in the liquor store; Abe the tobacconist; On Lok, my laundryman; Joseph, Bernard and Maurice in the grocery store at Ninth and Second Avenue; Harold the druggist; John, my mailman; Francy from whom I buy my newspaper, and Charles from whom I buy seeds for my Austrian garden.' Patronising? Maybe. Self-important? No. Generous? Yes.)

*

But he devoted himself above all to his work, which was poetry.

His friends and contemporaries tended to devote themselves to other things.

*

(Stephen Spender, for example, might be described as a poet who was too busy doing other interesting things – writing plays, autobiographies, journals, novels, translations and criticism; editing magazines, working for UNESCO, teaching, lecturing, and making friends with the famous – to have actually got round to writing any great poetry. In a letter to Spender in 1928, while they were still undergraduates at Oxford, Auden told him, 'Stephen, you are just not trying.' The truth is, he was probably trying too hard. Wading through the knee-deep Romanticism and the flood of poorly plumbed imitation Auden in his early verse, one eventually comes across a poem which stands out as a rock and a marker above all the others, the poem which begins:

> I think continually of those who were truly great.
> Who, from the womb, remembered the soul's history
> Through corridors of light, where the hours are suns,
> Endless and singing. Whose lovely ambition
> Was that their lips, still touched with fire,
> Should tell of the Spirit, clothed from head to foot in
>   song.

The 'truly great' haunt, taunt and eventually dement Spender's poetry, so that he ends up sounding like the sad old man down the pub with no money who's always talking about his rich and famous friends. I'm definitely not W. H. Auden. But please God, I'm not Stephen Spender.)

Every man's work shall be made manifest: for the day
shall declare it, because it shall be revealed by fire; and
the fire shall try every man's work of what sort it is.

(1 Corinthians 3:13)

*

For all its harping on fundamental themes, this stanza seems to
me to date the poem rather: it's maybe because the idea of
commuters pouring into the city in the early morning seems so
Eliot-y and early twentieth-century. The many changes in our
living and working habits over the past eighty years are the
consequence of all sorts of factors (globalisation, the rise of the
corporation, the growth in mechanised production, the expan-
sion of the service sector compared to the relative decline of
manufacturing, the development of networked computers – you
don't need me to tell you this stuff), which have helped to rede-
fine the shape and pattern of the average working life.

*

Or maybe it's not the poem that's dated at all, it's just me that's
getting older. Maybe it's because I am no longer an early-morn-
ing commuter but have become a helpless governor. (I am writ-
ing this, in fact, over a weekend, failing again to enjoy a weekend.
My wife and children are out and I'm here with my laptop, a
Wi-Fi connection and an inbox full of emails, repeating my
morning vow: 'I will not work this weekend.' I always work at the
weekend.)

*

Auden's governors are who? Pilate? Faceless bureaucrats?
Everyone's enemies in admin? Whoever they are, they are facing
some profound questions and difficulties.

Who can release them now,
Who can reach the deaf,
Who can speak for the dumb?

These are perhaps my least favourite lines in my least favourite stanza in the whole poem. They seem to me banal, deficient and silly.

(Though I can understand the impulse. When I first left school I went to work for Jesus, preaching good news to the poor, proclaiming release to the captive, testifying, as with great power the apostles gave witness to the resurrection of the Lord Jesus (Acts 4:33). I was also interested in restoring sight to the blind (Luke 4:18), casting out demons (Luke 9:1), making the lame walk (Matt. 15:31), cleansing lepers (Matt. 8:1–4), taking up poisonous serpents (Mark 16:18), feeding thousands (Luke 9:10–17) and raising the dead (John 11:1–43). I never quite managed to do any of those, fine ambitions though they are.)

Auden sounds here to me like a bad amateur theologian. In America he had started to read Kierkegaard, as well as Paul Tillich and Reinhold Niebuhr – who were good, professional theologians – and he eventually became rather churchy. You can read all about it in the biographies: the late Christian Auden is another phase in his development. There's no doubt he took it seriously.

But maybe in these lines he takes himself too seriously. Because the plea at the end of this stanza – basically, where are the healers? – rather implies that the poet might have an answer, which indeed he does. (The end of this stanza sets up the call to which the next is a response.)

*

Not that this is really a criticism. From where I'm standing, from my perspective, it's rather good if the poem takes a bit of a dive. If I've learnt anything reading Auden, it's how wearying unceasing brilliance can be, so much so that one cherishes any sign of weakness.

*

(Max Beerbohm, on Goethe in 'Quia Imperfectum': 'A man whose career was glorious without intermission, decade after decade, does sorely try our patience.')

*

This is an important lesson, which I have to learn again and again, in different ways with different writers.

(I've just been reading *Death in Venice*, for example, in the car, outside the school, waiting to pick up the children, on an unreasonably warm afternoon, and I am suddenly struck by a thought. Frustrated and disappointed by the many purple passages, the descriptions of sun and heat and the dream and the vision, it occurs to me, after thinking, momentarily, how much better the book would be without them, that the book would be nothing without them, or less than it is. The imperfections – which are considerable in this case – constitute the effect of reading the whole. In fact, they almost justify the rest.)

*

There are always faults and quirks in any work of art, there are always insufficiencies: art necessarily fails. Indeed, in a sense all art arises from error. (This has long been a philosophical objection to the artistic enterprise: Plato, in *The Republic*, contends that the ideal civilisation would banish artists because they distort the truth. And it's true, they do. We can only make art for the same reason we can make mistakes: which is because we can make the world as it is not. Art is, fundamentally, a misprision. An impression. A false impression. A confabulation. A concoction. A fiction.)

You don't have to be Hannah Arendt – although it might help – to see that the potential in failure, in deceit and in lying, is also the potential in art. In *Between Past and Future: Eight Exercises in Political Thought* (1968), Arendt claims that 'our ability to lie – but not necessarily our ability to tell the truth – belongs among the few obvious, demonstrable data that confirm human freedom'.

If I want Auden to be Auden, I have to let him go about his work.

If he wants to preach, sure, he can preach.

8

All I have is a voice
To undo the folded lie,
The romantic lie in the brain
Of the sensual man-in-the-street
And the lie of Authority
Whose buildings grope the sky:
There is no such thing as the State
And no one exists alone;
Hunger allows no choice
To the citizen or the police;
We must love one another or die.

AS OUR GREAT POET AUDEN SAID

Which brings us inevitably to this stanza.

The stanza.

The one that everyone talks about.

And I mean *everyone*.

I bump into an old friend on the street. They are not a bookish type, not at all. They ask me what I'm doing. I say I'm – still – writing a book about W. H. Auden. 'We must love one another or die, eh?' they say.

I'm talking to another friend, again definitely not a bookish type. They ask me how the book is going. I say fine. They ask, have I read Mitch Albom's *Tuesdays with Morrie*: they've just read it and it mentions Auden. They lend me the book. It's a sort of self-help memoir in which Albom writes about his trips to see his wise old professor, who's called Morrie:

> 'Love is so supremely important. As our great poet Auden said, "Love each other or perish."'
>
> 'Love each other or perish.' I wrote it down. Auden said that?

No, Auden didn't say that. Auden wrote, 'We must love one another or die.'

*

You can find these seven words – 'We must love one another or die' – quoted, misquoted, used, misused, discussed and pored over by literary critics, literary historians, in advertising and marketing materials, by writers and poets, and indeed by 'the sensual man-in-the-street'. There's really nothing you can say about 'We must love one another or die' that hasn't been said before. Nonetheless.

We must discuss 'We must love one another or die', or – well, I suppose that's the question, isn't it?

What's the alternative?

Or maybe, what are the consequences?

Auden's 'or' could mean both, or either.

*

I sometimes imagine meeting Auden and asking him about 'We must love one another or die'.

He says he has nothing to say to me about it, thank you, that he hasn't already said.

(The critic Hugh Kenner, who was very skilled at the art of winning friends and influencing people, recalls in his preface to *The Invisible Poet: T. S. Eliot* (1960) that 'At my one meeting with Mr. Eliot, I offered to complete a book on his literary career without pestering him.' When Kenner did inevitably pester, Eliot offered him just three pieces of information about his work: 'a summary of the contents of the *Ur-Waste Land*, so far as he could remember them', 'a gloss on the word "lot" in *Whispers of Immortality*', and the third, reveals Kenner, 'The third had reference to cheese.' Hard cheddar, perhaps?)

*

Over the years I have jotted down my notes and remarks on Auden's poetry in its multiple versions in multiple books, and on photocopies, purply old mimeographs and Gestetnered sheets – and I can safely say that the lines around this one stanza, in every book and on every copy, look like an Ordnance Survey map, one of those really detailed ones, at a scale of 1:25,000.

*

(Lots of people underline and squiggle in books. I'm hardly alone. You probably do it yourself. Coleridge outdid all of us with his effusions, a habit which almost developed into a second career: his marginalia were published during his lifetime; they were a source of income. It's a shame we can't all be Coleridge. Wordsworth, on the other hand, could hardly be bothered to write in books at all – and he cut his pages with a buttery knife. Merely contemplating the effort involved in Coleridge's note-making is overwhelming: the first part alone of the marginalia in the Bollingen *Collected Works*, volume 12, in three parts, consists of 879 pages. Coleridge was a bit like the graffiti artist who tags every wall and gable end in the neighbourhood – although obviously he was insinuating himself between the pages and into the margins of, say, Leibniz rather than throwing up his initials in six-foot-tall bubble-writing in a piss-stinking underpass. Personally, I have defaced and obscured the pages of my editions of Auden's books with so many notes in pen and pencil, and with so many faded Post-its, that I can now barely read them. I'm writing on Auden, literally, because it creates an illusion of intimacy: it's also a means of talking to myself, and a way, in the end, of erasing Auden. My Auden marginalia are a record of my own long, slow, sad self-development.)

*

Note, in my tiny handwriting, in the margins of 'September 1, 1939' in my copy of Robin Skelton's *Poetry of the Thirties*, which I used when I was teaching at the West London Institute of Further Education, from a tip-off by my friend David: 'John Ashbery, "Strange Things Happen at Night", from *And the Stars Were Shining* (1994), "We must double up, or die."'

Note, in my copy of the *Collected Poems*: 'Julian Barnes, *A History of the World in 10½ Chapters*.' It's a book I still have on the shelf. I look it up. In a chapter called 'Parenthesis', Barnes offers a brilliant short discussion of 'We must love one another or die' and the meaning of love.

Note, on photocopied teaching notes, period and provenance unknown: 'Mention Jarrell.' (This perhaps refers, self-regardingly, to my one and only contribution to accurate literary scholarship, my article 'Flouting Papa: Randall Jarrell and W. H. Auden', in *Auden Studies 3: 'In Solitude, for Company': W. H. Auden After 1940*, in which I point out that Auden's crucial revision of 'We must love one another or die' to 'We must love one another and die' may have been prompted by a passage in Randall Jarrell's novel *Pictures from an Institution*, published in 1954, predating Auden's correction by a year. As my children would say, big whoop.)

*

'All I have is a voice.' I have written in the margin of one of my copies of the poem, 'all I have is voices' (underlined three times).

As a rhetorical device, quotation can serve to
accommodate, to incorporate, to falsify (when wrongly
or even rightly paraphrased), to accumulate, to defend,
or to conquer – but always, even when in the form of a
passing allusion, it is a reminder that other writing serves

to displace present writing, to a greater or lesser extent,
from its absolute, central, proper place.

(Edward Said, *Beginnings*)

All we have is our voice: and that voice usually belongs to some-
one else. Freud, in the Strachey translation of *Civilization and its
Discontents*, remarks that 'Writing was in its origin the voice of an
absent person' – *persons*, one might say, underlining it at least
three times. (The philosopher Stanley Cavell has an interesting
remark about the voice in his autobiography, *A Pitch of Philosophy*.
Finding one's voice implies, he writes, the 'standing threat of not
finding it, or not recognizing it, or of its not being acknowl-
edged'. Finding one's voice also raises the question of what
Cavell calls 'plagiarism in human identity', the 'self-theft of
culture' in which the discovery of one's voice becomes an act of
vampirism. I'm very conscious that what I am doing is sucking
the lifeblood from Auden.)

*

On another copy of the poem, I have simply put a question
mark after the word 'voice'. I think what I meant to ask is, what
we do mean by 'voice', or what might it possibly involve: pitch,
pace, volume, pronunciation, stress, intonation, etc. And also,
what did Auden mean by 'voice'? We know that he was highly
attuned to the oral/aural/physical aspects of poetry. 'No poetry
[...] which when mastered is not better heard than read is good
poetry,' he announced in the introduction to *The Poet's Tongue* in
1935, and in later life, as he honed his skills on the poetry-read-
ing circuit, he re-emphasised this essential performative aspect
of verse:

One can never grasp a poem one is reading unless one
hears the actual sounds of the words, and its meaning
is the outcome of a dialogue between the words of the
poem and the response of whoever is listening to them.

(Auden, *Secondary Worlds*)

And again and again:

The characteristic style of 'Modern' poetry is an intimate
tone of voice, the speech of one person addressing one
person, not a large audience; whenever a modern poet
raises his voice he sounds phony.

(Auden, 'The Poet & The City')

Even the most formal and elevated styles of poetry are
more conditioned by the spoken tongue, the language
really used by the men of that country, than by anything
else.

(Auden, 'American Poetry')

As for his actual voice? 'He had the power', according to Stephen
Spender in *World Within World*, 'to make everything sound
Audenesque, so that if he said in his icy voice, separating each
word from the next as though on pincers, lines of Shakespeare
or of Housman, each sounded simply like Auden.' Stravinsky, in
the chapter on 'Writers' in his *Dialogues and a Diary*, provides a
kind of musical notation of his famous friends' conversational
styles. Aldous Huxley, 'too serenely high in tessitura', is repre-
sented in Stravinsky's notes as a trill, 'ppp' and an octave above
the stave. Auden's speech is rendered by a line with peaks and
troughs, as on an oscillograph. We know Auden wasn't exactly
mad keen on his voice himself. ('Who,' he asks in one of his late

little 'Shorts', 'upon hearing / a tape of his speaking voice, / is not revolted?' This revulsion, by the way, is not uncommon, because of the limited frequency response of recording and transmitting systems. I can never really 'hear' my voice.)

*

In his later life, on the circuit, Auden's voice became his instrument, a crucial part of his performance, his shtick. (At the Poetry International Festivals, for example, held at the South Bank Centre in London in the late 1960s and 1970s, Auden was the star. The Festivals were intended as an expression of global unity in which poets, famous and undiscovered, from all around the world, were allotted an equal time – twenty minutes – to contribute their words to a poetic 'universal language'. Between 1967 and 1973, Auden appeared at every Poetry International – the only poet to make such regular appearances – usually reading on the last night and drawing capacity crowds. Joseph Brodsky, who appeared with him at the Festival in 1972, recalled that Auden 'leaned on the lectern, and for a good half hour he filled the room with the lines he knew by heart. If I ever wished for time to stop, it was then, inside that large dark room on the south bank of the Thames.' I wish I could have been there. Last year my eldest son graduated from college in a ceremony held at the South Bank Centre and I wondered if Auden had ever crossed the walkway on the Hungerford Bridge – if so, this was probably the closest I'd ever come to walking in his footsteps.)

*

On another copy, next to 'All I have is a voice', I have written 'Really?' All I have is a voice? Clearly not. I have a lot of things apart from – in addition to – my voice.

*

And finally, on yet another copy, a note, a snippet from Carpenter's *Biography* – but what a snippet. Carpenter is discussing Auden's role in Germany after the war as a Bombing Research Analyst in the Morale Division of the US Strategic Bombing Survey, during which time he visited concentration-camp survivors in a hospital in Munich. In a letter to his friend Elizabeth Mayer he wrote, 'I was prepared for their appearance but not for their voices: they whisper like gnomes.'

*

As for the rest of the stanza, my notes are a terrible rat's nest, with multiple lines of connection that make no sense, or lead nowhere, or run off into long irrelevant detours, worse even than the rest.

From what I can make out, and without wishing to duplicate the work of others:

For 'folded lie', I have written 'Newspaper?', 'Fuller?', and then page references to various articles in the *New York Times* and *The Times* for 1939.

For 'The romantic lie in the brain', I have written, most clearly, 'See Mendelson, "Against the Devourer"' (which refers to a chapter in his book *Later Auden*).

For 'the sensual man-in-the-street', I have written 'the average man', 'the reasonable man in English law?', 'the man on the Clapham omnibus?' and 'Quetelet' (which of course refers to Adolphe Quetelet, and which relates to about two months' enjoyably pointless work in which I set out to discover the source of the phrase 'the sensual man-in-the-street' and all its possible cognates and related terms, tracing them back to this Quetelet, who of course I'd never heard of, but who turned out to be a classic example of the nineteenth-century universal man – a poet, astronomer, mathematician, statistician and sociologist who founded and directed the Brussels Observatory, was the permanent secretary of the Brussels Royal Academy of Science, Letters and Fine Arts, and somehow still found time to translate Byron into French and to write opera libretti – and who, in his book *Anthropométrie, ou Mesure des différentes facultés de l'homme* (1870), claimed that by using statistical charts and tables of growth showing the height and weight and other aspects and dimensions of select groups (the chest measurements of Scottish soldiers, for example), it was possible to arrive at 'the average of [...] individual constants [...] that I assign to a fictitious being whom I call the average man', or, in his words, 'l'homme moyen').

For 'the lie of Authority': again, a lot of nonsense mostly, recycling other people's ideas, but perhaps most amusingly, a recent note that reads, 'Sleaford Mods' "Kebab Spider"?', referencing a song which has absolutely nothing to do with Auden, but which I have been listening to on repeat in the final redraft of the redrafts of the rewrites, and which has the refrain 'Who knew, who knew, who knew / They got the experts in'.

For 'Whose buildings grope the sky': it's odd, I note, having the word 'grope' in the stanza of the poem that is talking about love. ('Auden back in the dive?' reads my note.) And then a reference to a book by someone called Sheila Sullivan, *Falling in Love: A History of Torment and Enchantment* (1999), which clearly caught my eye: 'The sex organs engorge, the skin tingles [...] the eyes dilate, the heart beats faster, the rate of breathing rises, and it is possible that the excited body also puts out aphrodisiac chemical odours.'

For 'And no one exists alone': I have copied out by hand a quote from Jerome J. McGann's book *The Beauty of Inflections: Literary Investigations in Historical Method and Theory* (1985),

which is a much better book than its title suggests, in which he
defines poetry as 'experience' and 'event':

> Poetry is, from the individual's point of view, a particular
> type of human experience; from a social point of
> view, however, it is an event. Criticism studies these
> experiences and events in their successive and interrelated
> apparitions. A work of poetry is not a thing or an object,
> nor should criticism conceive it as such; it is the result of
> an interactive network of productive people and forces.

And next to that I've written 'Bruno Latour' – a reference,
presumably, to Actor–Network Theory.

For 'Hunger allows no choice': one word, 'Hamsun', referring
to Knut Hamsun, the Norwegian author of the novel *Hunger*,
winner of the Nobel Prize for Literature, and an enthusiastic
Nazi, to whom Auden – fair play to him – wrote a scathing open
letter, which was published in the magazine *Common Sense* in
August 1940. I have a copy of the letter – from the Bodleian? the
British Library? – in a folder marked 'Hunger Allows No Choice'.
The folder contains absolutely nothing else.

> *Sir:*
> Where you are or what you are doing, I have no idea.
> Doubtless you are physically safe; having played your
> little literary part in their annihilation of Norwegian
> liberty and the destruction of Norwegian cities, your
> new masters, the 'youths with the jewelled eyes,' may
> be content for a while at least, to let you be. Unless a
> realization of what you have done has made you afraid to
> be alone, you may, for all I know, have retired once more
> to that farm which the proceeds of a literary career, that

might have been more honourable but could not have been more successful, has enabled you to purchase.

In the margins of my copy of this letter I have written a single word – which I could have written a thousand times on a thousand of these documents relating to Auden:

'Yes!'

WE MUST DIE ANYWAY

But as for the stanza's last crucial line, 'We must love one another or die':
No.
Just, no.

*

My notes relating to this line are too many.

'Love's limits are ample and great,' writes the very ample and great Robert Burton, in *The Anatomy of Melancholy*, 'and a spacious walk it hath.' My marginal notes on these seven words direct me to three manila folders on the shelf, containing years of notes on everything from *A Lover's Discourse* to *Antony and Cleopatra*, *As You Like It*, *Pride and Prejudice*, *The Allegory of Love*, *Love in the Western World*, *Love in the Time of Cholera*, *Bridget Jones's Diary*, *Dr Zhivago*, *Madame Bovary* … I have notes on falling in love, falling out of love, making love, forbidden love, love found, love lost, lovers' quarrels …

What did I ever think I was going to do with all this stuff?

It is – my God! – it's trash.

*

'Rereading a poem of mine,' wrote Auden in his foreword to Barry Bloomfield's vast *Bibliography* (1964) of his work, '"1st September 1939", after it had been published, I came to the line "We must love one another or die" and said to myself: "That's a damned lie! We must die anyway." So, in the next edition, I altered it to "We must love one another and die." This didn't seem to do either, so I cut the stanza. Still no good. The whole poem, I realised, was infected with an incurable dishonesty – and must be scrapped.'

*

Auden's brisk, surgical account of his revisions of the poem are both entertaining and misleading. As we know, throughout his career he took a stern approach to his own previous work, often rewriting and revising poems according to his changing ideas and – sometimes – in response to criticism from others.

His poem 'Spain 1937' is a famous example. First published in May 1937 as a five-page pamphlet, with the royalties from the sale going to the British Medical Committee in Spain, the poem had been written by Auden shortly after his return from Spain. In 1940, George Orwell wrote an essay in which he strongly objected to a line in the poem, 'The conscious acceptance of guilt in the necessary murder', claiming that such a comment could only have been written 'by a person to whom murder is at most a *word*'. He went on, 'Mr. Auden's brand of amoralism is only possible if you are the kind of person who is always somewhere else when the trigger is pulled.' Though objecting strongly to Orwell's criticism – he complained to friends that it was 'deeply unjust' – Auden nonetheless pulled the trigger on the controversial line. When he included 'Spain 1937' in *Another Time* (1940), he replaced the phrase 'necessary murder' with the more neutral 'fact of murder', and later still he refused to include the poem in any further editions of his work.

This sort of radical self-editing and meddling might be regarded as either valiant or deeply arrogant. Or perhaps both: courage often requires arrogance, if not vice versa.

*

But 'September 1, 1939' is a special case. 'September 1, 1939' is unlike any of the other poems that Auden revised. It is undoubtedly the most famous example in literary history of a writer attempting to revise his work, and of readers refusing to allow it. (Not only is it the most famous example; I can think of no other example. Again, you'll be sure to let me know.)

Auden may have attempted to hack up the poem and destroy it – but readers have saved it from dismemberment and death, time and time again, rediscovering it, reclaiming it.

The poem – and this phrase, 'We must love one another or die', in particular – won't die and never will, because people want it to be true.

The classic and unarguable objection to the line, of course, is that we die anyway. But the phrase simply can't be killed off.

'September 1, 1939', among other things, is the world's greatest zombie poem.

*

Auden was found dead in his hotel room in Vienna on 29 September 1973. Chester Kallman's stony and sinuous valedictory poem for the poet shudders into life at the discovery of his body: 'I found him dead / Turning icy-blue on a hotel bed'. Even those who were not as close to Auden as Kallman described the burden of readjusting to his death as a matter of physical necessity, the body of their language having consciously to reclothe itself in mourning: 'Suddenly, unexpectedly, we need the past tense,' wrote Clive James; 'He was a great poet,' wrote Joseph Brodsky, '(the only thing that's wrong with this sentence is its tense […]).'

In the way of such things, in death Auden was instantly granted his immortality: according to the *Times* obituary, 'W. H. Auden, for long the *enfant terrible* of English poetry, who has died at the age of 66, emerges finally as its undisputed master.'

> Why this desire in all of us that, after we have
> disappeared, the thoughts of the living shall now and
> again dwell upon our name? Our name. Anonymous
> immortality we cannot even escape. The consequences
> of our lives and actions can no more be erased than they
> can be identified and duly labelled – to our honour or
> our shame.
> 'The poor ye have always with you.' The dead, too.
> (Dag Hammarskjöld, *Markings*)

Auden's poetry haunts us because it seems to provide simple answers to individuals and cultures at times of crisis. This has happened a few times now – which makes it look like more than coincidence.

Let's take just a couple of examples.

'Dead poet is groovy due to hit movie'
(*The Sun*, 27 May 1994)

The 1994 film *Four Weddings and a Funeral* was a box-office hit in which Auden's poem 'Funeral Blues' was read as an oration at the funeral of a gay character, played by Simon Callow. Faber and Faber published a small paperback of ten of Auden's poems, titled *Tell Me the Truth About Love*, to coincide with the release of the film. There were reports of sales of over 275,000 copies, and Faber even decided to produce a long-awaited paperback edition of the *Collected Poems*. Some people were cynical about such profiteering: the *Guardian's* Diary (11 June 1994), for example, described it as 'a brilliantly circular scam – the book of the film of the poem from a book'. But the cynicism missed the point, as the poet James Fenton recognised in his analysis of the film's popularity:

> It seems that a large number of people, since the Aids
> epidemic, have become familiar with the experience
> of funerals at which a devastated boyfriend has to pay
> tribute to his prematurely dead lover. Though the death
> of the Callow character is actually caused by a heart
> attack, the emotional scene that ensues gains force
> from those kind of memories. So Auden's poem found
> an audience which needed it – nearly 60 years after its
> composition. Auden would have been surprised, and, I
> think, touched at the outcome.
>
> (James Fenton, 'Four weddings and a circle
> of poetry', *The Independent*, 30 May 1994)

*

The period 1979 to 1997 saw almost eighteen years of Conservative Party rule in Britain, which might be described as a crisis of another kind, and was certainly seen as such by the poet Glyn Maxwell, who on reading Auden's *The Orators* in 1989 was amazed to discover its relevance:

A world where doctors and headmasters elbow to market;
where material wealth is the index of human value, and
the quicker it's achieved, the greater the honour; where
the publication of pornography, propaganda, suicide
notes or glimpses of the erogenous zones of well-known
people are cherished freedoms; where good health and
water are sold to the people as two good things; where
bystanders are framed by policemen; where furious
conviction is rewarded by power or imprisonment
but nothing else; where a Prince, concerned with his
country's poverty, is asked to mind his own business, and
a Bishop branded political for the same reason; and –
well, just as strange.

(Glyn Maxwell, 'Echoes of *The Orators*')

During the early 1990s, history also seemed to be repeating itself
in Bosnia, and Auden's voice could be heard echoing throughout
the 1993 anthology *Klaonica: Poems for Bosnia*: in Michael Hulse's
'In Defence of Making Nothing Happen', James Sutherland-
Smith's 'Musée des Beaux Arts Revisited' and Joseph Brodsky's
'Bosnia Tune'.

*

And we have already discussed the impact of 'September 1,
1939' after the events of 9/11.

*

Auden's words – and not always his best words, his finest words
– have become part of the conversation of mankind.

As I understand it, the only apology for poetry worth considering is one which seeks to discern the place and quality of the voice of poetry in the conversation of mankind – a conversation where each voice speaks in its own idiom, where from time to time one voice may speak louder than others, but where none has natural superiority, let alone primacy. The proper context in which to consider poetic utterance, and indeed every other mode of utterance, is not a 'society' engaged in practical enterprise, nor one devoted to scientific enquiry; it is this society of conversationists.

(Michael Oakeshott, *The Voice of Poetry in the Conversation of Mankind*)

9

Defenceless under the night
Our world in stupor lies;
Yet, dotted everywhere,
Ironic points of light
Flash out wherever the Just
Exchange their messages:
May I, composed like them
Of Eros and of dust,
Beleaguered by the same
Negation and despair,
Show an affirming flame.

TWINKLING

The only way to atone for the sin of writing is to
annihilate what is written. But that can be done
only by the author; destruction leaves that which is
essential intact. I can, however, tie negation so closely
to affirmation that my pen gradually effaces what it has
written. In so doing it accomplishes, in a word, what is
generally accomplished by 'time' – which, from among
its multifarious edifices, allows only the traces of death to
subsist. I believe that the secret of literature is there, and
that a book is not a thing of beauty unless it is skilfully
adorned with the indifference of the ruins.

> (Georges Bataille, *L'Abbé C*,
> trans. Philip A. Facey)

I am teaching Chekhov, the short stories. The students are enjoy-
ing Chekhov: the pathos. We're looking at the endings, the way
in which Chekhov leaves the outcomes uncertain and the char-
acters in motion:

And it seemed as though in a little while the solution
would be found, and then a new and splendid life
would begin; and it was clear to both of them that
they had still a long, long way to go, and that the

most complicated and difficult part of it was only just
beginning.

('The Lady with the Dog')

And when he walked back to the tavern, looking at
the houses of the rich publicans, cattle-dealers, and
blacksmiths, he reflected how nice it would be to steal by
night into some rich man's house!

('The Horse Stealers')

The bass was singing in the hall. A little while after,
Kryukov's racing droshky was bumping along the dusty
road.

('Mire')

They did not heed each other; each of them was living in
his own life. The sheep were pondering, too.

('Happiness')

No one answered him, and they walked on in silence
with drooping heads.

('The New Villa')

'September 1, 1939' does not end like a Chekhov short story.

*

The New York World's Fair took place between April 1939 and
October 1940, occupying more than a thousand acres at Flushing
Meadows Park in Queens: it attracted more than 44 million visi-
tors. According to the official guide,

The eyes of the Fair are on the future – not in the sense of peering toward the unknown nor attempting to foretell the events of tomorrow and the shape of things to come, but in the sense of presenting a new and clearer view of today in preparation for tomorrow; a view of the forces and ideas that prevail as well as the machines.

To its visitors the Fair will say: 'Here are the materials, ideas, and forces at work in our world. These are the tools with which the World of Tomorrow must be made. They are all interesting and much effort has been expended to lay them before you in an interesting way. Familiarity with today is the best preparation for the future.'

The most popular exhibit at the Fair was a diorama designed by Norman Bel Geddes and sponsored by General Motors: it was called Futurama, a vision of the United States in 1960. Visitors to Futurama were seated on moving benches with built-in speakers which guided them through the exhibit. The magazine *Business Week* described it thus:

> More than 30,000 persons daily, the show's capacity, inch along the sizzling pavement in long queues until they reach the chairs which transport them to a tourist's paradise. It unfolds a prophecy of cities, towns, and countrysides served by a comprehensive road system. Somewhere in the rolling davenport a disembodied angel explains the elysium.
>
> ('Motoring at 100 M.P.H',
> *Business Week*, 29 September 1939)

In the final stanza of his poem, Auden becomes the disembodied voice of the elysium.

This is his vision.
This is Futurama, Auden style.

> The written word is far more powerful than simply a
> reminder: it re-creates the past in the present, and gives
> us, not the familiar remembered thing, but the glittering
> intensity of the summoned-up hallucination.
>
> (Northrop Frye, *The Great Code*)

He was, it has to be said, always rather prone to this sort of thing
– the big summing-up, th'angelic choir rejoicing, the great glit-
tering generalities. In a sense, it doesn't matter what he did with
the line 'We must love one another or die', because in the end
the whole poem swells to become a sort of secular sermon. It's
all a bit too much.

(George Orwell pointed out that in Auden's earlier work there
was always a bit of 'an atmosphere of uplift', and it never really
goes away. 'Teach the free man how to praise,' Auden writes in
'In Memory of W. B. Yeats'. In 'Making, Knowing and Judging',
he announces that 'There is only one thing that all poetry must
do; it must praise all it can for being and for happening.' After
his first meeting with Marianne Moore in 1939, he wrote her a
thank-you note that was also a fan letter, in which he enthused
that 'Like Rilke, you really do "praise".')

*

One might, if one were so inclined, trace a history of twinkliness
in Auden's work, which finds its fullest expression here in the
image of the ironic points of light flashing out messages from
the Just, but which can be found shining bright in his very first
surviving poem, written in 1922, aged just fifteen:

> The twinkling lamps stream up the hill
> Past the farm and past the mill
> Right at the top of the road one sees
> A round moon like a Stilton cheese.
>
> (Auden, 'California')

You get a hint of it also in 'A Walk After Dark' (1948), from his collection *Nones*:

> But the stars burn on overhead,
> Unconscious of final ends,
> As I walk home to bed,
> Asking what judgement waits
> My person, all my friends,
> And these United States.

These affirming flames were clearly an important part of Auden's vision of the world.

*

(I remember, I hadn't been to a big stadium concert in maybe twenty years and then I took my daughter to see Ed Sheeran, and towards the end of the concert he asked everyone to get out their phones and I thought, 'Does he want us to call someone?', but of course it was for everyone to switch on the lights on their phones: communication devices used as illumination devices. It was a reminder that networks of illumination and communication are also part of a vast network of control, the momentary flicker on our screens binding us together, but also connecting us to our provider.)

*

Not that Auden invented affirming flames, of course: the contrast between dark and light representing the difference between death and life and solitude and community, et cetera et cetera, is as old as literature itself. The Book of Genesis begins with darkness upon the face of the deep, until God lights it all up; and in John's Gospel, 'The light shineth in darkness; and the darkness comprehended it not'; and you can find the same sorts of image complex at work in Shakespeare, and in Milton – and in Alexander Pope. I don't think any scholars have identified Alexander Pope and his vision of 'Universal Darkness' in *The Dunciad* as a possible source for Auden's ironic points of light, but I wonder, could they be? Might they be?

> She comes! she comes! the sable Throne behold
> Of Night Primæval, and of Chaos old!
> Before her, Fancy's gilded clouds decay,
> And all its varying Rain-bows die away.
> Wit shoots in vain its momentary fires,
> The meteor drops, and in a flash expires.
> As one by one, at dread Medea's strain,
> The sick'ning stars fade off th'ethereal plain;
> As Argus' eyes by Hermes' wand opprest,
> Clos'd one by one to everlasting rest;
> Thus at her felt approach, and secret might,
> Art after Art goes out, and all is Night.

Maybe.

But then visions of light, in flashes and fires, come streaming everywhere in literature.

I've just been teaching Conrad, *Heart of Darkness*:

The sun set; the dusk fell on the stream, and lights began
to appear along the shore. The Chapman light-house, a
three-legged thing erect on a mud-flat, shone strongly.
Lights of ships moved in the fairway – a great stir of lights
going up and going down. And farther west on the upper
reaches the place of the monstrous town was still marked
ominously on the sky, a brooding gloom in sunshine, a
lurid glare under the stars.

And Conan Doyle, 'The Sign of Four':

It was a September evening, and not yet seven o'clock,
but the day had been a dreary one, and a dense drizzly
fog lay low upon the great city. Mud-coloured clouds
drooped sadly over the muddy streets. Down the
Strand the lamps were but misty splotches of diffused
light which threw a feeble circular glimmer upon
the slimy pavement. The yellow glare from the shop-
windows streamed out into the steamy, vaporous air
and threw a murky, shifting radiance across the crowded
thoroughfare. There was, to my mind, something eerie
and ghost-like in the endless procession of faces which
flitted across these narrow bars of light – sad faces and
glad, haggard and merry. Like all human kind, they
flitted from the gloom into the light, and so back into the
gloom once more. I am not subject to impressions, but
the dull, heavy evening, with the strange business upon
which we were engaged, combined to make me nervous
and depressed. I could see from Miss Morstan's manner
that she was suffering from the same feeling. Holmes
alone could rise superior to petty influences. He held his
open note-book upon his knee, and from time to time

he jotted down figures and memoranda in the light of his pocket-lantern.

I could go on. There are lots of other examples.

No more other examples, suggest my beta-readers – enough now of your affirming flames.

*

(My sister, who lives in Australia, persuades me I should buy a barbecue. I don't particularly like barbecues, either the food or the event. Christopher Isherwood tripped over a barbecue once and got an infection. I can't imagine Auden at a barbecue. I say, 'We have never had a barbecue,' which is not really an argument. My sister says, 'You're a long time dead,' which is not an argument either. But, nevertheless. We go to Homebase and buy a cheap one. 'The children will love it,' she says. I burn the chicken on the barbecue, because I'm too busy doing other things, like looking after the children. 'You have to watch it the whole time,' says my sister. Really? 'The whole time?' 'The whole time. It's not like an oven. You have to watch for flames.' I may not be cut out for barbecuing.)

> There is at the back of every artist's mind something like a pattern or a type of architecture. The original quality in any man of imagination is imagery. It is a thing like the landscape of his dreams; the sort of world he would like to make or in which he would wish to wander; the strange flora and fauna of his own secret planet; the sort of thing he likes to think about. This general atmosphere, and pattern or structure of growth, governs all his creations, however varied.
>
> (Auden, quoting G. K. Chesterton, *A Certain World*)

The general atmosphere of Auden's work? The pattern and structure of growth? The flora and fauna?

It's *all* affirming flames, wherever you look.

At different times and in different places, Auden's landscape of ideas features mystical experiences; and vivid apprehensions of nature; and longings for a lost Eden and a New Jerusalem; and of course the famous Vision of Dame Kind that he defines in his essay 'The Protestant Mystics' ('The basic experience is an overwhelming conviction that the objects confronting him have a numinous significance and importance, that the existence of everything he is aware of is holy. And the basic emotion is one of innocent joy, though this joy can include, of course, a reverent dread'); and 'There is less grief than wonder on the whole,' he writes in his poem 'Objects'; and it's all good, good, it's all all good.

And politicians love this sort of stuff.

*

'I have always thought', Auden wrote in 1962, 'one might learn much about the cultural history of a country by going through the speeches made by its public men over a certain period, in legislatures, in law courts, and at official banquets, and making a list of the books quoted from without attribution.'

*

Auden's words have been used without attribution in many speeches, most notably and disturbingly by American politicians: Anthony Hecht points out that Peggy Noonan borrowed the 'points of light' for the campaign speeches of President George Bush, and Edward Mendelson recalls a choice example from the 1960s when the phrase 'We must love one another or die' was adapted for a campaign advertisement for Lyndon

Johnson's 1964 election campaign. (In England, Auden's words have tended to be put to rather more prosaic public uses. The 1993 Annual Report for the Transport Users' Consultative Committee for Western England, for example, recorded the suggested development of twenty-eight park-and-ride stations providing a shuttle service to urban centres, and made its point with a quotation from Auden.)

*

(President Roosevelt, in his address at the opening of the World's Fair, echoing the official line, added a few twinkles of his own that sound just like bad Auden: 'The eyes of the United States are fixed on the future. Our wagon is hitched to a star. But it is a star of good will, a star of progress for mankind, a star of greater happiness and less hardship, a star of international good will, and above all, a star of peace. May the months to come carry us forward in the rays of that hope.' Those rays of hope carried forth until 7 December 1941, when the attack on Pearl Harbor finally brought the United States into World War II.)

*

It's precisely because Auden does not specify who are the Just, or what is the exact nature of their messages, that politicians have been able to borrow his phrases for their own purposes – you can take the words and bend them and shape them according to your needs.

The time may have come for me to claim them for my own purposes.

I suppose that's what I've been doing here all along.

National identity can be a benign influence only if
it is tolerant of ambivalence, or multiple affiliation.
Individuals who simultaneously are English, British,
European, and have some overall sense of global
citizenship, may regard one of these as their overriding
identity, but this need not prevent them accepting the
others too. Xenophobic nationalism is the opposite: the
nation is 'one, indivisible'. It is culturally protectionist,
assuming the nation has a 'destiny' – that it is not only
set apart from but superior to other nations. But nations
don't have destinies and all nations, without exception,
are 'mongrel nations'. The nation is not something given
in nature, and whatever remote connections they may
have to earlier ethnic communities, nations are a product
of relatively recent history. They have all been built from
a diversity of cultural fragments.

(Anthony Giddens, *The Third Way:
The Renewal of Social Democracy*)

We want to participate, we want to debate, we want to
make our voices heard in public, and we want to have
a possibility to determine the political course of our
country. Since the country is too big for all of us to come
together and determine our fate, we need a number of
public spaces within it. […] [I]f only ten of us are sitting
around a table, each expressing his opinion, each hearing
the opinions of others, then a rational formation of
opinion can take place through the exchange of opinions.
There, too, it will become clear which one of us is best
suited to present our view before the next higher council,
where in turn our view will be clarified through the
influence of other views, revised, or proved wrong. […]

> In this direction I see the possibility of forming a new
> concept of the state.
>
> (Hannah Arendt, *Crises of the Republic*)

But just a reminder – to myself, as much as to anyone, before we get carried away with all this – a reminder about the exact nature of Auden's points of light.

They're ironic.

In his book *The Alluring Problem*, the poet D. J. Enright suggests that irony provides us with 'a way of making statements, not unlike that of poetry, which through the unexpectedness and the avoidance of head-on assertion had a stronger chance of discomposing, if not winning over, the person addressed'.

An ironic point of light might be ironic in a number of senses: it might, for example, be signalling an ironic message.

A secret message.

A nod and a wink.

Whatever it is, it is worth bearing in mind that the messages exchanged by the Just are not necessarily head-on assertions. They're not statements. They're *ironic* points of light.

> In the late fifties a wire-service transmitted a greatly
> exaggerated report of Auden's death, and one college
> organized a memorial service before a correction arrived,
> reading 'Auden not dead.'
>
> (Edward Mendelson, *W. H. Auden, 1907–1973*)

If you're really looking for the living flame of Auden and his work, I suggest looking elsewhere, away from the bright shiny lights of the Just.

*

(Edward Lear, in Auden's poem, 'became a land', and Auden himself has become a street – actually three streets named after him in Austria – and there are various memorials dotted around the world. A tablet in Christ Church Cathedral, another in Westminster Abbey, plaques at 1 Montague Terrace, Brooklyn, and at the hotel in Vienna where he died. According to Derek Walcott, 'A great writer can make even tourism happen,' and during the 1950s, according to Harold Norse, in the wake of Auden, the island of Ischia became 'an Anglo-American literary colony', a popular literary hang-out. These days, you can also visit Auden's house in Kirchstetten, which is the closest thing there is to an actual Auden Museum – Wienerstrasse 32, 3062 Kirchstetten; visits by appointment only – which really is ironic, because although Auden was awarded the Staatspreis, the most prestigious Austrian literary prize, he knew little if anything of Austrian literature, and Austrian writers were little interested in him. Asked if he wanted to meet Auden, the novelist Thomas Bernhard politely declined. There should really be an Auden museum on 52nd Street.)

*

But never mind the big statements and the monuments: by far the most astonishing aspect of Auden's afterlife has been the continual flood of poems to, for and about him. Little flashes and flames.

It's like people lighting candles for Jim Morrison at Père-Lachaise.

*

The poems addressed to Auden are remarkable for both their abundance and their variety. Auden's work features in other people's poems in a number of ways, as one might expect –

through allusion, quotation, imitation, parody and pastiche. Quotations from Auden occur as prompts to poems, within poems and in the margins of poems, as epigraphs and as notes. Some poets, meanwhile, use Auden's own forms as a means of addressing him: Anna Adams's *A Reply to Intercepted Mail* (1979), for example, is a verse-letter to Auden in the rhyme-royal of his own 'Letter to Lord Byron'. Francis Spufford's 'A Letter to Wystan Auden, from Iceland' is the same, as is David Grant's *Letter to W. H. Auden* (1993).

The most common tributes to Auden are the personal poems from friends and admirers wishing him birthday greetings: Edmund Wilson and Louise Bogan's 'To Wystan Auden on his Birthday', Geoffrey Grigson's 'To Wystan Auden, 1967', Charles Causley's 'Letter from Jericho', William Meredith's 'Talking Back'.

After his death, there were poems recording and remembering encounters: Anne Rouse's 'Memo to Auden', Lincoln Kirstein's *'Siegfriedslage'*, Roy Fuller's 'Visiting the Great'.

His death also prompted a number of elegiac summings-up and assessments, and poets have continued to mine this vein: Robert Greacen's 'Auden', Derek Walcott's 'Eulogy to W. H. Auden', Clive James's 'What Happened to Auden', Elizabeth Jennings's 'Elegy for W. H. Auden', Karl Shapiro's 'W.H.A.', Carol Ann Duffy's 'Alphabet for Auden'. Other poets have written indirectly in praise of his inspiring influence (Richard Wilbur's 'For W. H. Auden', Thomas Kinsella's 'Dedication'), or about their discovery of his work (Christy Brown's 'W. H. Auden').

But if I had to pick my favourite? The pilot light?

James Schuyler – the great overlooked Schuyler, the greatest, in my opinion, of the New York School of poets, who worked for a while as Auden's assistant – produced what I think is the finest elegy for Auden.

It is sprawling, delightful, and sad.

And this is just a fragment.

    So much
to remember, so little to
say: that he liked martinis
and was greedy about the wine?
I always thought he would live
to a great age. He did not.
Wystan, kind man and great poet,
goodbye.

A NEW CHAPTER
IN MY LIFE

Suddenly, it's over.

> I'm astounded whenever I finish something. Astounded
> and distressed. My perfectionist instinct should inhibit
> me from finishing; it should inhibit me from even
> beginning. But I get distracted and start doing something.
> What I achieve is not the product of an act of my will
> but of my will's surrender. I begin because I don't have
> the strength to think; I finish because I don't have the
> courage to quit. This book is my cowardice.
> (Fernando Pessoa, *The Book of Disquiet*,
> trans. Richard Zenith, 2001)

I am not the person I was when I started writing this book twenty-five years ago.

We make certain assumptions about the inviolable and unchanging nature of the human subject.

We are wrong.

> For we are all insulted by
> The mere suggestion that we die
> Each moment and that each great I
> Is but a process in a process

Within a field that never closes;
As proper people find it strange
That we are changed by what we change,
That no event can happen twice
And that no two existences
Can ever be alike; we'd rather
Be perfect copies of our father,
Prefer our *idées fixes* to be
True of a fixed Reality.

(Auden, New Year Letter)

Each great I is but a process in a process – and no two existences can ever be alike.

It turns out I am definitely not W. H. Auden.

But I'm not even myself any more.

*

I started writing this book so long ago that I had no children. Now my children have all left home.

I started writing this on 3M 3.5-inch diskettes, double-sided, high-density, formatted for use with IBM PS/2 (models 30, 286, 50, 60, 70, 80) and compatible systems using DOS 3.3 and higher. I am finishing it on my Mac AirBook.

I started writing this with a thirty-inch waist – and then a thirty-two, a thirty-four, and after that I'm afraid I stopped counting. At least my height remains more or less constant, at five foot eight.

When I started this book I was still a young man, with everything before me. Now, I am a small, round middle-aged man, with less time before me than behind me – and however long that's going to be, I will never be W. H. Auden.

A person at least knows one thing about his future, that
however different it may be from his present, it will
be his. However he may have changed he will still be
himself, not somebody else.

(Auden, 'Making, Knowing and Judging')

If I had to describe what on earth I think I've been doing for all
these years, returning constantly to this poem, on and off, again
and again, I would probably say that I've been dreaming it, and
that this book is simply my recounting of that dream.

Then she thought, (in a dream within a dream, as it
were,) how this same little Alice would, in the after-time,
be herself a grown woman: and how she would keep,
through her riper years, the simple and loving heart of
her childhood: and how she would gather around her
other little children, and make their eyes bright and eager
with many a wonderful tale, perhaps even with these very
adventures of the little Alice of long ago …

(Lewis Carroll, *Alice's Adventures Under Ground*)

Or perhaps the recounting of a parable:

You cannot tell people what to do, you can only tell them
parables; and that is what art really is, particular stories
of particular people and experiences, from which each
according to his immediate and particular needs may
draw his own conclusions.

(Auden, 'Psychology and Art To-day')

In Woody Allen's film *Midnight in Paris* – the last great Woody Allen film – the main character travels back in time to hang out in Paris with the likes of Gertrude Stein. I know that if I was able to travel back in time to hang out in New York with Auden in 1939 – at the Dizzy Club, or in Brooklyn, wherever, we would not have got on. Wrong looks, wrong class, wrong type.

*

(On my one trip to New York many years ago, I tried to retrace Auden's footsteps. I had lists, addresses, everything.

> The city does not consist of this, but of relationships
> between the measurements of its space and the events
> of its past [...] As this wave from memories flows in,
> the city soaks it up like a sponge and expands [...]
> The city, however, does not tell its past, but contains it
> like the lines of a hand, written in the corners of the
> streets, the gratings of the windows, the banisters of the
> steps, the antennae of the lightning rods, the poles of
> the flags, every segment marked in turn with scratches,
> indentations, scrolls.
>
> (Italo Calvino, *Invisible Cities*)

I saw nothing, felt nothing, experienced nothing. I was in entirely the wrong place. I know only the Auden of the poem.)

*

I started reading poetry in my teens.

I can offer no simple explanation for this activity – no one in my family had shown any interest in poetry before, and no one has shown any interest since.

And why do I read it now?

(Honestly? Often because I am tired of reading slight, sad stories about slightly sad people, who are vaguely troubled by their slightly sad lives and who face some minor crisis which prompts them to reassess their priorities and to learn a little about themselves and others, so that in the end everything is vaguely OK again. If I wanted to read that, I could go back and read Chekhov. I am entirely out of love and out of touch with most contemporary fiction.)

> The purpose of art is to impart the sensation of things
> as they are perceived and not as they are known. The
> technique of art is to make objects 'unfamiliar,' to make
> forms difficult, to increase the difficulty and length
> of perception because the process of perception is an
> aesthetic end in itself and must be prolonged. Art is a way
> of experiencing the artfulness of an object; the object is
> not important.
>
> (Viktor Shklovsky, 'Art as Technique')

Even now, though, I'm not sure what to do with a poem.

Is it even a thing, poetry, that you can *do* something with? I don't know.

But I'll tell you what I do know, after all these years: I thoroughly dislike it.

> I, too, dislike it: […]
> Reading it, however, with a perfect contempt for it,
>   one discovers that there is in
> it, after all, a place for the genuine.
>
> (Marianne Moore, 'Poetry')

Everyone dislikes it, even poets.

Why?

Because poetry embarrasses and humiliates us. It makes us feel weak and small, and it encourages in us false and sentimental ideas and emotions. Poetry can bully us, and it can mock us, it can mislead us and it can lead us astray. And we have to acknowledge this, if we want to grant poetry its proper place in our lives, its appropriate place – if, that is, we don't want to spend twenty-five years in thrall to its power.

*

If I have learnt anything from Auden, it is that poetry does not necessarily uplift and sublimate and make things good.

> The primary function of poetry, as of all the arts, is to
> make us more aware of ourselves and the world around
> us. I do not know if such increased awareness makes us
> more moral or more efficient. I hope not. I think it makes
> us more human, and I am quite certain it makes us more
> difficult to deceive.
>
> (Auden, introduction to *Poems of Freedom*)

There are other poets – lots of poets – who have meant a lot to me. Marianne Moore. Ivor Gurney. Swift, Langland, Frank O'Hara, Elizabeth Bishop, Charles Simic, Vladimir Mayakovsky. But would I write a book about any of them? I wouldn't: I couldn't.

Thinking back, then, why did I ever think I could write a book about Auden?

*

In the late 1980s and early 1990s I was working in Foyles Bookshop, on the Charing Cross Road in London. I loved working in Foyles: I liked meeting the sales reps, and opening up the big boxes of books; I liked the tea trolley that came round in the morning and again in the afternoon; and I liked hiding from the customers and pretending I was busy. Also, I earned more money, hour for hour, working in Foyles than I ever had before or I ever have since. It was good: life was sweet. Unfortunately, though, the old employment policy at Foyles ensured that everyone was fired within two years – something to do with insurance and pensions. When my two years was coming to an end, I had no plan, of course, and no career in mind. I thought about doing teacher training, graduate-trainee schemes. I wrote letters, received application forms. I failed to get any jobs or to be accepted on any courses, and eventually I took the last route open to me: I applied to do a PhD. It took me a while to choose what I wanted to study but in the end I settled on Auden as my proposed subject because (a) I knew I wanted to study something in the twentieth century (easier, so I thought); (b) I didn't want to do novels (too many themes); (c) or plays (too much talking); and (d) of the major twentieth-century poets, I already knew I didn't like Eliot (too humourless) or Pound (too anti-Semitic), and to be absolutely honest, Auden was one of the only other major twentieth-century poets I'd heard of, and I knew he was somehow left-wing and had something to do with the 1930s, which was good because I myself was a member of the Labour Party and was deeply opposed to fascism. Also, I liked the look of his face.

To my surprise, I was accepted to study for a PhD, and was given a grant, which left only one problem: I hadn't actually read any W. H. Auden. So, on my last day at Foyles, I used my staff discount (25 per cent) to buy a copy of the *Collected Poems* and on the first day of term, back at college in my mid-twenties, I sat down at my desk with my sharpened pencils, my big pad of paper and an Amstrad computer with a daisy-wheel printer, and started to work my way through my new copy of Auden's *Collected*.

*

Before finishing this book, I thought I would sit down one more time with the *Collected Poems*, and work my way through the whole lot again, pencil and notebook in hand, repeating the experiment – giving myself up unto the work without guides, commentaries or notes, as utterly guileless, as unarmed and as innocent as I was back then, in order to try and work out that most crucial and compelling of all critical questions: was it really worth me devoting all that time to?

*

So I settle down again, with the fresh new edition of the *Collected Poems*, the American Modern Library edition, stitched, cloth-bound, 'set in a digitized version of Janson, a typeface that dates from about 1690 and was cut by Nicholas Kis, a Hungarian working in Amsterdam'. The previous *Collected Poems* (1991), my old copy, had been revised and reset from the original 1976 edition and was one of those squat Faber books with a tessellated, Pentagram-designed cover, enough to put off all but the most determined of readers before even getting to the poems.

And on into the book. Mendelson, Auden's executor, the keeper of the flame, has added a new 'Note' to his earlier preface, which is warm, welcoming and short, and which clearly sets out to reposition Auden, not as a heartless brainbox, but as the great twentieth-century poet of love: 'His poems bear witness to the close connection between intelligence and love.' (It's a shame, then, that the *Collected Poems* begins with 'Paid on Both Sides', Auden's 1928 show-off play, which is a kind of revenge tragedy featuring dream sequences, soliloquies, a Chorus, Father Christmas, and characters called Bo, Po and 'The Man-Woman'. It all seems extremely portentous and strained. I'd forgotten about 'Paid on Both Sides', but it's forgivable. Auden was twenty-one when he wrote it. When I was twenty-one – well.)

Rather than representing the poems as they appeared in the original collections – as Peter McDonald has done in his edition of Louis MacNeice's *Collected Poems*, for example – Mendelson has again chosen to honour Auden's own habit of radically editing and then rearranging his poetry in roughly chronological order by period, with each period reflecting what Auden believed was 'a new chapter in my life'. Thus, Part II of the *Collected Poems*, rather than presenting all of the poems from Auden's first full collection, *Poems* (1930), gathers together instead all of those poems from the period 1927–1932 which Auden himself wished to preserve; there are exactly thirty-eight of them. And they are, admittedly, fantastic. No one could possibly deny the brilliance of Auden's early crack-of-doom phrase-making, which maps the mythic and the psychological onto a landscape. 'Who stands, the crux left of the watershed, / On the wet road between the chafing grass.' When reading these early poems, what one is responding to is not just the intellectual showiness but the sheer *sexiness* of Auden's language, as in the post-coital conclusion to 'Consider this and in our time': 'To disintegrate on an instant in the explosion of mania / Or lapse for ever into a classic fatigue.'

Next comes 'Letter to Lord Byron', which is a jollity. Then poems from the period 1933–1938, the glory years, the years of 'Out on the lawn I lie in bed', and 'Paysage Moralisé' and 'Night Mail' and 'Musée des Beaux Arts', the famous thirties poems of social conscience. (Though you won't find the most famous of

Auden's poems from the period here – 'Spain 1937', or indeed 'September 1, 1939' – because Auden decided he disagreed with their sentiments in later life, and Mendelson accordingly excludes them; the *Collected Poems* is very much a *Collected* rather than a *Complete* Auden.)

Then there's *New Year Letter* (1940), a long verse-letter in couplets, and it's here that one begins perhaps for the first time to become really irritated by Auden's pomposity, by the spiritual wrangling and the grand gestures: 'Under the familiar weight / Of winter, conscience and the State, / In loose formations of good cheer, / Love, language, loneliness and fear.' This paternal tone – from a poet only then in his thirties – penetrates deeper in the poems from the period 1939–1947, whose titles alone give some indication of their grand ambitions: 'In Memory of W. B. Yeats', 'In Memory of Sigmund Freud', 'At the Grave of Henry James'. For better or for worse, this is undoubtedly Auden's most quotable period; this is where you'll find 'poetry makes nothing happen' and 'the treason of all clerks'. This is also where you'll find 'The Fall of Rome', which may contain Auden's most perfect stanza:

Altogether elsewhere, vast
Herds of reindeer move across
Miles and miles of golden moss,
Silently and very fast.

But, next: *For the Time Being* ('A Christmas Oratorio') and *The Sea and the Mirror* ('A Commentary on Shakespeare's The Tempest'), fertile ground for academics, anathema to the general reader. *The Age of Anxiety* ('A Baroque Eclogue'), written in alliterative lines, whose title is perhaps more memorable than any of its contents. Then the poems from the period 1948–1957, displaying Auden at his most formally inventive and intellectually promiscuous: poems in syllabics about history and western culture. *Dichtung und Wahrheit* ('An Unwritten Poem'), Auden's meditation on the meaning of love, gets a section to itself, which perhaps exaggerates its significance. And then the poems of 1958–1971 and 1972–1973: chatty, worldly and wry.

So, in total, overall, reading them all the way through again, in retrospect, is it any good?

No. Absolutely not.

Good is not the word.

*

('But of works of art little can be said': Robert Louis Stevenson, 'Books Which Have Influenced Me', 1882.)

*

There are some things we will never know. Did Livia poison her husband, Emperor Augustus? Did Gandhi really travel on a train between Johannesburg and Durban reading Ruskin's *Unto This Last* in 1904 and resolve to change his life, simple as that? Are our thoughts distinct from physiological processes? Is there life after death, and if so, will it be like Doris Stokes used to say it was, all hugs and hot tea and flannelette pyjamas? Why has a cow got four legs? Why bother?

But some things are for sure.

W. H. Auden was a great *great* poet.

In one of the *Dream Songs*, John Berryman writes of Robert Frost, 'For a while here we possessed / an unusual man.'

*

My wife asks, what does it feel like, to have finished? The only thing in my life that has lasted longer than my interest in Auden is my marriage. What does it feel like to have finished?

I say that it feels like I've escaped.

*

(At the end of Irvine Welsh's novel *Trainspotting*, the Kierkegaard-quoting heroin-addict Mark Renton gives his mates the slip: 'Now, free from them all, for good, he could be what he wanted to be. He'd stand or fall alone.')

*

Finally, I am escaping from the poem, and the poem is escaping from me. I have entertained it for twenty-five years, and it has entertained me. Now we are both free to go about our business.

*

Sometimes, in desperation over the years, I have imagined giving up, not just this work on Auden, but work on everything, giving up entirely. Writers who admit to this desire – Larkin, say ('Beneath it all, desire of oblivion runs'), or Beckett ('sleep till death / healeth / come ease / this life disease'), E. M. Cioran – are regarded by some as self-despisers, yet this yearning for ultimate escape seems to be an instinct as common and as natural as the instinct for self-preservation, and may sometimes even lead us towards self-knowledge and self-respect.

It is a testament to Auden that in my despair over Auden, Auden continued to keep me company.

*

The logic of escape demands that one escapes 'from' some place – or something or somebody – 'to' some other place, and in order to do so, one undertakes a journey in between.

So where was I before?

Where am I now?

And what was the journey in between?

*

D'you know, I really can't say.

All I've done is finish the preparation.

Maybe now I can begin.

TWENTY-FIVE YEARS' WORTH OF READING

I have included everything here that seemed relevant.

Abbott, Craig S., *Marianne Moore: A Reference Guide* (Boston, Mass., 1978).

Abrams, M. H., 'Structure and Style in the Greater Romantic Lyric' (1965), repr. in Harold Bloom, ed., *Romanticism and Consciousness: Essays in Criticism* (New York, 1970).

Adams, Anna, *A Reply to Intercepted Mail (a Verse-Letter to W. H. Auden)* (Liskeard, Cornwall, 1979).

Aiken, Conrad, *Selected Letters of Conrad Aiken*, ed. Joseph Killorin (New Haven, 1978).

Allott, Kenneth, *Poems* (London, 1938).

Alvarez, A., *The New Poetry* (1962; rev. edn Harmondsworth, 1966).

Amis, Kingsley, *Memoirs* (London, 1991).

Amis, Martin, 'A Poetic Injustice', the *Guardian*, Weekend, 21 Aug. 1993.

Ansen, Alan, *The Table Talk of W. H. Auden*, ed. Nicholas Jenkins (London, 1991).

Appleyard, Bryan, *The Pleasures of Peace: Art and Imagination in Post-war Britain* (London, 1989).

Aquarius, Roy Fuller Special Issue, 'Roy Fuller – a Tribute', 21/22 (1993).

Arendt, Hannah, *The Human Condition* (Chicago, 1958).

—, *Crises of the Republic* (New York, 1972).

Ash, John, *The Goodbyes* (Manchester, 1982).

Ashbery, John, interview with Peter Stitt (1980), repr. in George Plimpton, ed., *Poets at Work* (London, 1989).

Atkinson, Donald, *A Sleep of Drowned Fathers* (Calstock, Cornwall, 1989).

Atlas, James, *Delmore Schwartz: The Life of an American Poet* (New York, 1977).

—, 'New Voices in American Poetry', *New York Times Magazine*, 3 Feb. 1980.

Auden, W. H., *Poems* (London, 1930).

—, *The Orators: An English Study* (1932).

—, ed., *The Poet's Tongue: An Anthology*, with John Garrett (London, 1935).

—, *Look, Stranger!* (London, 1936).

—, *Letters from Iceland*, with Louis MacNeice (London, 1937).

—, *Another Time* (London, 1940).

—, *The Double Man* (New York, 1941).

—, *New Year Letter* (London, 1941), British edn of *The Double Man*.

—, 'The Rewards of Patience', *Partisan Review*, 9:4 (July/Aug. 1942).

—, 'New Poems', *New York Times*, 15 Oct. 1944.

—, 'Squares and Oblongs', in Charles D. Abbott, ed., *Poets at Work* (New York, 1948).

—, *The Enchafèd Flood* (1950; repr. London, 1985).

—, *Collected Shorter Poems 1930–1944* (London, 1950).

—, *Nones* (New York, 1951).

—, *The Shield of Achilles* (New York, 1955).

—, *Making, Knowing and Judging* (Oxford, 1956).

—, ed., *The Faber Book of Modern American Verse* (London, 1956).

—, 'Miss Marianne Moore, Bless Her!', *The Mid-Century*, 5 (Fall 1959).

—, *Homage to Clio* (London, 1960).

—, review of *A Marianne Moore Reader*, *The Mid-Century*, 36 (Feb. 1962).

—, *The Dyer's Hand* (London, 1963).

—, 'A Literary Transference', in A. J. Guérard, ed., *Hardy: A Collection of Critical Essays* (Englewood Cliffs, N.J., 1963).

—, 'Homage to Marianne Moore on Her Seventy-Fifth Birthday', *Proceedings of the American Academy of Arts and Letters and the National Institute of Arts and Letters*, 2:13 (1963).

—, *The Faber Book of Aphorisms* (London, 1964).

—, *About the House* (New York, 1965).

—, *Secondary Worlds* (London, 1968).

—, *Academic Graffiti* (London, 1971).

—, *A Certain World: A Commonplace Book* (London, 1971).

—, 'Louise Bogan 1897–1970', *Proceedings of the American Academy of Arts and Letters and the National Institute of Arts and Letters*, 2:21 (1971).

—, *Epistle to a Godson* (London, 1972).

—, *Forewords and Afterwords*, selected by Edward Mendelson (London, 1973).

—, 'Larkin's Choice', the *Guardian*, 29 Mar. 1973.

—, 'Marianne Moore 1887–1972', *Proceedings of the American Academy of Arts and Letters and the National Institute of Arts and Letters*, 2:23 (1973).

—, *Thank You, Fog* (London, 1974)

—, 'Sue', Sycamore Broadsheet 23 (Oxford, 1977).

—, *The English Auden: Poems, Essays and Dramatic Writings 1927–1939*, ed. Edward Mendelson (London, 1977).

—, *Plays and Other Dramatic Writings 1928–1938*, with Christopher Isherwood, ed. Edward Mendelson (London, 1989).

—, *Collected Poems*, ed. Edward Mendelson, 2nd edn (London, 1991).

—, *Libretti and Other Dramatic Writings 1939–1973*, with Chester Kallman, ed. Edward Mendelson (Princeton, 1993).

—, *Juvenilia: Poems 1922–1928*, ed. Katherine Bucknell (London, 1994).

—, *Tell Me the Truth About Love: Ten Poems by W. H. Auden* (London, 1994).

—, *Collected Poems*, ed. Edward Mendelson, rev. edn (London, 2007).

Austin, J. L., 'A Plea for Excuses', *Proceedings of the Aristotelian Society*, n.s. 57 (1956–57).

Bachelard, Gaston, *Water and Dreams: An Essay on the Imagination of Matter*, trans. Edith R. Farrell (1914; repr. Dallas, 1983).

Baker, Nicholson, *U & I* (London, 1991).

Barker, George, *Poems* (London, 1935).

Barthes, Roland, *Camera Lucida* (1980), trans. Richard Howard (1981; repr. London, 1984).

Bar-yaacov, Lois, 'The Odd Couple: The Correspondence between Marianne Moore and Ezra Pound, 1918–1939', *Twentieth Century Literature*, 34:4 (Winter 1988).

Bateson, F. W., 'Auden's (and Empson's) Heirs', *Essays in Criticism*, 7:1 (Jan. 1957).

Bawer, Bruce, 'Louise Bogan's Angry Solitude', *New Criterion*, 3:9 (May 1985).

—, *The Middle Generation* (Hamden, Conn., 1986).

Bayard, Pierre, *Comment parler des livres que l'on n'a pas lus?* (Paris, 2007).

—, *Comment parler des lieux où l'on n'a pas été?* (Paris, 2012).

Bayley, John, *The Romantic Survival: A Study in Poetic Evolution* (London, 1957).

—, 'The Verse of Accomplishment', *TLS*, 27 Aug. 1982.

—, 'We Shall Not Be Moved', *London Review of Books*, 2–15 Feb. 1984.

—, 'Larkin and the Romantic Tradition', *Critical Quarterly*, 26:1/2 (Spring 1984).

—, *Selected Essays* (Cambridge, 1984).

—, 'Aardvark', *London Review of Books*, 22 Apr. 1993.

Beach, Christopher, *ABC of Influence: Ezra Pound and the Remaking of American Poetic Tradition* (Berkeley, 1992).

Beach, Joseph Warren, *The Making of the Auden Canon* (Minneapolis, 1957).

Beaton, Cecil, *The Wandering Years, Diaries: 1922–1939* (London, 1961).

Bennett, Alan, *Objects of Affection* (London, 1982).

—, 'Alas! Deceived', *London Review of Books*, 25 Mar. 1993.

Bergonzi, Bernard, *Reading the Thirties: Texts and Contexts* (London, 1978).

Berryman, John, *The Freedom of the Poet* (New York, 1976).

—, *Collected Poems 1937–1971*, ed. Charles Thornbury (London, 1990).

Bethea, David M., *Joseph Brodsky and the Creation of Exile* (Princeton, 1994).

Birchall, Ian, *'The smallest mass party in the world': Building the Socialist Workers Party, 1951–1979* (London, 1981).

Bishop, Elizabeth, *Collected Prose*, ed. Robert Giroux (London, 1984).

Blackburn, Robin, 'Marxism and Aesthetics – A Reply to James Fenton', *New Statesman*, 22 June 1979.

Blair, John G., *The Poetic Art of W. H. Auden* (Princeton, 1965).

Blanshard, Frances, *Portraits of Wordsworth* (London, 1959).

Blond, Anthony, *The Book Book* (London, 1985).

Bloom, Harold, *The Anxiety of Influence* (New York, 1973).

—, *A Map of Misreading* (New York, 1975).

—, *Poetry and Repression: Revisionism from Blake to Stevens* (New Haven, 1976).

—, *Agon: Towards a Theory of Revisionism* (New York, 1982).

—, ed., *Marianne Moore: Modern Critical Views* (New York, 1987).

Bloomfield, B. C., *W. H. Auden: A Bibliography* (Charlottesville, Va., 1964).

—, *W. H. Auden: A Bibliography 1924–1969*, 2nd edn, with Edward Mendelson (Charlottesville, Va., 1972).

Bogan, Louise, review of Moore's *What Are Years*, *New Yorker*, 1 Nov. 1941.

—, review of Hecht's *A Summoning of Stones*, *New Yorker*, 5 June 1954.

—, review of Moore's *Fables*, *New Yorker*, 4 Sept. 1954.

—, *Collected Poems 1923–1953* (New York, 1954).

—, *Selected Criticism* (New York, 1955).

—, *A Poet's Alphabet: Reflections on the Literary Art and Vocation*, ed. Robert Phelps and Ruth Limmer (New York, 1970).

—, trans., *The Sorrows of Young Werther* and *Novella*, with Elizabeth Mayer (New York, 1971).

—, *What the Woman Lived: Selected Letters of Louise Bogan 1920–1970*, ed. Ruth Limmer (New York, 1973).

Boland, Eavan, 'Undersongs of Another Life', *PN Review*, 14:2 (1987).

Bold, Alan, ed., *W. H. Auden: The Far Interior* (London, 1985).

Boly, John R., *Reading Auden: The Returns of Caliban* (Ithaca, N.Y., 1991).

Booth, James, *Philip Larkin: Writer* (Hemel Hempstead, 1992).

Bowles, Gloria, *Louise Bogan's Aesthetic of Limitation* (Bloomington, Ind., 1987).

Boyers, Robert, ed., *Contemporary Poetry in America* (New York, 1974).

Bradbury, Malcolm, and Richard Ruland, eds, *From Puritanism to Postmodernism: A History of American Literature* (London, 1991).

Brecht, Bertolt, *Poems 1913–1956*, ed. John Willett and Ralph Manheim (London, 1976).

Brett, Simon, ed., *The Faber Book of Parodies* (London, 1984).

Brewer, Charlotte, 'The Second Edition of the *Oxford English Dictionary*', *Review of English Studies*, 44:175 (Aug. 1993).

Bristol, Michael D., *Shakespeare's America, America's Shakespeare* (London, 1990).

Britten, Benjamin, *Letters from a Life: The Selected Letters and Diaries of Benjamin Britten*, vol. 2, 1939–1945, ed. Donald Mitchell (London, 1991).

Brodsky, Joseph, *Less Than One: Selected Essays* (1986; repr. Harmondsworth, 1987).

—, Nobel Prize Speech, *Index on Censorship*, 17:2 (Feb. 1988).

Brown, Christy, *Collected Poems* (London, 1982).

Brown, Stewart, ed., *The Art of Derek Walcott* (Bridgend, 1991).

Browne, Ray B., and Donald Pizer, eds, *Themes and Directions in American Literature* (Lafayette, Ind., 1969).

Brownjohn, Alan, *Philip Larkin* (Harlow, 1975).

Bucknell, Katherine, 'Freelance', *TLS*, 19 May 1989.

Bucknell, Katherine, and Nicholas Jenkins, eds, *W. H. Auden: 'The Map of All My Youth': Early Works, Friends, and Influences*, Auden Studies 1 (Oxford, 1990).

—, eds, *W. H. Auden: 'The Language of Learning and the Language of Love': Uncollected Writings, New Interpretations*, Auden Studies 2 (Oxford, 1994).

Burt, Stephen, '"September 1, 1939" Revisited: Or, Poetry, Politics, and the Idea of the Public', *American Literary History*, 15.3 (Fall 2003).

Caesar, Adrian, *Dividing Lines: Poetry, Class and Ideology in the 1930s* (Manchester, 1991).

Callaghan, John, *British Trotskyism: Theory and Practice* (Oxford, 1984).

Callan, Edward, *Auden: A Carnival of Intellect* (Oxford, 1983).

Callinicos, Alex, *Trotskyism* (Milton Keynes, 1990).

Cameron, Deborah, ed., *The Feminist Critique of Language: A Reader* (London, 1990).

Carlson, Michael, 'The War of Memory', *The Spectator*, 9 Oct. 1982.

Carpenter, Humphrey, *W. H. Auden: A Biography* (London, 1981).

Caudwell, Christopher, *Poems* (London, 1939).

Chambers, Harry, ed., *An Enormous Yes: In Memoriam Philip Larkin (1922–1985)* (Calstock, Cornwall, 1986).

Chekhov, Anton, *Select Tales of Tchehov*, trans. Constance Garnett (London, 1927).

Clausen, Jan, *A Movement of Poets: Thoughts on Poetry and Feminism* (New York, 1982).

Collins, Martha, ed., *Critical Essays on Louise Bogan* (Boston, Mass., 1984).

Connolly, Cyril, *Enemies of Promise* (London, 1938).

—, 'Comment', *Horizon*, 2:12 (Dec. 1940).

Conquest, Robert, ed., *New Lines: An Anthology* (London, 1956).

—, *The Abomination of Moab* (London, 1979).

Corcoran, Kelvin, 'Spitewinter Provocations: An Interview on the Condition of Poetry with Peter Riley', *Reality Studios*, 8:1–4 (1986).

Corcoran, Neil, *English Poetry since 1940* (Harlow, 1993).

Costello, Bonnie, *Marianne Moore: Imaginary Possessions* (Cambridge, Mass., 1981).

—, *The Plural of Us: Poetry and Community in Auden and Others* (Princeton, 2017).

Coward, Noël, 'Don't Let's Be Beastly to the Germans', in Barry Day, ed., *Noël Coward: The Complete Lyrics* (Woodstock, N.Y., 1998).

Cowley, Malcolm, *The Literary Situation* (New York, 1955).

—, *The Flower and the Leaf: A Contemporary Record of American Writing since 1941*, ed. Donald W. Faulkner (New York, 1985).

Creeley, Robert, *The Collected Essays of Robert Creeley* (Berkeley, 1989).

Cross, Amanda, *Poetic Justice* (1970; repr. London, 1993).

Cunningham, Valentine, *British Writers of the Thirties* (Oxford, 1988).

—, 'Sublime Rhyme a Dime', *Observer*, 13 Feb. 1994.

Cutrer, Thomas W., *Parnassus on the Mississippi* (Baton Rouge, 1984).

Daiches, David, *The Present Age: After 1920* (London, 1958).

Davidson, Michael, *The World, the Flesh and Myself* (London, 1962).

Davie, Donald, *Brides of Reason* (Oxford, 1955).

—, *Thomas Hardy and British Poetry* (London, 1973).

—, *Kenneth Allott and the Thirties* (Liverpool, 1980).

Day, Roger, *Larkin* (Milton Keynes, 1987).

Day Lewis, C., *From Feathers to Iron* (London, 1931).

—, writing as Nicholas Blake, *A Question of Proof* (London, 1935).

—, *The Buried Day* (London, 1960).

Day-Lewis, Sean, *C. Day-Lewis: An English Literary Life* (London, 1980).

Delaney, Paul, *Tom Stoppard: The Moral Vision of the Major Plays* (Basingstoke, 1990).

Department for Education, *English for ages 5 to 16* (London, 1993).

Derrida, Jacques, *The Post Card: From Socrates to Freud and Beyond*, trans. Alan Bass (London, 1989).

Donoghue, Denis, ed., *Seven American Poets from MacLeish to Nemerov: An Introduction* (Minneapolis, 1975).

Drabble, Margaret, 'Heroes and Villains', *The Independent*, Magazine, 16 Mar. 1991.

Dreyfus, Hubert L., and Paul Rabinow, eds, *Michel Foucault: Beyond Structuralism and Hermeneutics* (Chicago, 1982).

Driver, Paul, 'Upstaging', *London Review of Books*, 19 Aug. 1993.

Duffy, Carol Ann, *Standing Female Nude* (London, 1985).

Duncan, Robert, *The Years as Catches: First Poems (1939–1946)* (Berkeley, 1966).

Dunn, Douglas, *Dante's Drum-kit* (London, 1993).

Durrell, Lawrence, *Cities, Plains and People* (London, 1946).

Eagleton, Terry, *Exiles and Émigrés: Studies in Modern Literature* (London, 1970).

Eco, Umberto, *Reflections on The Name of the Rose*, trans. William Weaver (London, 1985).

Edmunds, Lowell, *Martini, Straight Up: The Classic American Cocktail* (Baltimore, 1998).

Ehrenpreis, Irvin, 'At the Poles of Poetry', *New York Review of Books*, 17 Aug. 1978.

Eliot, T. S., *To Criticize the Critic* (London, 1965).

Ellmann, Mary, *Thinking About Women* (London, 1968).

Ellmann, Richard, ed., *The New Oxford Book of American Verse* (New York, 1976).

Engel, Bernard F., 'A Disjointed Distrust: Marianne Moore's World War II', *Contemporary Literature*, 30:3 (Fall 1989).

Engell, James, and David Perkins, eds, *Teaching Literature: What is Needed Now* (Cambridge, Mass., 1988).

Enright, D. J., *Poets of the 1950's: An Anthology of New English Verse* (Tokyo, 1955).

Everett, Barbara, 'Philip Larkin: After Symbolism', *Essays in Criticism*, 30:3 (July 1980).

—, *Poets in Their Time* (London, 1986).

Ewart, Gavin, 'Auden', *Quarto*, 7 (June 1980).

—, 'Larkin About', *Poetry Review*, 72:2 (June 1982).

—, *The Complete Little Ones: His Shortest Poems* (London, 1986).

—, 'Roy Fuller – Partly Personal', *Poetry Review*, 81:4 (Winter 1991/92).

Farnan, Dorothy J., *Auden in Love* (London, 1984).

Feldman, Gene, and Max Gartenberg, eds, *Protest* (London, 1959).

Fenton, James, *Our Western Furniture* (Oxford, 1968).

—, 'Common at Cnidos', *New Statesman*, 21 Aug. 1970.

—, 'The Instructive Analogies', *New Statesman*, 5 Mar. 1971.

—, 'Popular Rising', *New Statesman*, 19 Mar. 1971.

—, 'The Longest Strike (cont.)', *New Statesman*, 27 Aug. 1971.

—, 'Ulster: The Other Terror', *New Statesman*, 5 Nov. 1971.

—, *Terminal Moraine* (London, 1972).

—, 'Rhubarb and Sugar Candy', *New Statesman*, 11 Aug. 1972.

—, 'What is a Marxist?', *New Statesman*, 13 Oct. 1972.

—, 'Johnsoniana', *New Statesman*, 11 May 1973.

—, 'In Search of Cambodia's War', *New Statesman*, 9 Nov. 1973.

—, 'Showing My Hand', *New Statesman*, 14 June 1974.

—, 'Against Honesty', *New Statesman*, 23 Aug. 1974.

—, 'Advice to Poets', *New Statesman*, 20 Sept. 1974.

—, 'Auden's Last Bow', *New Statesman*, 27 Sept. 1974.

316

—, 'Poetry and Self-Regard', *New Statesman*, 6 Dec. 1974.

—, 'A Foreigner in London', *New Statesman*, 12 Sept. 1975.

—, 'Democracy and Shirley Williams', *New Statesman*, 28 Jan. 1977.

—, 'A Man Blind of One Eye', *New Statesman*, 26 Aug. 1977.

—, 'Hullo to the Labour Party', *New Statesman*, 16 Sept. 1977.

—, 'Nostalgie de la Guerre', *New Statesman*, 7 Apr. 1978.

—, 'Of the Martian School', *New Statesman*, 20 Oct. 1978.

—, 'The Means of Production', *New Statesman*, 25 May 1979.

—, 'Marxism and Aesthetics', *New Statesman*, 20 July 1979.

—, trans., *Rigoletto*, English National Opera Guide 15 (London, 1982).

—, 'The Manifesto Against Manifestoes', *Poetry Review*, 73:3 (Sept. 1983).

—, *The Memory of War and Children in Exile: Poems 1968–1983* (Harmondsworth, 1983).

—, *You Were Marvellous: Theatre Reviews from the Sunday Times* (London, 1983).

—, 'Birds and Beads', *Poetry Review*, 74:1 (Apr. 1984).

—, 'James Fenton in Conversation with Grevel Lindop', *PN Review*, 11:2 (1984).

—, trans., *Simon Boccanegra*, English National Opera Guide 32 (London, 1985).

—, *Manila Envelope* (Quezon City, Philippines, 1989).

—, *All the Wrong Places: Adrift in the Politics of Asia* (London, 1989).

—, 'Ars Poetica', *Independent on Sunday*, 28 Jan. 1990.

—, 'Some Mistakes People Make About Poetry', *New York Review of Books*, 25 Mar. 1993.

—, 'War in the Garden', *New York Review of Books*, 24 June 1993.

—, *Out of Danger* (Harmondsworth, 1993).

—, *Poetry Book Society Bulletin*, 159 (Winter 1993).

—, 'Four Weddings and a Circle of Poetry', *The Independent*, 30 May 1994.

—, 'Auden's Shakespeare', *New York Review of Books*, 23 Mar. 2000.

—, 'Auden's Enchantment', *New York Review of Books*, 13 Apr. 2000.

Ferenczi, Sandor, *Thalassa: A Theory of Genitality* (1938; repr. London, 1989).

Ferguson, Peter, 'Philip Larkin's *XX Poems*: The Missing Link', *Agenda*, 14:3 (Autumn 1976).

Ferguson, Suzanne, *The Poetry of Randall Jarrell* (Baton Rouge, 1971).

Firchow, Peter, 'The American Auden: A Poet Reborn?', *American Literary History*, 11:3 (Fall 1999).

Fisher, Mark, ed., *Letters to an Editor* (Manchester, 1989).

Fitzgerald, Robert, 'The Poetic Responsibility', *New Republic*, 26 Apr. 1948.

Fletcher, John, 'Our Man in New York', *The Spectator*, 13 Dec. 1969.

Flood, Alison, 'Unseen W. H. Auden Diary Sheds Light on Famous Poem and Personal Life', the *Guardian*, 26 June 2013.

Foden, Giles, 'Compass of Dismay', the *Guardian*, 7 Dec. 1993.

Ford, Boris, ed., *The Pelican Guide to English Literature*, vol. 7: *The Modern Age* (2nd edn, London, 1966).

Foucault, Michel, *The Archaeology of Knowledge*, trans. A. M. Sheridan Smith (London, 1972).

Fowler, Russell T., 'Charting the "Lost World": Rilke's Influence on Randall Jarrell', *Twentieth Century Literature*, 30:1 (Spring 1984).

Frank, Elizabeth, *Louise Bogan: A Portrait* (New York, 1985).

Fraser, G. S., *The Modern Writer and His World* (London, 1953).

—, 'Phantoms and Objects', *New Statesman and Nation*, 18 Dec. 1954.

—, *Vision and Rhetoric: Studies in Modern Poetry* (London, 1959).

—, 'Auden: The Composite Giant', *Shenandoah*, 15:4 (Summer 1964).

—, *A Stranger and Afraid: The Autobiography of an Intellectual* (Manchester, 1983).

French, Sean, 'W. H. Auden on the Production Line', *New Statesman and Society*, 25 Aug. 1989.

—, 'The Red Pen and the Golden Word', *The Observer*, Review, 2 Jan. 1994.

Freud, Sigmund, *The Standard Edition of the Complete Psychological Works of Sigmund Freud*, trans. and ed. James Strachey, in collaboration with Anna Freud, assisted by Alix Strachey, Alan Tyson and Angela Richards, 24 vols (London, 1953–74).

Fuller, John, 'Randall Jarrell', *The Review*, 16 (Oct. 1966).

—, *A Reader's Guide to W. H. Auden* (London, 1970).

—, *Epistles to Several Persons* (London, 1973).

—, 'Pleasing Ma: The poetry of W. H. Auden', Kenneth Allott Lecture 1992, unpublished typescript.

—, *W.H. Auden: A Commentary* (London, 1998).

—, *The Worm and the Star* (London, 1993).

Fuller, Roy, 'New Year' & 'Poem', *New Verse*, 19 (Feb./Mar. 1936).

—, unpublished letters to Julian Symons, 1937–39 (in possession of John Fuller).

—, 'Recent Verse', *New English Weekly*, 8 Dec. 1938.

—, 'Poem', *Poetry* (Chicago), 54:2 (May 1939).

—, *Poems* (London, 1939).

—, *The Middle of a War* (London, 1942).

—, *A Lost Season* (London, 1944).

—, *With My Little Eye* (London, 1948).

—, 'Byron', *The Listener*, 7 Oct. 1948.

—, ed., *Byron for To-day* (London, 1948).

—, *Epitaphs and Occasions* (London, 1949).

—, *Counterparts* (London, 1954).

—, *Fantasy and Fugue* (London, 1954).

—, review of Spender's *The Making of a Poem*, *London Magazine*, 2:11 (Nov. 1955).

—, review of Wain's *A Word Carved on a Sill*, *London Magazine*, 3:8 (Aug. 1956).

—, *Brutus's Orchard* (London, 1957).

—, 'Mood of the Month – VII', *London Magazine*, 5:11 (Nov. 1958).

—, review of Murch's *The Development of the Detective Novel*, *London Magazine*, 6:1 (Jan. 1959).

—, *The Ruined Boys* (London, 1959).

—, *Collected Poems: 1936–1961* (London, 1962).

—, 'Ten Comments on a Questionnaire', *London Magazine*, n.s. 4:8 (Nov. 1964).

—, 'Life?', *The Listener*, 12 Oct. 1967.

—, 'Virtuoso Fiddling: Marianne Moore's Syllabics', *TLS*, 30 May 1968.

—, 'Poetry in my Time', *The Listener*, 27 June 1968.

—, 'Views', *The Listener*, 18 July 1968.

—, 'The Isis Interview', interview with Tony Holden, *Isis*, 12 Feb. 1969.

—, 'Views', *The Listener*, 27 Feb. 1969.

—, 'From Blackheath to Oxford', *London Magazine*, n.s. 8:12 (Mar. 1969).

—, 'At the Picnic', *New Statesman*, 26 Sept. 1969.

—, *The Carnal Island* (London, 1970).

—, 'Views', *The Listener*, 11 Mar. 1971.

—, *Owls and Artificers: Oxford Lectures on Poetry* (London, 1971).

—, 'The Need for the Non-Literary', *TLS*, 10 Nov. 1972.

—, 'W. H. Auden, 1907–1973', *The Listener*, 4 Oct. 1973.

—, 'Poet's Prose', *London Magazine*, n.s. 13:4 (Oct./Nov. 1973).

—, *Professors and Gods: Last Oxford Lectures on Poetry* (London, 1973).

—, 'Langham Diary', *The Listener*, 18 Apr. 1974.

—, 'Short Measure', *TLS*, 31 Jan. 1975.

—, *From the Joke Shop* (London, 1975).

—, 'Lancastrian Syllabics', *TLS*, 10 Sept. 1976.

—, 'A Good Job We Were Young', *New Review*, 3:28 (July 1976).

—, 'Taxpayers, the Arts and Big Balloonz', *Encounter*, 49:4 (Oct. 1977).

—, Letter to *Encounter*, 49:6 (Dec. 1977).

—, *The Other Planet* (Richmond, Surrey, 1979).

—, *The Reign of Sparrows* (London, 1980).

—, *Souvenirs* (London, 1980).

—, *Vamp Till Ready: Further Memoirs* (London, 1982).

—, *The Individual and His Times: A Selection of the Poetry of Roy Fuller*, ed. V. J. Lee (London, 1982).

—, *Home and Dry: Memoirs III* (London, 1984).

—, *Subsequent to Summer* (Edinburgh, 1985).

—, *New and Collected Poems* (London, 1985).

—, 'Roy Fuller in Conversation with Brian Morton', *PN Review*, 12:6 (1986).

—, *The World Through the Window: Collected Poems for Children* (London, 1989).

—, *Available for Dreams* (London, 1989).

—, *Stares* (London, 1990).

—, *Spanner and Pen: Post-war Memoirs* (London, 1991).

—, *Last Poems* (London, 1993).

Fussell, Paul, *Poetic Meter and Poetic Form* (New York, rev. edn, 1979).

Garfitt, Roger, 'Intimate Anxieties', *London Magazine*, n.s. 15:5 (Dec. 1975/Jan. 1976).

Gelpi, Albert, *A Coherent Splendor: The American Poetic Renaissance, 1910–1950* (Cambridge, 1987).

Gershwin, Ira, *Lyrics on Several Occasions* (London, 1977).

Giddens, Anthony, *The Third Way: The Renewal of Social Democracy* (London, 1998).

Gilbert, Sandra M., and Susan Gubar, *The Madwoman in the Attic: The Woman Writer and the Nineteenth-Century Literary Imagination* (New Haven, 1979).

—, eds, *Shakespeare's Sisters: Feminist Essays on Women Poets* (Bloomington, Ind., 1979).

—, *No Man's Land: The Place of the Woman Writer in the Twentieth Century*, vol. 1: *The War of the Words* (New Haven, 1988).

Gitzen, Julian, 'A Tour of the Pitt-Rivers Museum', *Helix*, 17 (1984).

Goethe, Johann Wolfgang, *Selected Verse*, ed. David Luke (Harmondsworth, 1964).

Goldensohn, Lorrie, *Elizabeth Bishop: The Biography of a Poetry* (New York, 1992).

Gooch, Brad, *City Poet: The Life and Times of Frank O'Hara* (New York, 1993).

Goodridge, Celeste, *Hints and Disguises: Marianne Moore and Her Contemporaries* (Iowa, 1989).

Goodwin, K. L., *The Influence of Ezra Pound* (London, 1966).

Gopnik, Adam, 'The Double Man', *New Yorker*, 23 Sept. 2002.

Gowrie, Grey, 'Accomplishing Auden: The Later Poems in Context', *Agenda*, 31:4–32:1 (Winter/Spring 1994).

Grant, David, *Letter to W. H. Auden* (Axminster, 1993).

Graves, Robert, 'These Be Your Gods, O Israel!', *Essays in Criticism*, 5:2 (Apr. 1955).

Gray, Richard, *American Poetry of the Twentieth Century* (London, 1990).

Gray, Simon, 'Otherwise Enraged: A Paranoid View of Reviewing', *TLS*, 2 Sept. 1983.

Greacen, Robert, *A Bright Mask* (Dublin, 1985).

Green, Henry, *Pack My Bag* (London, 1952).

Grigson, Geoffrey, ed., *Poetry of the Present: An Anthology of the Thirties and After* (London, 1949).

Grobel, Lawrence, *Conversations with Capote* (New York, 1985).

Groddeck, Georg, *The Book of the It* (London, 1935).

Grubb, Frederick, *A Vision of Reality: A Study of Liberalism in Twentieth-Century Verse* (London, 1965).

Gunn, Thom, interview with Ian Hamilton, *London Magazine*, n.s. 4:8 (Nov. 1964).

Hadlock, Richard, *Jazz Masters of the Twenties* (New York, 1965).

Haffenden, John, *Viewpoints: Poets in Conversation with John Haffenden* (London, 1981).

—, ed., *W. H. Auden: The Critical Heritage* (London, 1983).

Hagenbüchle, Helen, *The Black Goddess: A Study of the Archetypal Feminine in the Poetry of Randall Jarrell* (Zurich, 1975).

Hall, Donald, 'Dry Farming', *New Statesman*, 9 July 1960.

—, *Marianne Moore: The Cage and the Animal* (New York, 1970).

Hamilton, Ian, review of Fuller's *Buff*, *London Magazine*, n.s. 5:3 (June 1965).

—, 'Profile: Professor of Poetry – Ian Hamilton Writes about Roy Fuller', *The Listener*, 5 Dec. 1968.

—, *A Poetry Chronicle: Essays and Reviews* (London, 1973).

—, *Robert Lowell: A Biography* (London, 1983).

—, 'Ian Hamilton in Conversation with Peter Dale', *Agenda*, 31:2 (Summer 1993).

Hammarskjöld, Dag, *Markings*, trans. Leif Sjöberg and W. H. Auden (London, 1964).

Hampson, Robert, and Peter Barry, eds, *New British Poetries: The Scope of the Possible* (Manchester, 1993).

Harmon, William, 'Larkin's Memory', *Sewanee Review*, 98:2 (Spring 1990).

Hartley, Anthony, 'Poets of the Fifties', *The Spectator*, 27 Aug. 1954.

—, 'New Verse', *The Spectator*, 24 Dec. 1954.

—, *A State of England* (London, 1963).

Hartley, George, ed., *Philip Larkin 1922–1985: A Tribute* (London, 1988).

Heaney, Seamus, *The Government of the Tongue: The 1986 T. S. Eliot Memorial Lectures and Other Critical Writings* (London, 1988).

The Heath Anthology of American Literature, vol. 2 (Lexington, Mass., 1990).

Hecht, Anthony, 'Once Removed', *Kenyon Review*, 9:2 (Spring 1947).

—, *A Summoning of Stones* (New York, 1954).

—, 'A Few Green Leaves', *Sewanee Review*, 67:4 (Autumn 1959).

—, 'On the Methods and Ambitions of Poetry', *Hudson Review*, 18:4 (Winter 1965/66).

—, 'An Interview with Anthony Hecht', Philip L. Gerber and Robert J. Gemmett, *Mediterranean Review*, 1:3 (Spring 1971).

—, 'John Crowe Ransom', *American Scholar*, 49:3 (Summer 1980).

—, *Obbligati: Essays in Criticism* (New York, 1986).

—, *Collected Earlier Poems* (Oxford, 1991).

—, *The Transparent Man* (Oxford, 1991).

—, *The Hidden Law: The Poetry of W. H. Auden* (Cambridge, Mass., 1993).

Hecht, Anthony, and John Hollander, eds, *Jiggery-Pokery: A Compendium of Double Dactyls* (New York, 1967).

Hendry, J. F., and Henry Treece, eds, *The White Horseman: Prose and Verse of the New Apocalypse* (London, 1941).

Hewett, R. P., ed., *A Choice of Poets: An Anthology of Poets from Wordsworth to the Present Day* (London, 1968).

Hewison, Robert, *In Anger: Culture in the Cold War 1945–60* (London, 1981).

Hoffman, Daniel, 'The Poetry of Anguish', *The Reporter*, 22 Feb. 1968.

—, ed., *Harvard Guide to Contemporary American Writing* (Cambridge, Mass., 1979).

Hoffpauir, Richard, *The Art of Restraint: English Poetry from Hardy to Larkin* (Newark, 1991).

Hollander, John, 'W. H. Auden', *Yale Review*, 77:4 (Summer 1988).

Holley, Margaret, *The Poetry of Marianne Moore: A Study in Voice and Value* (Cambridge, 1987).

Hollinghurst, Alan, 'Best Things', *London Review of Books*, 20 Aug. 1981.

Homberger, Eric, 'Roy Fuller: "In the Paralysis of Class"', *Poetry Nation*, 6 (1976).

—, *The Art of the Real: Poetry in England and America since 1939* (London, 1977).

Horovitz, Michael, ed., *Children of Albion: Poetry of the Underground in Britain* (Harmondsworth, 1969).

Howard, Richard, *Alone with America: The Art of Poetry in the United States since 1950* (London, 1970).

Hulse, Michael, 'The New Line of Wit', *Helix*, 17 (1984).

Hulse, Michael, David Kennedy and David Morley, eds, *The New Poetry* (Newcastle, 1993).

Hynes, Samuel, *The Auden Generation: Literature and Politics in England in the 1930s* (London, 1976).

Illich, Ivan, *H2O and the Waters of Forgetfulness* (London, 1986).

Isherwood, Christopher, *Lions and Shadows: An Education in the Twenties* (London, 1938).

Isis, 6 Nov. 1968.

—, 'Poetry Elections '68', 20 Nov. 1968.

—, 'Editorial', 26 Feb. 1969.

Iyer, Pico, 'Putting Faces to Writers', *TLS*, 28 June 1991.

James, Clive, 'Auden's Achievement', *Commentary*, 56:6 (Dec. 1973).

—, *At the Pillars of Hercules* (London, 1979).

—, 'What Happened to Auden', *New Yorker*, 2 Nov. 1992.

Jardine, Lisa, 'Saxon Violence', the *Guardian*, 8 Dec. 1992.

Jarrell, Randall, 'The Rage for the Lost Penny', in *Five Young American Poets* (Norfolk, Conn., 1940).

—, *Blood for a Stranger* (New York, 1942).

—, *Little Friend, Little Friend* (New York, 1945).

—, *Losses* (New York, 1948).

—, *The Seven-League Crutches* (New York, 1951).

—, *Poetry and the Age* (1953; London, 1955).

—, *Pictures from an Institution: A Comedy* (London, 1954).

—, *Selected Poems* (New York, 1955).

—, *The Woman at the Washington Zoo* (New York, 1960).

—, *A Sad Heart at the Supermarket* (New York, 1962).

—, *The Bat-Poet* (1963; repr. Harmondsworth, 1977).

—, *The Animal Family* (New York, 1965).

—, *The Lost World* (New York, 1965).

—, *The Complete Poems* (1969; London, 1971).

—, *The Third Book of Criticism* (1969; London, 1975).

—, *Jerome: The Biography of a Poem* (New York, 1971).

—, *Kipling, Auden & Co.: Essays and Reviews 1935–1964* (New York, 1980).

—, *Randall Jarrell's Letters*, ed. Mary Jarrell (London, 1986).

Jenkins, Nicholas, 'The Queen's Masque', *TLS*, 20 May 1988.

Jennings, Elizabeth, *Growing-Points* (Cheadle, 1975).

Johnson, Paul, 'Lucky Jim's Political Testament', *New Statesman and Nation*, 12 Jan. 1957.

—, 'Farewell to the Labour Party', *New Statesman*, 9 Sept. 1977.

Jones, Ernest, *Sigmund Freud: Life and Work*, vol. 2 (London, 1955).

Jones, Peter, and Michael Schmidt, eds, *British Poetry Since 1970: A Critical Survey* (Manchester, 1980).

Joyce, James, *A Portrait of the Artist as a Young Man* (1916; definitive text, ed. Richard Ellmann, London, 1968).

Kalstone, David, *Becoming a Poet: Elizabeth Bishop with Marianne Moore and Robert Lowell* (London, 1989).

Kavanagh, Patrick, 'Auden and the Creative Mind', *Envoy*, 5:19 (June 1951).

Kavanagh, P. J., 'Roy the Lion and Unicorn George', *The Spectator*, 7 Dec. 1991.

Kenner, Hugh, *A Homemade World: The American Modernist Writers* (New York, 1975).

Kerman, Joseph, 'Auden's *Magic Flute*', *Hudson Review*, 10:2 (Summer 1957).

Kermode, Frank, *The Genesis of Secrecy: On the Interpretation of Narrative* (Cambridge, Mass., 1979).

—, 'Oldham', *London Review of Books*, 22 May 1980.

Kinsella, Thomas, *Poems from Centre City* (Dublin, 1990).

La Fontaine, Jean, *Fables* (12 vols, 1668–1694; 1 vol. edn, Paris, 1966).

Larkin, Philip, *The North Ship* (1945; repr. London, 1966).

—, *Jill* (1946; repr. London, 1964).

—, 'No More Fever', *Listen*, 2:1 (Summer 1956).

—, 'What's Become of Wystan?', *The Spectator*, 15 July 1960.

—, 'Philip Larkin Writes …', *Poetry Book Society Bulletin*, 40 (Feb. 1964).

—, interview with Ian Hamilton, *London Magazine*, n.s. 4:8 (Nov. 1964).

—, interview with John Horder, 'Poet on the 8.15', *The Guardian*, 20 May 1965.

—, *All What Jazz* (1970; rev. edn London, 1985).

—, 'Words for Music, Perhaps', *TLS*, 27 Feb. 1981.

—, *Required Writing: Miscellaneous Pieces 1955–1982* (London, 1983).

—, *Collected Poems*, ed. Anthony Thwaite (London, 1988; rev. edn 1990).

Larrissy, Edward, *Reading Twentieth-Century Poetry: The Language of Gender and Objects* (Oxford, 1990).

Läutner, Alfred, 'The Nine Lives of *Poetry International*', *New Review*, 1:5 (Aug. 1974).

Lawrence, D. H., *Fantasia of the Unconscious* (London, 1923).

Lea, Sydney, *The Burdens of Formality: Essays on the Poetry of Anthony Hecht* (Athens, Ga., 1989).

Leapman, Michael, 'Engrossing Record of Auden's Vigour and Achievement', *The Times*, 9 Dec. 1980.

Lear, Edward, *The Complete Nonsense of Edward Lear*, ed. Holbrook Jackson (London, 1947).

Leavis, F. R., *New Bearings in English Poetry: A Study of the Contemporary Situation* (1932; rev. edn 1950; repr. London, 1963).

Lee, Christopher, *Under the Sun* (London, 1948).

Lehman, David, *The Last Avant-Garde: The Making of the New York School of Poets* (New York, 1998).

Lehmann, John, ed., *New Writing*, 1 (Spring 1936).

—, ed., *The Craft of Letters in England: A Symposium* (London, 1956).

—, *I Am My Brother: Autobiography II* (London, 1960).

Leithauser, Brad, 'Poet for a Dark Age', *New York Review of Books*, 13 Feb. 1986.

Levi, Peter, *The Art of Poetry* (New Haven, 1991).

Levin, Harry, *Memories of the Moderns* (New York, 1980).

The Listener, 'The Intellectual and the Wireless', 30 Oct. 1929.

Logue, Christopher, *New Numbers* (London, 1969).

Lomas, Herbert, 'The American Auden', *PN Review*, 16:5 (1989).

Longley, Edna, 'Larkin, Edward Thomas and the Tradition', *Phoenix*, 11/12 (Autumn/Winter 1973/74).

—, 'Seedy Menagerie', *Poetry Review*, 74:1 (Apr. 1984).

—, 'MacNeice and After', *Poetry Review*, 78:2 (Summer 1988).

—, *Louis MacNeice: A Study* (London, 1988).

Lowell, Robert, *Notebook* (London, 1970).

Lowell, Robert, Peter Taylor and Robert Penn Warren, eds, *Randall Jarrell 1914–1965* (New York, 1967).

Lucas, John, ed., *The 1930's: A Challenge to Orthodoxy* (Brighton, 1978).

—, 'The Bluff Masks of Old Buff', *TLS*, 7 Mar. 1980.

Lucie-Smith, Edward, *British Poetry Since 1945* (Harmondsworth, 1970).

MacDiarmid, Hugh, *Lucky Poet: A Self-Study in Literature and Political Ideas* (London, 1943).

—, 'Metaphysics and Poetry', interview with Water Perrie (1974), repr. in Alan Riach, ed., *Hugh MacDiarmid: Selected Prose* (Manchester, 1992).

—, *Selected Prose*, ed. Alan Riach (Manchester, 1992).

Mackintosh, Paul St. John, 'Ironing out Auden's Wrinkles', *Contemporary Review*, 260:1515 (Apr. 1992).

MacNeice, Louis, *Poems* (London, 1935).

—, 'Traveller's Return', *Horizon*, 3:14 (Feb. 1941).

Makolkin, Anna, *Name, Hero, Icon: Semiotics of Nationalism through Heroic Biography* (Berlin, 1992).

Martin, Robert K., *The Homosexual Tradition in American Poetry* (Austin, Tex., 1979).

Matthiessen, F. O., ed., *The Oxford Book of American Verse* (New York, 1950).

Maxwell, Glyn, 'Echoes of *The Orators*', *Verse*, 6:3 (Winter 1989).

—, 'Random Thoughts on my Debt to Auden', *Agenda*, 31:4–32:1 (Winter/Spring 1994).

McArthur, Tom, ed., *The Oxford Companion to the English Language* (Oxford, 1992).

McCarthy, Mary, *Occasional Prose* (London, 1985).

McClatchy, J. D., 'Anatomies of Melancholy', *Grand Street*, 6:1 (Autumn 1986).

McConnell-Ginet, Sally, Ruth Borker and Nelly Furman, eds, *Women and Language in Literature and Society* (New York, 1980).

McDiarmid, Lucy, *Saving Civilization: Yeats, Eliot, and Auden Between the Wars* (Cambridge, 1984).

—, *Auden's Apologies for Poetry* (Princeton, 1990).

McGann, Jerome J., *The Beauty of Inflections: Literary Investigations in Historical Method and Theory* (Oxford, 1985).

McHenry, Eric, 'Auden on Bin Laden', *Slate*, 20 Sept. 2001. https://slate.com/culture/2001/09/auden-on-bin-laden.html.

Mendelson, Edward, 'Editing Auden', *New Statesman*, 17 Sept. 1976.

—, *W. H. Auden, 1907–1973: An Exhibition of Manuscripts, Books, and Photographs Selected from the Henry W. and Albert A. Berg Collection of English and American Literature* (New York, 1976).

—, *Early Auden* (London, 1981).

—, 'The Fading Coal vs. The Gothic Cathedral or What to Do about an Author both Forgetful and Deceased', *Text*, 3 (New York, 1987).

—, 'The Secret Auden', *New York Review of Books*, 20 Mar. 2014.

—, *Later Auden* (London, 1999).

Meyer, Michael, and Sidney Keyes, eds, *Eight Oxford Poets* (London, 1941).

Meyers, Jeffrey, 'Randall Jarrell and German Culture', *Salmagundi*, 61 (Fall 1983).

Miles, Barry, *Ginsberg: A Biography* (1989; London, 1990).

Miller, Charles H., *Auden: An American Friendship* (New York, 1983).

Miller, Edward D., *Emergency Broadcasting and 1930s American Radio* (Philadelphia, 2003).

Mitchison, Naomi, 'Young Auden', *Shenandoah*, 18:2 (Winter 1967).

—, *You May Well Ask: A Memoir 1920–1940* (London, 1970).

Mizener, Arthur, review of Moore's *Fables*, *Kenyon Review*, 16:3 (Summer 1954).

Moi, Toril, ed., *The Kristeva Reader* (Oxford, 1986).

Mole, John, 'Hearts of Darkness', *TLS*, 2 Apr. 1982.

—, 'Conceit and Concern', *Encounter*, 64:1 (Jan. 1986).

—, *Passing Judgements: Poetry in the Eighties* (Bristol, 1989).

Montefiore, Jan, '"Undeservedly Forgotten": Women Poets and Others in the 1930s', *PN Review*, 20:3 (Jan.–Feb. 1994).

Moore, Marianne, *Selected Poems* (London, 1935).

—, *What Are Years* (New York, 1941).

—, *Collected Poems* (London, 1951).

—, trans., *The Fables of La Fontaine* (New York, 1954).

—, *Predilections* (London, 1956).

—, 'Logic and "The Magic Flute"', *Shenandoah*, 7:3 (Summer 1956).

—, *A Marianne Moore Reader* (New York, 1961).

—, *Complete Poems* (1968; rev. edn London, 1981).

—, *The Complete Prose of Marianne Moore*, ed. Patricia C. Willis (London, 1987).

Morrison, Blake, *The Movement: English Poetry and Fiction of the 1950s* (1980; repr. London, 1986).

—, *Dark Glasses* (London, 1984).

—, 'Tending the Flame', *Bookseller*, 26 May 1989.

Morrison, Blake, and Andrew Motion, eds, *The Penguin Book of Contemporary British Poetry* (Harmondsworth, 1982).

Motion, Andrew, 'Veils and Veins', *New Statesman*, 9 May 1980.

—, 'Remembering', *New Statesman*, 20 Mar. 1981.

—, *Philip Larkin* (London, 1982).

—, 'An Interview with James Fenton', *Poetry Review*, 72:2 (June 1982).

—, *Natural Causes* (London, 1987).

—, *Philip Larkin: A Writer's Life* (London, 1993).

Muldoon, Paul, *Meeting the British* (London, 1987).

Murphy, Rosalie, ed., *Contemporary Poets of the English Language* (London, 1970).

Neill, Edward, 'Modernism and Englishness: Reflections on Auden and Larkin', *Essays and Studies*, 36 (1983).

New Verse, 26–27, Auden Double Number (Nov. 1937).

Nitchie, George W., *Marianne Moore: An Introduction to the Poetry* (New York, 1969).

Norse, Harold, *Memoirs of a Bastard Angel: A Fifty-Year Literary and Erotic Odyssey* (New York, 1989).

The Norton Anthology of American Literature (3rd edn, New York, 1989).

The Norton Anthology of English Literature, vol. 2 (5th edn, New York, 1986).

The Norton Anthology of Poetry (3rd edn, New York, 1983).

Novak, Michael Paul, 'Love and Influence: Louise Bogan, Rolfe Humphries, and Theodore Roethke', *Kenyon Review*, 7:3 (Summer 1985).

O'Brien, Sean, review of *The English Auden*, *Poetry Review*, 68:1 (Apr. 1978).

—, 'Chosen by our Politics', *Poetry Review*, 71:1 (June 1981).

—, 'The Auden Regeneration', *Sunday Times*, Review, 31 July 1994.

O'Hanlon, Redmond, *Into the Heart of Borneo: An Account of a Journey Made in 1983 to the Mountains of Batu Tiban with James Fenton* (Edinburgh, 1984).

O'Hara, Frank, *The Collected Poems of Frank O'Hara*, ed. Donald Allen (New York, 1972).

—, *Early Writing*, ed. Donald Allen (Bolinas, Calif., 1977).

Olsen, Tillie, *Silences* (London, 1980).

Orwell, George, ed., *Talking to India* (London, 1943).

Osborne, Charles, 'The Day of the Funeral', *London Magazine*, n.s. 15:1 (Apr./May 1975).

—, *W. H. Auden: The Life of a Poet* (London, 1980).

—, *Letter to W. H. Auden and Other Poems 1981–1984* (London, 1984).

Ostriker, Alicia, 'What Do Women (Poets) Want?: H. D. and Marianne Moore as Poetic Ancestresses', *Contemporary Literature*, 27:4 (Winter 1986).

—, *Stealing the Language: The Emergence of Women's Poetry in America* (London, 1987).

Parini, Jay, ed., *The Columbia History of American Poetry* (New York, 1993).

Paulin, Tom, *Thomas Hardy: The Poetry of Perception* (1975; 2nd edn Basingstoke, 1986).

—, *A State of Justice* (London, 1977).

—, *Ireland & the English Crisis* (Newcastle, 1984).

—, letter to the editor, *TLS*, 6 Nov. 1992.

—, *Minotaur: Poetry and the Nation State* (London, 1992).

Penguin Modern Poets 13 (Harmondsworth, 1969).

The Penguin New Writing, 18 (July/Sept. 1943).

Perloff, Marjorie, review of Hecht's *The Hard Hours*, *Far Point*, 2 (Spring/Summer 1969).

Peterson, Douglas L., 'The Poetry of Louise Bogan', *Southern Review*, 19:1 (Jan. 1983).

Piper, David, *The Image of the Poet* (Oxford, 1982).

Plath, Sylvia, *Letters Home: Correspondence 1950–1963*, ed. Aurelia Schober Plath (London, 1976).

—, *Collected Poems*, ed. Ted Hughes (London, 1981).

Plimpton, George, ed., *Poets at Work* (London, 1989).

PN Review, 'Poets' Round Table: "A Common Language"': Joseph Brodsky, Seamus Heaney, Les Murray, Derek Walcott, 15:4 (1989).

'Poetry International 1970', National Sound Archive 1531–1532.

Popper, Karl, *The Logic of Scientific Discovery* (1959; rev. edn, London, 1968).

Porter, Cole, *The Complete Lyrics of Cole Porter*, ed. Robert Kimball (London, 1983).

Porter, Peter, 'Philip Larkin: the Making of a Master', *The Independent*, 8 Oct. 1988.

—, 'Provinces Plenty, London Nil', *Independent on Sunday*, 30 May 1993.

—, 'The Magician & The Censor', *Poetry Review*, 83:4 (Winter 1993/94).

Pound, Ezra, *ABC of Reading* (London, 1934).

—, *The Letters of Ezra Pound 1907–1941*, ed. D. D. Paige (London, 1951).

Pritchard, William H., *Randall Jarrell: A Literary Life* (New York, 1990).

Pygge, Edward, 'Problems in Auden', *New Review*, 1:9 (Dec. 1974).

Rajan, B., ed., *Focus 5: Modern American Poetry* (London, 1950).

Redmond, John, 'Irish Poetry after Auden: The influence of W. H. Auden on Patrick Kavanagh, Derek Mahon, and Paul Muldoon', MA thesis, University College Dublin, 1990.

Regan, Stephen, *Philip Larkin* (Basingstoke, 1992).

Replogle, Justin, *Auden's Poetry* (London, 1969).

Revolutionary Democratic Group, *The Politics of the SWP* (Exeter, 1987).

Rexroth, Kenneth, *The New British Poets: An Anthology* (Norfolk, Conn., 1949).

Rich, Adrienne, *Adrienne Rich's Poetry*, ed. Barbara Charlesworth Gelpi and Albert Gelpi (New York, 1975).

—, *On Lies, Secrets, and Silence: Selected Prose 1966–1978* (New York, 1979).

Ricks, Christopher, 'Poets Who Have Learned Their Trade', *New York Times Book Review*, 2 Dec. 1979.

Ricks, Christopher, and William L. Vance, eds, *The Faber Book of America* (London, 1992).

Roberts, Michael, ed., *New Country* (London, 1933).

Robinson, Alan, *Instabilities in Contemporary British Poetry* (Basingstoke, 1988).

Robinson, Peter, *In the Circumstances: About Poems and Poets* (Oxford, 1992).

Rodden, John, *The Politics of Literary Reputation: The Making and Claiming of 'St. George' Orwell* (Oxford, 1989).

Roden, Claudia, *Coffee* (London, 1977).

Roessel, David, 'Pangolins and People: A Study of Marianne Moore and her Notes', *English Language Notes*, 27:3 (Mar. 1990).

Roethke, Theodore, *Selected Letters of Theodore Roethke*, ed. Ralph J. Mills (Seattle, 1968).

Rorty, Richard, J. B. Schneewind and Quentin Skinner, eds, *Philosophy in History* (Cambridge, 1984).

Ross, Alan, 'A Lament for the "Thirties" Poets', *Poetry Quarterly*, 10:2 (Summer 1948).

Rossen, Janice, *Philip Larkin: His Life's Work* (Hemel Hempstead, 1989).

Rouse, Anne, *Sunset Grill* (Newcastle, 1993).

Sagetrieb, Marianne Moore Special Issue, 6:3 (Winter 1987).

Salus, Peter H., and Paul B. Taylor, eds, *For W. H. Auden: February 21, 1972* (New York, 1972).

Sander, August, *August Sander: Photographs of an Epoch 1904–1959* (New York, 1980).

Sansom, Peter, *Everything You've Heard is True* (Manchester, 1990).

Sargeant, Winthrop, 'Humility, Concentration, and Gusto', *New Yorker*, 16 Feb. 1957.

Savage, D. S., *The Personal Principle: Studies in Modern Poetry* (London, 1944).

Scammell, William, 'Crossing the Lines', *Poetry Review*, 79:3 (Autumn 1989).

—, 'Word-Painting', *London Magazine*, n.s. 31:9/10 (Dec. 1991/ Jan. 1992).

Scannell, Vernon, *Not Without Glory: Poets of the Second World War* (London, 1976).

Scarfe, Francis, *Auden and After: The Liberation of Poetry 1930–1941* (London, 1942).

Schmidt, Michael, 'Poetry Professor', letter to the editor, *TLS*, 29 May 1969.

Schuyler, James, 'Wystan Auden', *TLS*, 28 Mar. 1975.

Schwartz, Delmore, *Selected Essays of Delmore Schwartz*, ed. Donald A. Dike and David H. Zucker (Chicago, 1970).

Schweik, Susan, 'Writing War Poetry Like a Woman', *Critical Inquiry*, 13:3 (Spring 1987).

Scupham, Peter, 'Grisaille and Millefleurs', *Poetry Review*, 76:3 (Oct. 1986).

Sellers, Susan, ed., *Delighting the Heart: A Notebook by Women Writers* (London, 1989).

Shapiro, Karl, *Essay on Rime* (London, 1947).

—, *In Defense of Ignorance* (New York, 1960).

—, *Randall Jarrell* (Washington, 1967).

—, *Collected Poems 1940–1978* (New York, 1978).

Shaw, Arnold, *52nd Street: The Street of Jazz* (New York, 1977).

Shaw, Robert B., ed., *American Poetry Since 1960: Some Critical Perspectives* (Cheadle, 1973).

Shaw, Roy, 'The Arts Council and Poetic Injustice', *Encounter*, 49:5 (Nov. 1977).

—, 'The Arts Council Debate', *Encounter*, 49:6 (Dec. 1977).

Shenandoah, 'A Tribute to W. H. Auden on His Sixtieth Birthday', 18:2 (Winter 1967).

Shetley, Vernon, 'Take But Degree Away', *Poetry* (Chicago), 137:5 (Feb. 1981).

Shklovsky, Viktor, 'Art as Technique' (1917), in L. T. Lemon and M. J. Reis, eds, *Russian Formalist Criticism: Four Essays* (Lincoln, Neb., 1965).

Showalter, Elaine, ed., *The New Feminist Criticism: Essays on Women, Literature and Theory* (London, 1986).

Sidnell, Michael J., *Dances of Death: The Group Theatre of London in the Thirties* (London, 1984).

Silver, Keith, 'Dinosaurs', *PN Review*, 18:2 (Nov./Dec. 1991).

Simpson, Eileen, *Poets in Their Youth: A Memoir* (New York, 1982).

Simpson, Louis, *Studies of Dylan Thomas, Allan Ginsberg, Sylvia Plath and Robert Lowell* (London, 1979).

Sinfield, Alan, *Literature, Politics and Culture in Postwar Britain* (Oxford, 1989).

Sisson, C. H., *English Poetry 1900–1950: An Assessment* (rev. edn, Manchester, 1981).

—, 'With the Woolwich', *London Review of Books*, 18 July 1985.

Skelton, Robin, ed., *Poetry of the Forties* (Harmondsworth, 1968).

Skinner, Quentin, 'The Limits of Historical Explanations', *Philosophy*, 41:157 (July 1966).

Slatin, John M., *The Savage's Romance: The Poetry of Marianne Moore* (Pennsylvania, 1986).

Sloterdijk, Peter, *Terror from the Air* (Cambridge, Mass., 2009).

Smith, Ken, and Judi Benson, eds, *Klaonica: Poems for Bosnia* (Newcastle, 1993).

Smith, Stan, 'Two Unknown Holograph Poems by W. H. Auden and C. Day Lewis', *Notes and Queries*, n.s. 36:2 (June 1989).

Smith, Steven, 'The Curious Generation of Roy Fuller', *London Magazine*, n.s. 33:7/8 (Oct./Nov. 1993).

Sontag, Susan, *Illness as Metaphor* (1978; repr. Harmondsworth, 1983).

Spears, Monroe K., 'Auden in the Fifties: Rites of Homage', *Sewanee Review*, 69:3 (Summer 1961).

—, *The Poetry of W. H. Auden: The Disenchanted Island* (New York, 1963).

—, *Auden: A Collection of Critical Essays* (Englewood Cliffs, N.J., 1964).

Spender, Stephen, 'The Importance of W. H. Auden', *London Mercury*, 39:234 (Apr. 1939).

—, 'The Year's Poetry, 1940', *Horizon*, 3:14 (Feb. 1941).

—, *W. H. Auden: A Memorial Address* (London, 1973).

—, *Love–Hate Relations: A Study of Anglo-American Sensibilities* (London, 1974).

—, ed., *W. H. Auden: A Tribute* (London, 1974).

—, *Journals 1939–1983*, ed. John Goldsmith (London, 1985).

—, *The Temple* (London, 1988).

Spender, Stephen, and Donald Hall, eds, *The Concise Encyclopedia of English and American Poets and Poetry* (London, 2nd rev. edn, 1970).

Spiegelman, Willard, *The Didactic Muse: Scenes of Instruction in Contemporary American Poetry* (Princeton, 1989).

Spufford, Francis, 'A Letter to Wystan Auden, from Iceland', *London Review of Books*, 21 Feb. 1991.

Stanford, Derek, *Inside the Forties: Literary Memoirs 1937–1957* (London, 1977).

Stapleton, Laurence, *Marianne Moore: The Poet's Advance* (Princeton, 1978).

Stevenson, Anne, 'Sylvia Plath, Elizabeth Bishop and the Romantic Iconography of the Mind', *Poetry Review*, 79:2 (Summer 1989).

—, 'Passacaglias of Pain', *Poetry Review*, 81:1 (Spring 1991).

Stravinsky, Igor, and Robert Craft, *Dialogues and a Diary* (New York, 1963).

Symons, Julian, *The Second Man* (London, 1943).

—, 'The Double Man', in B. Rajan and Andrew Pearse, eds, *Focus*, 2 (London, 1946).

—, 'Early Auden', *Shenandoah*, 18:2 (Winter 1967).

—, *The Thirties and the Nineties* (Manchester, 1990).

Tambimuttu, ed., *Festschrift for Marianne Moore's Seventy-Seventh Birthday* (New York, 1964).

Taylor, Henry, 'Forms of Conviction', *Southern Review*, 27:1 (Winter 1991).

Thomas, Dylan, and John Davenport, *The Death of the King's Canary* (London, 1976).

Thorpe, Adam, 'Near as a Rainbow to Rain', *The Observer*, 26 Dec. 1993.

Thurley, Geoffrey, *The Ironic Harvest: English Poetry in the Twentieth Century* (London, 1974).

Thwaite, Anthony, ed., *Larkin at Sixty* (London, 1982).

—, *Poetry Today: A Critical Guide to British Poetry* (Harlow, 1985).

—, ed., *Selected Letters of Philip Larkin 1940–1985* (London, 1992).

Timms, David, *Philip Larkin* (Edinburgh, 1973).

TLS, 'A Critical and Descriptive Survey of Contemporary British Writing for Readers Oversea', 25 Aug. 1950.

—, 'Poetic Observation', review of Fuller's *Counterparts*, 10 Sept. 1954.

—, 'Unamerican Editions', review of Hecht's *The Hard Hours*, 23 Nov. 1967.

—, 'The Larkin Letters', 6 Nov.–4 Dec. 1992.

Tolley, A. T., *The Poetry of the Forties* (Manchester, 1985).

—, *My Proper Ground: A Study of the Work of Philip Larkin and Its Development* (Edinburgh, 1991).

Tomlinson, Charles, 'The Middlebrow Muse', *Essays in Criticism*, 7:2 (Apr. 1957).

—, ed., *Marianne Moore: A Collection of Critical Essays* (Englewood Cliffs, N.J., 1969).

Trotter, David, *The Making of the Reader: Language and Subjectivity in Modern American, English and Irish Poetry* (Basingstoke, 1984).

Tudeau-Clayton, Margaret, and Martin Warner, eds, *Addressing Frank Kermode: Essays in Criticism and Interpretation* (Basingstoke, 1991).

Tully, James, ed., *Meaning and Context: Quentin Skinner and his Critics* (Cambridge, 1988).

Tymieniecka, Anna-Teresa, ed., *Poetics of the Elements in the Human Condition: The Sea* (Dordrecht, 1985).

Unwin, Stanley, *The Truth about Publishing* (London, 1926).

Vansittart, Peter, *In the Fifties* (London, 1995).

Vendler, Helen, *The Music of What Happens: Poems, Poets, Critics* (London, 1988).

Wain, John, *Mixed Feelings* (Reading, 1951).

Walcott, Derek, *The Arkansas Testament* (London, 1988).

Ward, Geoff, *Statutes of Liberty: The New York School of Poets* (Basingstoke, 1993).

Warner, Rex, *Poems* (London, 1937).

Wasley, Aidan, 'Auden and Poetic Inheritance', *Raritan*, 19:2 (Fall 1999).

Watson, George, 'Larkin Ascending', *American Scholar*, 57:3 (Summer 1988).

—, *British Literature since 1945* (Basingstoke, 1991).

Watts, Emily Stipes, *The Poetry of American Women from 1632 to 1945* (Austin, 1977).

Waugh, Evelyn, *Put Out More Flags* (London, 1942).

Wellek, René, *Concepts of Criticism* (New Haven, 1963).

The W. H. Auden Society Newsletter, 1988–.

Widdowson, Peter, *Hardy in History: A Study in Literary Sociology* (London, 1989).

Widgery, David, ed., *The Left in Britain 1956–1968* (Harmondsworth, 1976).

Wilbur, Richard, *New and Collected Poems* (London, 1989).

Williams, David G., 'The Influence of W. H. Auden on the Work of Peter Porter', *English*, 41:169 (Spring 1992).

Williams, Melanie L., 'Then and Now: The Natural/Positivist Nexus at War: Auden's "September 1, 1939"', *Journal of Law and Society*, 31:1 (Mar. 2004).

Williams, Oscar, ed., *The New Pocket Anthology of American Verse* (New York, 1955).

Willoughby, Martin, *Post Cards* (London, 1989).

Wilson, Edmund, *Classics and Commercials: A Literary Chronicle of the Forties* (New York, 1950).

—, *Letters on Literature and Politics 1912–1972*, ed. Elena Wilson (London, 1977).

—, *The Fifties*, ed. Leon Edel (London, 1986).

Wilson, Robert A., *Auden's Library* (New York, 1975).

Wittgenstein, Ludwig, *Tractatus Logico-Philosophicus*, trans. C. K. Ogden (1921; repr. London, 1990).

Woodhead, Chris, *Nineteenth and Twentieth Century Verse* (Oxford, 1984).

Woods, Gregory, *Articulate Flesh: Male Homo-Eroticism and Modern Poetry* (New Haven, 1987).

Wright, Stuart, *Randall Jarrell: A Descriptive Bibliography 1929–1983* (Charlottesville, Va., 1986).

Zim, Larry, Mel Lerner and Herbert Rolfes, *The World of Tomorrow: The 1939 New York World's Fair* (New York, 1988).